American Farm Collectibles

Identification and Price Guide
2nd Edition

❧ Russell E. Lewis ❧

©2007 by Russell E. Lewis

Published by

krause publications

An Imprint of F+W Publications

700 East State Street • Iola, WI 54990-0001
715-445-2214 • 888-457-2873
www.krausebooks.com

Library of Congress Catalog Number: 2006935444

ISBN: 978-0-89689-459-4

Designed by David Jensen

Edited by Kristine Manty

Photos by Russell E. Lewis

Printed in China

Dedication

This book is dedicated to my wife Wendy, my sons Justin and Rob, my brothers Gord and Ron, and to my parents, Gerald and Marian Lewis. Farming is about tradition and, without these folks, I would have none. Without my parents, I never would have had the opportunities afforded to me for farming and for education. Without my brothers, models for success would be fewer. Without my wife, I could not do what I do now. Without my sons, what hope is there for the future?

As a child, my father was known to family and friends as "Bob-the-White-Horse." He played for hours on end that he was the Percheron draft horse named Bob on my grandfather's farm. He hooked himself up to a crate with binder-twine harness and completed a variety of farm duties daily. This pattern of play set the stage for a life dedicated to farming and being in a position to pass down a tradition to his family. I dedicate this book to his memory and to all of the hard working farming men and women like him who have made American farming the most productive in the world.

Contents

A Century on the Farm

The second edition of this book on collectible items related to farming and farming households in America includes photographs and illustrations in full color. Pricing information has also been updated when needed, but most pricing has not changed much in the past three years other than going up with general inflation and even faster in a few select areas, such as a larger increase in fine duck decoys and some other items. Tractor values have actually flattened out some in the past three years since the first edition due to economic issues in our nation and especially in the American farm community.

This book covers items of a collectible nature related to farming in North America from the period beginning shortly after the Civil War until approximately 1965. Many of our current farming collectibles were invented prior to 1900 and examples are still readily found for sale, with some of the items still in use on farms. These dates correspond to the beginning impact of the industrial revolution on farming in America and the manufacture of many items that have now today become collectibles and antiques of interest to many, not just farmers and those raised on the farm. Also, you never know where you may find an item of interest. In July of 2006, for instance, while buying a duck decoy collection, I also picked up a nice original wooden handle drill and bit for boring holes in barn post and beam construction.

I found this nice antique wooden drill and bit for post and beam construction while buying a duck decoy collection in Grand Rapids, Mich., in July 2006, $75+.

The time period selected represents the evolution from a truly agrarian society to an urban society in America. Many people now find farm collectibles of interest partly due to the "romantic" ideal of an agrarian society. As a life-long farmer, I know that not all aspects of farming are as ideal as we like to think. However, I also know that this is an area of great interest to the general public and I hope this book is helpful in identifying and pricing farm related antiques and collectibles.

Not much has been written in this field, and nothing in the past 10 years. Only a handful of earlier works, now out of print, deal with this field and the field is so large that many books could be written about the area, basically covering each chapter in this book. But this is a beginning, a guidepost if you will. Or should I say a "corner post."

This is not a book just about tractors! Tractors are of course included, but many fine guides exist on full-size tractors that are referred to in the text. I have included items related to tractors and implements as part of the book in the fields of advertising and toys and Chapter 12 gives a brief overview on collectible tractors from the classic era of tractor development, the 1930s-1960s. I was fortunate to have Tractor Supply Co. stores sell the first edition of this book and it found its home on the shelves amongst many fine books on tractors.

Why should you listen to me? I have been farming since shortly after birth. I was the Gold Star State Dairy Farmer for the Future Farmers Association in Michigan in 1965, one of 22 youths selected for their knowledge and ability in farming out of a pool of 22,000 at the time, and the only youth selected for dairy farming. I still farm. I raise draft horses and North Country Cheviot, Oxford and Scottish Blackface sheep with my wife, Wendy, and have raised and milked Jerseys, Ayrshires, Brown Swiss, Holsteins, Milking Shorthorns and even one Guernsey!

I have also spent many a Saturday the past 35 years attending the ever present "farm auction" to look for treasures needed for farming or collecting. I've amassed so many items over the years that I have had three fairly large farm auctions myself, one holding the record for "buyer's numbers," at nearly 500 buyers, for some time.

Also, as an anthropologist, I spent years working with and writing about the Old Order Amish and living within their communities in Indiana and Michigan while studying their agricultural techniques and the energy efficiency of horse agriculture.

This familiarity with the older equipment used by the Amish simply added to my interest in farm antiques and collectibles.

This is our dairy barn built by the Peters family in 1876 and still sound. The dairy cup and stanchions shown in Chapter 7, Page 136, are from this barn. The original Centennial Farm sign, at right, indicates the age of the farm. These signs are themselves collectible, as discussed in Chapter 3. The farm was in the Peters family from the time of a grant by the U.S. government in 1876 until they sold it to us in 2001. If it could only tell stories!

I'm still an active farmer and raise three different kinds of sheep, along with draft horses.

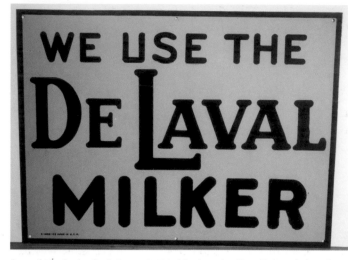

One of the lucky finds for us is this black and yellow DeLaval sign that is virtually new from old stock found in an old hardware store in Bay City, Mich., in the past 20 years. The store was a DeLaval dealership and had a box of 12 of these signs still with the shipping paper attached new in the box, $50-$150. More signs in our collection are featured in Chapter 3.

Recently when it was time to put a new roof on our large dairy barn, only the Amish were able to take on this task locally, as most "modern roofers" did not want to deal with the height or the liability insurance issues for their employees.

My wife and I collect some items related to farming, especially tin dairy equipment signs, such as DeLaval, Surge, etc. Our house seems to be full of items related to farming and agriculture, chickens, sheep, tins, etc. I personally saw the transition from horse agriculture to tractor agriculture in our community as a child, and I recall the last time the Lewis family ever used horses to thresh grain and the threshing dinner afterward. As a growing boy, one of my neighbors, Neff Fisk, used to allow me to drive his team either on the way to my one-room country school or on the return home, as he continued using horses his entire life.

All of these things have contributed to my interest in farming collectibles and antiques. Many of the items of interest have been well covered in books about tractors or implements, but many of the smaller items have not been specifically covered in a book about farm collectibles, although many of these items do appear scattered throughout other references on collectibles at times. It is hoped that this one book will become the basic text of farming collectibles and give easy access to all types of farm collectibles in one source. As mentioned earlier, it is a mere beginning and I hope it has a long and wonderful life of revisions, additions, and expansions.

The book is in the format familiar to collectors, with photos, descriptions of items, history and dates of items, and values presented. There is also general information on dating and values. In addition, included are suggested farm museums and living villages to help you learn more and view items of interest.

The book is broken into the following chapters:

An Interview with the Experts: This section includes a detailed pricing of recent auction values from "on-site farm auctions" conducted by an auctioneer with 25 years experience conducting farm and country auctions. Art Smith has been auctioning since 1981 and has specialized in farm items during his entire career. He has numerous antique dealers that follow his sales due to the quality of items he sells and he has extensive knowledge of the values on farm collectibles, which he generously shares in this section. There are also brief comments from other experts in the field to give the collector additional information regarding values and their ideas regarding farm collectibles.

Finding, Dating and Pricing Items: This section includes tips on collecting, valuation, using the Internet as a collecting and research tool, building a collection and more. There is also a section on dating items that should be used in conjunction with the data provided in the book and the final chapter showing at least 65 years of advertising of farm items.

Farming in Print: Print items related to farming such as manuals, pamphlets, magazines, advertisements, calendars, etc., are covered in this section. Many of the manuals for tractors and farm equipment have become both highly collectible and highly priced. This section also briefly introduces the reader to books of a collectible nature related to farming.

Farming in advertising: This section includes non-print advertising items such as "give-away" items from farm quipment dealers, seed companies, dairy companies and commodity companies (tobacco, cotton, etc.), and the all-important role of tin signs on the farm and in collecting. Items include everything from ashtrays to tape measures.

Small Scale Farming and Children's Recreation: This section includes the development of farm toys and related collectibles designed for children. Of course, there are books already out on toys and even farm toys; however, this chapter attempts to expand on these books and cover additional areas and at least introduce the reader to the importance of farm toys and related child items.

Farm Implements: An introduction to non-tractor implements and their collectibility are featured in this chapter. Over the past 35-40 years, collectors have purchased cream separators and scalding kettles to become garden flower pots, windmills as yard decorations, one-row cultivators to sit in the yard, scythes to hang on the garage wall, hog scrapers because they look interesting even though most people did not know what they were, wool carders, etc. Also included is a discussion of old implement seats and their values.

Farm Tools: This section concentrates on smaller tools of the farming trade, including wrenches, hammers, shovels, rakes, hoes, etc. Again, there are books on the market dealing with some of these items, but nothing specifically about farming tools and some of the special wrenches and items needed to repair farm implements, such as the items needed to repair chains and sickle bars.

Horse Hardware and Stable Items: This section includes the ever-growing popularity of collecting what we term horse hardware: items related to horse harnesses. This includes old collars, hames, ivory rings, bells, buckles, decorative brass, tugs, and even complete sets of harnesses. It also includes antique tongues for farm equipment made by a particular company, such as Deere or International Harvester, and implements to care for horses such as picks, combs, halters, brushes, and tack boxes, as well as barn and stable-related collectibles for other farm animals.

The Farm Kitchen/Household: Covered in this chapter are items related to preparation and preservation of food that were not unique to farms but of special importance to them given their isolation from "store bought" food in many cases. Again, this is not unique on the market but is an overview of important items and some items overlooked in the past. It includes canning items, pie safes, Hoosiers, early refrigerators, small utensils, etc. I have also included other items related to farm households that fit best in this category, such as household shutters, doors, windows, bells, lightning rods and other decorative or functional items found on the farmstead.

The Farm Garden: This section includes the one field still lasting into today's economy in large scale: the garden companies and their seeds. There are many items of interest in this field: advertising specifically related to seeds and gardening, early gardening tools, seed packages, catalogs, and the comeback of "heritage or antique seed varieties" in recent years. Seed display units from old hardware stores are in demand, as are calendars and "give-away" items from seed companies. Not a lot of data is available for this one category but what is clear is that interest is growing for items of a vintage nature related to gardening and I am sure that this section will expand as revisions are made to this book in the future.

Farm Recreation: Some of the special advertising that went into selling hunting, fishing and other recreational items specifically to the farming community is featured in this chapter. Hunting especially was often a necessity to the farmer to provide needed food and was commonly seen as an extension of food production. With this in mind, many companies marketed items to farmers in a different fashion and this is examined as to its collectible value. Examples include the marketing of crow and owl decoys to deter the crows as pests, and predator calls to eliminate those "bad" animals from your farm.

Many fine books are already available that cover hunting and fishing collectibles (I have authored more than 10 books in this field to date) but I wanted to include a brief chapter on the subject to make certain that all new collectors are aware of the growing value of fishing lures, shot-shell boxes, duck decoys, game calls, old wooden skis, old croquet sets, and other recreational items.

Farm Organizations: Collectible items from organizations such as The Grange, 4-H and FFA are the focus of this chapter. Most American farmers have been members of some form of organization or cooperative and each of these groups in turn have produced items that have become collectible by their scarcity or design, such as toy tractors endorsed by the FFA. Many items in this category have an unknown market value at this time, but as our demand increases for farm memorabilia, it is anticipated that we shall see an increase in the trading of pins, awards and certificates in much the same way as similar fraternal society and military items have increased in value over the recent years.

Collectible Tractors: This section concentrates on tractors from 1930 to 1965, with coverage in photos and values of the most commonly collected vintage tractors, including Allis-Chalmers, Case, Ford, John Deere, and Oliver. I have also included some valuation comments from collectors, restorers, dealers and users of vintage tractors.

There are many fine books in print on tractors; however, I have concentrated on tractors most likely to be collected by those of us baby boomers in our 50s and 60s.

A History of Farm Advertising: A review of many of the items that are now collectible is completed in this chapter by reprinting a number of advertisements from farm publications dating from 1903 until about 1965. Of special interest are reproduced ads from the 1903-1905 period that show most of the items found in this book.

You can get both an idea of how old many of the collectible items are and the fact that many farm items did not change greatly once invented in the late 1800s or early 1900s, for instance fence stretching tools, feeding equipment and implements, until the advent of the tractor in the 1920s. Also, a review of the *Montgomery Ward Farm Catalog* of 1964 demonstrates that many of the early 1900s items are still in use and demand.

This should also assist you in dating items to prevent you from buying "antique items" that are really only a few years old—many of the items passed off online as "antique" are really only 30 years old and may not be all that rare. Of course, some of the more recent items are still highly collectible but the buyer should be aware of how long many of the farm items of a collectible nature were actually manufactured. It is difficult to tell a hoof pick from 2003 from a 1965 one, for instance. At any rate, this chapter is offered as a great way to familiarize yourself with changes through the ages of American agriculture.

An Interview with "the Expert(s)"

In preparation for the final manuscript revisions, I was fortunate enough to spend a few hours with an old friend and expert in the field of farm collectibles and antiques, Art Smith. Art is an auctioneer who has been specializing in "good old country auctions" since 1981. He is an award-winning auctioneer for his talents and one of the most respected of all local auctioneers due to his honesty and knowledge of the items. I have hired Art for three major farm auctions during the past 15 years and have attended dozens of his auctions as a buyer. Art and his wife, Kim, are now in business together, along with their son, Noah, and they maintain a great site at http://www.artsmithauctions.com that details all future and many past farm auctions. You can learn a great amount about values by simply going to this site and examining the excellent quality of photos of items that have sold over the past few auctions.

We spent one morning going over recent and upcoming sales and discussing values on items and what items recently sold for at auction. We also discussed the fact eBay and other online auctions have really only helped local auction markets because now people attend farm auctions to buy items to resell online. Art believes that farm auction prices have only gone up due to online sales, contrary to what was often believed when online auctions first began in the mid-1990s.

Art was also kind enough to share with me some of his personally owned farm collectibles and treasures, featured in many photos throughout the book. Regardless of your experience, there are always surprises in valuation when speaking with someone of Smith's experience. My two big surprises that day were the values placed on "hit and miss" engines (see photos in Chapter 12, Page 240) from the early 1900s and the advertising pencils given away by farm dealerships known as "bullet pencils." Hit and miss engines easily bring upward of $3,000 and bullet pencils are currently selling for $25 to $100 depending on condition, locale, age of dealership, proximity of sale site to the former dealership, etc.

I was also surprised to see there is not as much interest in some of the horse hardware items as I expected. Interest is there, but it is just not as constant as on some of the major farm collectibles. Values on horse hardware items appear to have hit a valley at this time. Another thing to note is that values on old tractors have not kept up with the increased values on older implements. The valuation of horse hardware and tractors may have reached a temporary peak because these are some of the more obvious farm collectibles, and those most interested have already purchased what they want. It is likely that the values on old tractors and horse hardware will again increase, but it is difficult to anticipate when this may occur. Horse items have risen some in the past three years.

I would also like to note the assistance that Brian Taylor of Burnip's Equipment, my local New Holland dealer, has given me in terms of tractor valuation and trends. Taylor had a major sale in 2002 and noted with interest the high values on antique implements in his sale compared to the antique tractors. He had numerous examples of both and by far the biggest surprise was the high value assigned to many implements by the buyers. In a recent interview with him, he indicated that prices for Ford 8Ns, 9Ns, Farmall Ms, Super Ms, Hs, John

Art Smith.

A Ford 8N that has been fully restored is owned by Burnips Equipment of Burnips and Big Rapids, Mich., **$4,000+** in this condition.

Jerry Paulsen and a Cub tractor he restored. More photos of his Cub are featured in Chapter 12, Page 225.

Deere As, Bs, and other common older tractors have really not gone up significantly during the past 25 years and may have even gone down recently. Prices realized at a 2006 auction held by Smith seems to confirm that prices are even higher yet again for the old plows and equipment compared to prices for older tractors being more level.

The fully restored 8N located at Burnip's Equipment in Big Rapids, Mich., as an example, would be worth a little more than the normal top end auction price of about $2,500 due to its pristine condition. However, many 8Ns may be purchased for $1,500 to $2,000 in the marketplace. Farmall Ms now seldom bring even $1,500, unless exceptionally clean; an H may only bring $950 to $1,200 and a Super M a bit more than an M. And so it goes with the John Deere versions, with the exception that there seems to be a premium price paid because it is a John Deere, but even As and Bs are going for only $900 to $1,500 in most cases. However, Taylor indicated how the prices of antique farm implements are only increasing in value at this time and items such as hit and miss engines are skyrocketing. Also, a rare tractor such as a Farmall MTA will still command a good price.

I would also like to thank the assistance of Jerry Paulsen and the hospitality shown by him and his wife, Carol, in allowing me into their home for a photo session of some of his toy collection and related farm collectibles. Jerry has worked his entire career in the farm tractor and implement field and spent a number of years at both Allis-Chalmers and Ford dealerships, including the Ford dealership where we purchased our first Ford 5000 in Cedar Springs, Mich. He also owned a store dedicated simply to farm toy collectibles and has a large collection of Ertl and Precision tractors yet today. Finally, he began restoring both tractors and garden tractors in recent years and is very familiar with pricing in these two areas as well.

One of the most phenomenal collections of general farm collectibles is owned by David and Kelley VanAlstine and I first noticed it while driving by their lovely home a few years ago. I dropped by and they were kind enough to give me a guided tour and extended an invitation into their home full of country and farm collectibles and antiques and gave me the opportunity to photograph items for this book. The VanAlstine family owns literally hundreds of farm collectibles and they have also been very wise in their purchases, with many "bargains" being found by keeping eyes and ears open for items others failed to value as highly as most of us would. Some of the prices they paid for items were frankly shockingly low due to their knack for finding "deals," but they also realize the value in the items. The photos from their collection have been shown throughout the book and without their contribution, the book would be missing many rare items, such as the two early wooden butter churns shown in Chapter 8, Page 152.

Also, I want to thank my colleague and good friends, Dr. Terry Nerbonne and his wife, Andie, for allowing me to photograph some of their antique and collectible farm items from their barn. Most of the items shown were present in the barn when the farm was purchased by Terry and the pristine condition of some of the items is amazing due to the dry storage conditions in his barn. I could not believe the horse "fly-chasers," as I call them, found in the harness room—an item, fragile at that, from the 1920s-1930s in perfect shape! He also has a very rare walk-behind drill that he picked up at a farm auction and excellent examples of hay grapples and track mechanisms for hay storage.

When the 1st edition of this book came out, he laughed at me calling his items the Nerbonne Collection, as the items, for the most part, were simply part of the farm he bought. However, he did add some items and regardless, needs to be thanked by us all for protecting and preserving some rare historical items we may now enjoy in print.

Lastly, I need to remember the tolerance my wife has shown for invading our own country home to take photos of our personal items and to clutter the house with photos, items and manuscript while working on this fun project. She has tolerated six years of fishing lures, duck decoys and farm antiques being strewn throughout our home as I write away in the privacy of my den. Most spouses would not tolerate this with such compassion as she has shown and for this I thank her. Maybe I need to build a barn just for collectibles and seriously consider doing just that from time to time. She also conducted research on 1800s and early 1900s items by examining early publications for advertisements to be used in the 1st edition of this book. Without Wendy this book could not have been completed.

Regarding your own education on farm collectibles, the best advice is for you to go to as many local auction sales as possible to see first hand what items sell for and to make yourself aware of any local idiosyncrasies related to pricing of farm collectibles. By viewing half a dozen local auctions, you will get the feel for the market and the items described in this chapter will become easily recognizable if not already known.

I have organized this chapter according to the same categories as in the main part of the book and listed prices and item descriptions and dates sold, if known. Photographs of many of the items are featured throughout the book and many are also illustrated in Chapter 13 in advertising reprints.

Print items

Farm manuals ranged from a low of $12.50 to a high of $240 at a local farm auction in western Michigan. The high item was a manual for an International Harvester Corporation "hit and miss" engine from 1913. Many other manuals from the 1930s-40s sold for $40 to $120 each, including manuals for Oliver, a Case 1952 D owner's manual, a 1932 DeLaval catalog, a John Deere 1937 Type E engine manual, many John Deere tractor and equipment manuals from the 1930s-40s, an early AC combine manual, etc.

Advertising items for Ford and Massey Ferguson tractors and equipment dating from the 1940s-1970s sold for $5 to $40 per item at the same sale; most of the advertising items sold for $12.50 to $25 each. Included in these items were a number of "note book calendars," a popular give away by dealerships, grain and seed companies, and others. Magazines of more recent vintage on collecting "Gas Engines" and "Antique Tractors" sold for $5 each in most cases at the same auction.

Books at the auction did not fare so well and most sold for only a dollar or two. Exceptional books from the 1800s still did well but common farm books from the post 1900 period do not bring much at sales of this nature. However, a mid-1800s county atlas is expected to bring a few hundred dollars at an upcoming sale, so interest does exist for the better, earlier, rarer books.

Postcards from recent auctions and online sales reach prices of $10, with some commonality and occasionally a card will sell for $35-$50. Only exceptionally early cards, rare scenes, or very detailed cards will exceed these figures.

Advertising items

Oil companies have produced many items now collectible and many people collecting farm items are also interested in early oil company labels and advertising. Chapter 3 has a fine example of an excellent buy made by Art Smith: an original Standard Oil Household polish tin. Also, oil cans with labels are collectible and a Mobil Oil can sold for $15, six oilers (household and farm type) sold for $95, and a New York Railroad lantern sold for $50.

A stand from a hardware store, used to measure rope, sold for $25 and an Allis-Chalmers pith helmet sold for $140. Feedbags with advertising sold for $5 to $10, depending on condition and the area of the mill. Cream and milk cans with local advertising sold for $15 to $50. A Winchester calendar from 1899 sold for $130 and magazines and calendars sold in general for the same as sporting items: e.g. $10 each for items in the 1940s with prices quickly going up for each 10 years older. A John Deere bullet pencil sold for $75, as it advertised a local dealership. Manuals such as DeLaval and others sold for up to $75. Wooden rulers and "walking sticks" used to measure items bring from $20 to $40 each.

Children's items

Sleds from the 1950s sold from $20 to $40 at a farm auction in Michigan. At another farm auction in

Children's items: Arcade cast iron trucks are selling for **$400 to $500** at farm auctions and the Auburn rubber tractors usually fetch around **$75**, if in decent condition. Farm toys vary too much in price to give a complete range, but toy tractors and implements are always in demand and create a lot of bidding competition for the most part. Good condition Ertl tractors always bring at least half of their book value and sometimes more, if rare. The little cast iron Arcade motorcycles like the one shown in Chapter 4, Page 75, are worth up to **$75 each**.

Michigan, a much older (1920s) red child's sleigh sold for $150. Common 1940s-50s sleds brought at least $35. A child's wheelbarrow sold for a surprisingly low $12.50. A little wooden wagon, likely from the 1930s, brought $35.

Farm implements

An Oliver walking plow sold for $140, an old ensilage cutter brought $40, a double beam potato plow brought $40, and steel wheels sold for $8 each to $12.50 each.

At an Amish farm sale in western Michigan, a walking cultivator brought $25, an old Oliver wooden wheel grain drill sold for $90, a Papec silo filler brought $300 (much more than another sale, where a number of them were being sold at once), an IHC Model 7 hay mower brought $275, a New Idea four steel wheel manure spreader brought in $975, a nice McCormick Deering grain binder sold for $775 (this is about what corn binders also bring), steel wheels sold for $12.50 to $20 each, a corn binder sold for $900, a hammer mill sold for $300, a dumpy rake brought $35, and a running gear on steel sold for $120.

At another farm auction, a 1916 IHC hit and miss engine sold for $5,200 and a Fairbanks-Morse one from the same era sold for $3,400. A fanning mill only sold for $20 and platform scales brought around $50. A primitive wooden two-section spike tooth drag sold for $40 and a most unusual item, an antique steam engine whistle, sold for $240 at the same sale. One-row walking cultivators sold for $75 to $100 and riding cultivators sell for $150 to $450 each, depending on brand and condition; a high price I have seen was a McCormick for $450.

An American Seeding Co. (the company made hand corn planters, too) five-hole walking grain drill on wheels

IHC Famous

A 1916 IHC Famous hit and miss engine, **$5,200.**

sold for $260. This is similar to the larger grain drill of Terry Nerbonne's shown in Chapter 5. An Oliver cast iron seat sold for $225 at the same auction.

Farm tools

At a local farm sale, an antique barn beam drill, used to make the holes for the pegs in construction of barns, sold for $70—many times what they were selling for a few years ago. At the same sale, a cant hook sold for $12, two hand corn planters sold for $15 and $17.50 each, a hand potato planter sold for $22.50, old wooden planes sold for $40 each, a mattock sold for $7.50, nice old pulleys sold for $12.50 each, a clinker grabber (to remove unburned coal from a stove) sold for $12.50, a bean sorter brought $20, a Cyclone brand seeder sold for $15, a scythe sold for $35, a broad axe brought $30, a draw shave fetched $7.50, a bull leader (one grabbed the ring with this lead stick device) sold for $9, hay knives sold for $10 to $20 and corn knives sold for $15 to $30 each.

Additional prices included a lanyard scale selling for $22.50, cross-cut saws selling for $17.50 to $30 each, Ford wrenches selling for $10 to $30 each, a barrel-mounted corn sheller selling for $40, milk cans selling for up to $150 in an Amish community (where they are still used to take milk to the local cheese factory), with ornamental type milk cans selling for $15 to $30 each, cream cans selling for $40 to $50, silage forks bringing up to $40 each (people are buying them to use on bark for landscaping), a saw set sold for $3, an IHC wrench sold for $20, hog scrapers sold for about $5 to $10 unless exceptionally clean, hand-held corn picks (hand huskers) sold for $5 most of the time, cream separators sold from $20 to $220 for one in perfect working order, a wooden 55-gallon barrel sold for $27.50, a hand-sharpening grinder sold for $40, and hand cultivators, wheelbarrows and mowers sold for a few dollars to about $25 each, tops.

At the Amish farm sale, an Ashley milk can cooler sold for $100, a milk strainer sold for $25, and milk cans brought $20 to $125 each. The glass chicken waterers from the 1940s sold for $75 each and some interesting barn items included hay spears for $10 to $15, a hay grappling hook for $35, a manure truck for $17.50 and barn roof rails for the hay track selling for $5 per eight-foot section.

Horse hardware

A cowbell (steel, not brass) sold for $15 and a cast iron horse weight, used to tie a horse down, sold for $45. Brass horse weights usually command more than $200 each. An ox yoke sold for $110 at the same sale.

At an Amish farm sale, a set of sleigh bells brought $150 and collars brought from $5 to $100 depending on condition. Some of the spreaders with ivory rings brought up to $40 each and harnesses sold for only about $100 per set but were nothing fancy. The high horse item at the sale was an open-top buggy selling for $900.

Farm kitchen

Ice tongs sold for $10, an old egg crate for $7, wooden shutters for the home sold for $65 for four short ones and $180 for four longer ones, a No. 4 farm bell sold for $170 and another smaller bell sold for $100, and a canner (a simple graniteware water bath) sold for $10.

Additional prices included sad irons, only bringing $5 to $15 each unless very unusual, rug beaters bringing $10 to $30, a gristmill for flour making in the kitchen selling for $80, old brass fans bringing $50, and kitchen scales selling for $15 to $25. An unusual item was a kerosene-powered slide projector selling for $400, wool cards bringing $20 to $25 each and lightning rod globes selling for up to $65 each at sales. A hand coffee grinder sold for $130 and two Hoosiers sold for $950 and $1,050 each, respectively. Pie safes are averaging about $225 each and old refrigerators (wooden ones) sell well, with a Leonard Oak Ice Box selling for $600 at a farm sale.

Always popular are the colored handled kitchenware items selling for at least $5 each unless found in a box lot. Apple peelers sell for $50 to $60 each according to Smith, while cherry pitters with fewer moving parts only bring $25 to $40 each. The once crazy high prices for green canning jars are all but gone, with jars selling for $3 to $5 each if old and in great condition. Some of the school-size bells bring in $350 or better at farm auctions.

Farm garden

A nice old birdbath from the 1940s sold for $170. Lawn sprinklers made from die-cast material on wheels sell for $75 to $100 easily at farm auctions. The human neck yokes used to carry water to the house sell for about $5 each, since not many good memories are attached to these. Hog scalding kettles sell for $100 to $150 and are now used nearly exclusively for planters.

Windmills are selling for nearly $2,000 if in decent shape and complete. Art Smith sold one in 1992 that was about 75 percent complete for $650 and he believes they would start at $1,000 today for the same condition. According to discussions with other collectors, 100-percent complete windmills start at $1,500 and go up quickly from there. Just two piles of windmill parts at a recent auction sold for $125 per pile.

An interesting farmstead item was a Leader brand maple syrup evaporator selling for $1,850 at an Amish auction in Michigan. Maple syrup making is still fairly big business here in Michigan and these items hold their value. The same is true for bee equipment: even if old and collectible, it is often still used.

Farm recreation

Two Community Newhouse wolf traps sold for $150 each and a homemade bear trap sold for $180. Bear traps often sell for $500 or more each depending on make and condition. It is not often any more that bidders are not competing for traps, shell boxes, gun loading equipment, guns, fishing items, and snowshoes at farm auctions.

Smith has sold individual fishing lures for up to $500 each and has a large following for his competitive gun auctions when included in one of his sales. Lang's Antique Tackle Auction holds the world record for pricing at $125,000 in 2005 for a Haskell Minnow. There are not many of those around so do not expect to find one in a "box lot" at the local auction.

Vintage tractors

My guess is that tractors bring more at one of Smith's auctions than the current market value, due to the competitive spirit and the large following he has. However, he did sell a Ford 2000 for $7,900 at a Michigan auction and a 1952 JD Model 60 (gas) for $3,100 at the same auction. He reports that older tractors normally sell within the $1,200 to $2,000 range depending on the condition and models. This would be a little better than the current prices seen at many auctions, but I would expect them to be higher at his auctions as mentioned.

Summary

The foregoing is just a brief scratching of the surface of current auction values according to what I learned speaking with Art Smith. Hopefully it shows the direction of items at this time in our history and will give the beginning collector an idea of values.

Of course, what makes any auction fun is that you can sometimes find items really "cheap" and at other times if caught in the auction frenzy will pay far more than market value to beat out the other person or because the item is needed to fill a collection.

Prices are sometimes volatile in collecting any item and this is true for farm collectibles as well. The prices given are for examples and general information and should not be seen as a guarantee of future values—they are simply a guide based upon past performance.

The most often forgotten item is the importance of condition, condition, condition. Authors writing about collecting stress its importance but then buyers often forget how important it is when trying to sell their own items. An item in pristine condition will always bring a premium price and you must remember that point. On the other hand, items in poor condition not only will not sell for much, they also will not go up in value.

In my opinion, it is always better to invest more money in quality than quantity and I hope readers will keep in mind the important role of condition when examining photos and prices in this book and when making purchases.

❧ Chapter 1 ❧

Finding, Dating, and Pricing Items

Prior to breaking down the specific sales data on farm collectibles and antiques, it is necessary to give a few precautionary words on collecting these items and also to attempt to give some dating hints for the uninitiated. As an attorney, I am very familiar with the term caveat emptor, which simply means that the buyer should be aware. Also, we have the term carpe diem, which means to seize the day. Sometimes when you are attempting to seize the day (the item), you forget to be aware! This brief introduction is to remind all of you to be aware when attempting to build your collection with that all-important item for it.

First, remember that not all souls are pure in the antiques and collectible business; most are or try to be, but many are very willing to skin you alive and sell you back your own skin. I have witnessed more than one person willing to dupe buyers in the area of sporting collectibles and now I have observed many in the farm collectibles business equally willing to stretch the truth. However, with a little knowledge, most of the "sucker tricks" can be avoided. Here are some things to be aware of in the farming collectibles field. Most observations are based upon a review of thousands of online auction listings and the wording used in them. In addition, some of the comments are based upon observations made at auctions and at flea markets.

Many online auctions do whatever possible to claim an item to be "antique," e.g. 100 years old or more to get in that special legal category. Some of the antique category tricks I have noticed include the following:

• "The gentleman I purchased this from was 85 and he claimed his dad played with this item making it over 100 years old" (variations include aunt, uncle, grandmother, grandfather, neighbor, etc.). When you encounter such a general description, it usually is "made-up" by the seller and not based upon fact or reality. If I am selling something from a person with a claimed age, I support it with facts, not generalizations.

• "This item came from a farm sale in _____ and all of the items are very old." Again, mere puffery, as lawyers call it, and there are not any facts to support the age of the item.

• "This is from an Amish farm." This is a fairly commonly used attempt to mislead potential buyers, as it seems to indicate that Amish farm items are all old. Of course, some well could be with the culture dating back to 1691 (I wrote my thesis on the Amish and have published extensively about their culture); however, most of the farm items sold online as "old Amish items" can be purchased in Wana Hardware—a large hardware store owned by a Mennonite family in Shipshewana, Ind., serving the local Old Order Amish community—or some such place today. Two recent examples stick out in my mind. The first was a canning bath lift tray made of simple steel which is still used in canning baths all over the world being sold as "from an old farm estate"—the same lift can be purchased in our local hardware store, if not at Wal-Mart. The second was a common Cyclone seeder that was supposedly old for two reasons: it was Amish and it had a patent date of 1925. Neither claim makes an item old.

• The Cyclone seeder leads to another common area of fraud: patent dates. Patent dates simply indicate when something was patented, applied for a patent, or in some cases when an item had a patent pending. It is as though if you find an 1865 coin in an archaeology dig, you know the site is at least as recent as 1865 but you do not yet know the age. An 1865 coin indicates the possibility of some age to the site, but the coin could have been dropped in either 1985 or 1865. An item with a patent date of 1898 does not mean it is from 1898. In the fishing lure arena, Skinner fluted spinners have very early patent dates and Skinner continued to use them through the 1950s on its lures. Old patent dates help prove the date of the patent, not the age of the item. More information on using patents as a tool starts on P. 16.

• Artificial weathering is another area of caution in any collecting field. Dealers that are not honest have often purposely left duck decoys out in a field during winter to "age" them. The same things can be done with farm and farming collectibles with wooden parts or metal parts that will "age" when exposed to bad weather. I am sad to report a certain dealer that had "weathered" a "primitive" apothecary took in a friend of mine at a flea market. It was a very nice looking unit (made about one year before purchased) that was clearly "aged" in the field. My friend assumed the dealer was telling the truth and failed to check the item carefully for construction techniques that would have shown its true age.

• "I am not really sure what it is, but I was told it was used for _____ on old farms and it is at least _____ years old." Again, this is a nice way to add fluff to a listing that likely has a common item or one not even related to historical agriculture.

These examples are not all of the tricks the unscrupulous have up their sleeves, but they cover most of the obvious tricks used for online auction listings and even in some other settings. A little common sense and a careful reading of the description and examination of the photos, or lack of photo details, usually will protect the buyer. But remember, caveat emptor.

Now, with the above in mind, how do you tell the age of an item? Solid research is the only solution. There are certain things you can learn with a little exposure to farming and farm collectibles, but some details will take significant research. There are some general time periods that will become obvious with a little exposure to the field and others we are all still learning to date with more accuracy. For instance, with the exception of some large steam tractors, tractor-related items do not gain significance until the early 1900s and horse-drawn equipment is still the mainstay in the 1800s and really through the 1940s in some regions of America. Many of us recall the last team of horses in the neighborhood still being used in the 1950s or even the 1960s in my case (non-Amish, that is). Our family used horses in the mid-50s for the last time.

Diesel power was not significant as an agricultural influence until the 1930s and really was not common until the post-war era of the early 1950s. Small farms did not purchase their first diesel tractor until the 1960s, or the 1950s at the earliest for most. This helps date oil industry-related items, such as cans. Milking machines became commonplace only in the 1950s, with earlier ones existing but being far more rare on farms. Milk was shipped in cans commonly through the early 1960s, with bulk tanks replacing cans in the 1960s in most areas and the cream cans of the pre-Depression era giving way to larger milk cans in the 1930s-1960s. Some areas only shipped cream without milk cans being used at all.

The introduction of certain materials, such as Tenite 1 and Tenite 2, plastics developed during World War II and just before, are clear indicators of a post-war item in most cases; early Tenite 1 was unstable and can be a sign of an item's age—1935-1941 in many cases. The addition of better plastic components was common in the 1940s as plastic, and then nylon, were seen as "miracle materials" and many manufacturers figured ways to

Identification marks on this butter churn indicate it was made by Union Mfg. Co. of Toledo, Ohio. These marks prove invaluable in determining the age of the item. This churn is valued at **$300+**. *VanAlstine Collection.*

incorporate these lighter materials into many items. Of course, some items were completely replaced by plastic items in the 1940s and 1950s.

Toys show a good evolution of materials from wood to early rubber to cast iron to other forms of steel and tin and improved rubber, then vinyl and nylon and finally plastic replacing most earlier materials. A cast iron Arcade toy farm tractor is older and we know it simply by the materials used to cast the toy. One of the misleading articles mentioned was a tin lithograph barn made by Marx Toys and a set of Auburn Vinyl animals being touted as "over 100 years old." Neither of these materials existed 100 years ago and both items are dated from the early 1950s.

The most valuable way to learn to date an item is to handle as many items as possible, go to shows, visit reputable dealers, go to auctions, read club literature, visit Internet sites, talk to people, etc. The following list is not comprehensive but is certainly a good overview of how to date items that are collectible:

1. Catalogs and magazines. These are invaluable aides to dating items. However, catalogs themselves are too expensive for the average collector to acquire just for dating purposes. Magazines, on the other hand, are very affordable and can assist you in determining the first year of production of an item, short production run identification, and trends in manufacturing. I have identified many items only by scanning through old magazines and seeing the "only" advertisement ever run by a small company. It is common to still find magazines from the 1950s for only a few dollars each in mint condition, with earlier magazines increasing in value greatly for each 10-year period covered. Catalogs of manufacturers are also fairly inexpensive for the 1950s but increasing fast, with earlier catalogs easily

fetching $50 on up for the 1930s-40s and much more for earlier ones. They have not yet reached the prices seen for sporting collectibles catalogs, but they will not stay this inexpensive for too long as interest grows in farm collectibles and antiques. See also number 7, Benchmarks.

2. Club literature. Another wonderful source of data is literature of the various tractor, toy tractor, toy, hardware and kitchen collector clubs. In addition, old issues of newsletters and club magazines can assist you in identifying "unknown" items.

3. Packaging. This is a big clue in dating if you are lucky enough to find an item in its box or on its card. The first thing to look at is the address to determine if a Zip Code is present. The cartoon character Zippy started introducing the Zip Code for the U.S. Postal Service in 1963 and the Zip Code started appearing immediately on some packaging. However, the lack of a Zip Code may also simply mean the company used up "in stock" packaging first or simply failed to comply with new postal regulations. The lack of a Zip Code is not a guarantee that an item is pre-1963, but it is one possible indicator. Also, I have noted that many companies used the Zip Code on a coupon or mailing label but not on the front of a package or catalog for the first few years of the 1960s. So again, beware; lack of Zip Code was often only a sign of a company being slow to react to new postal regulations and/or the layout department not being real creative and using old copy for catalogs and advertisements.

4. Package colors and materials. These also evolved and are an obvious indication of approximate time of manufacture. Items packed in wooden crates are normally older than items found in cardboard boxes and the crates marked with a stencil painted label are older than others. Labels such as fruit crate labels ended for the most part by the 1950s and would indicate an approximate age of the item. Also look at the box construction itself, with many of the cardboard boxes being dated by the maker even when the contents were not dated. Also, some catalogs and magazines showed the packaging and this would assist dating a found item if the package is still present. Regardless of the packaging, items can usually be dated to a range of years, at the very least by the package type and/or color. Of course, addresses on the packaging may also help date a company if you know the various locations of the company.

5. Handle items. The most important way to date an item is to handle as many that you already know the dates on and can learn to compare by examination of similarities and differences. This is one of the main advantages to the many collectibles and antiques shows you can attend. You are able to walk around, pick up items, ask questions, make comparisons, learn, and not spend a cent. I know I have spent many days as an

instructor, e.g. set up to sell items, for others to learn from my experience and have enjoyed the opportunity to teach others what I have learned. Most people who do the shows also enjoy teaching you about the items they have for sale, so go, ask, learn, and maybe even buy an item or two. As for me, I no longer go to shows in anticipation of selling, as I believe the Internet is a far superior tool for that avenue. However, I still enjoy seeing thousands of collectible items in one spot and it is a great social activity, too.

6. Company names and packaging. As indicated in No. 4, one way to help date an item is to examine its packaging and note the full company name, which often changed through the years, and the complete address of the company.

7. Benchmarks. What I refer to as benchmarks include literature or advertising introducing an item as "new." But beware, as some companies used the designation "new" for more than one year to sell their products. A review of numerous company and wholesale catalogs from 1901 through 1987 when researching for my fishing lure books demonstrated this over and over again. These can be catalogs, magazine advertisements, company brochures, call box inserts, separate wholesaler fliers or advertisements, or company histories. I think that the wisest investment the new collector can make is that once a direction for the collection has been decided upon, purchase the company catalog for the particular year of the beginning of the collection, if available. Then, attempt to follow the changes in following years through catalogs and advertising in trade magazines and popular literature. Research and collecting must both have a beginning and once you have this foundation, the rest of your collection is built on the strength of knowledge of your product. Two of the best sources for post-war collecting are the Sears and Montgomery Wards farm catalogs each company produced apart from their general catalogs. I recall going to the special farm store one of these large chains had in Grand Rapids as a boy and being dazzled at all of the farm equipment. These early catalogs document as well as any source what was available and when, from the post-war period up until the 1960s.

8. Oral history. As a former working anthropologist and folklorist, I long ago learned the importance of paying attention to oral history and seeking out "informants" when attempting to learn the history of an area or subject. This is no different in farm and farming collectible history. I have included an interview with an experienced farm auctioneer as an example in this book. How many of us have listened to stories told by our fathers, mothers, grandparents, aunts and uncles only now to find they are no longer here to jot those memories down? It is most important to the future of farming history and farm collectibles that we document all we are able to about the history of items by seeking out individuals with knowledge and writing down what they have to say while the information is still available. I have learned much of my information through discussions with farmers, family members, collectors, jobbers and retailers in the trade and I can only hope that others are also documenting all they are able to while it is still fresh in the minds of those involved.

9. Patents, trademarks, trade names and copyrights. One final way to date an item is to complete a patent search for it on the U.S. Patent and Trademark Office Web site, http://www.uspto.gov, by entering the appropriate data. The site is quite easy to use and will result in finding great details on an individual piece. Sometimes the only information about an item we have is the patent number printed on it and this will result in a complete history of the item by entering the number in the search process. There are limitations on certain searches unless you know the patent number and keep in mind that the patent year only indicates when the item was actually granted a patent; sometimes this is years after an item was "used in commerce." It is also possible to conduct trademark, trade name and copyright searches for items; however, this is a bit more complicated than entering the patent number. Trademark and trade name searches are conducted through the U.S. Patent and Trademark Office and copyright searches would be completed through the Library of Congress, the organization in charge of protecting copyrighted material in the United States. You can go from the http://www.uspto.gov site to the copyright site, http://lcweb.loc.gov/copyright/, and it tells you how to go about searches. Also, keep in mind that if you are printing items for publication, some of the materials on the U.S. Government sites are protected by copyright and you will need permission to reprint certain items for publication.

Finding items

As I said, it is tougher and tougher to find items "on the street," so to speak. However, it can still happen and I use every available technique known to find items for my collections. Every once in a while I get lucky and find a good item for a low price. But it all takes work and diligence to be successful. The ones finding items with the most regularity are not just "lucky" they are also "industrious." I know one picker who is always finding great things but he is out of bed early, at estate sales to get number 1, and works at least four days a week finding items, etc. Also, he is willing to pay for an item. Many people think that items are out there at ridiculously low prices just waiting to be discovered. Trust me, this is the exception and not the norm. The norm is that an estate dealer prices items fairly with enough profit margin left for the dealer to also make a dollar or two. Thus, items at estate sales are not "cheap," but are fairly priced in most instances.

The point is that I have a real issue with those who do not want to pay a fair price for an item. Sure, we all like bargains if found, but please do not always try to beat down prices when someone has an item for sale.

In the same fashion, if you are asked the actual value of an item, I believe it is our ethical duty as collectors and dealers to tell the truth the best we know it. In other words, if I go to a garage sale and see a tin sign hanging on the wall not in the sale but the owners are willing to sell it, I should be prepared to tell them the value when asked. This is not to say we have to tell people the value of an item that is already priced, as I do not think this is necessary. But if someone is relying upon our knowledge and experience and we are after something of theirs that is not already priced, we have a duty to be honest about the value in that situation. Of course, I am not suggesting it is only fair to pay full retail for an item; only that the seller has a right to know the full retail if asking. Each of us will make our own decisions on how much to pay but we should be duty-bound to be fair and ethical in all of our dealings. I know that in my own experiences this has only resulted in positive repeat dealings with people and me having access to collections denied others desiring the same access.

How do you find items? A complete list could be quite long, but I will attempt to summarize:

- Dealers
- Antiques shops and malls
- Farm and household auctions
- Flea markets
- Advertising in local papers
- Advertising in regional magazines
- Advertising in retirement homes
- Telling each and every friend of your interests
- Buying advertising space on a billboard
- Visiting shows dedicated to farming collectibles
- Visiting areas rich in agricultural history
- Visiting Internet sites where you can buy/sell/learn about farming collectibles and antiques
- Visiting living agricultural museums and historical museums
- Going to auctions dedicated to farming collectibles
- Joining every organization related to farming collectibles
- Joining a local organization dedicated to collecting
- Giving lectures on the topic to community service groups
- Giving lectures on the topic to local school groups
- Developing a network of collector-to-collector exchanges
- Lots of footwork, phone calling, emailing, and other contacts
- Training and using a quality picker or pickers to assist you

Using the Internet in collecting

I have been involved in higher education for nearly 37 years as a professor and administrator and only wish I would have had a microprocessor and the Internet when conducting research for my earlier professional writings. My students can find answers to many questions in less time today than it took me to drive or walk to the library. What does this mean for collecting? A lot.

The Internet became a viable tool for selling and buying collectibles and antiques beginning in 1995 with the birth of many online auction houses. Only a few remain today and most of the market is consumed and controlled by only one: eBay. I have researched pricing for antiques and collectibles online extensively since 1998, and concentrated on looking for farm collectibles for sale since 2003 on eBay. These items were found under a number of related categories and I marveled that an entire farming collectible collection, including an 1800s Studebaker wagon, could be purchased without leaving my chair at my computer desk.

This was no surprise to me, though, as I make a substantial number of sales per year on eBay and use it as a tool on a weekly, if not daily, basis. However, for many, this is a bewildering area still not trusted or understood. But even if you do not buy even one farming collectible or antique over the Internet, it is still a great tool to learn about farms, farm history, and farming antiques and collectibles. More and more dealers, auction houses and publishers are making online sites available for all of us to visit and expand our knowledge regarding their products. Even many collectors are sharing their collections and knowledge online by adding technically accurate listings of items, with references given to major research works to verify it. Many of the items I have purchased online over the years had detailed factual data related to manufacture and time period of the items, and even were supported by references in some instances.

You can buy and sell on the Internet with confidence if only a few simple rules are followed. The first and most important rule is to deal only with those dealers with a positive reputation. This is the same for online dealers or those with storefronts. Just as you usually select a mechanic or an attorney based upon reputation, you should also select a dealer the same way. With online dealers, "feedback" information can easily be checked to determine how others have fared in their dealings. If all others are happy with the service, the timeliness of delivery, the quality of the items, the proper description of the items sold, etc., then it is likely you are dealing with a reputable individual or company. If the individual or company still lacks feedback, positive or negative, I would not spend a large amount of money in my purchases from them. But, if someone has sold a number of related farm collectibles or antiques in the past year and all feedback is positive, it is likely you are safe in your dealings with that person/company.

There are additional ways to guarantee your satisfaction with more expensive items. Make sure you know the seller's return policies and that you can live with them. Also, for a $3,000 item, will the seller accept funds being escrowed to a third party until the transaction is completed? If not, that is not a guarantee of problems, but it does give you more options for very valuable items if the funds may be held in escrow. Also, most auction services and electronic payment services (such as PayPal) are now offering guarantees that may be purchased at the time of electronic payment. For a $12 item this is not necessary in most instances; however, it would be one more assurance for a $3,000 item.

Finally, the best guarantee is based upon past dealings with the seller personally by the buyer; you then know first hand if you are satisfied with the past performance of a seller and with the product(s) supplied. I buy and sell thousands of dollars worth of sporting collectibles per year on the Internet and have had only one really unpleasant experience and that is not a bad record with more than eight years of direct online sales experience and an additional three supplying inventory to another seller.

So, my advice to all with access to a computer and the Internet is to learn to use it as a tool at the very least. Also, it is a great way to find items that trips to the local antiques store would take years to accomplish. Any item on the Internet is available to anyone for looking and buying and it allows us to fill in our collections far more easily and rapidly than any other technique, albeit at a more costly price in many cases. Yet, at the same time, there can be bargains had when a seller lists an item with which he/she is not familiar or during times of a soft economy. I can attest to the fact that I have found some real buys on the Internet for both reasons. The most important advice is to learn by experience and have fun along the way.

John Deere hit and miss engines from the 1910s or early 1920s are among farm antiques that have appreciated greatly in value over the past few years. They're worth **$2,000 or more**.

The Internet is also an invaluable research tool and should be used to learn more about your collecting interests. One great site to visit and then visit the actual place is: http://www.alhfam.org, the site for the Association for Living History, Farm and Agricultural Museums. ALHFAM is the clearing house and society for information about many items related to early farm life in America and this site will lead you to many links and great information. Currently there are 125 member institutions listed in its information base and you can find locations, hours, and special collections by a visit to the site. There are more than 80 international Web site links also given. Whether it is the great and extensive Greenfield Village or one of the smaller but wonderful sites such as Conner Prairie in Indiana, you can learn much about historical agriculture through the Web site itself and then visits to the museums. Most land grant universities, such as Michigan State, Cornell, Penn State and most others, also have museums and major research collections on farming.

Value trends

Gone are the days of a $5 DeLaval or Surge tin sign being found at the local antiques shop, for the most part anyway. Bargains can still be found in unique situations, but overall most dealers now know the value of good farming collectibles, if they can identify them. Thus, even novice dealers easily identify advertising items due to the additional printed information on the item; however, you could at the same time find a tool or implement not identified because the items are not marked or the markings are coded and the dealer does not know the meaning.

Also, estate sales can have some bargains. For instance, I went to a neighborhood estate sale and picked up two Ford wrenches for $1.50 because the dealer used masking tape to place the price on the wrenches and covered up the trademark on the wrenches, but I noticed the "D" and bought them. I also picked up a very old Crescent brand 12-inch wrench for only $3.50 in excellent shape. The dealers were not specialists in tools, so priced these items cheaply compared to glassware and kitchen items. But if a dealer has resources available on prices, the prices will not be so low for the most part.

Values in antiques and collectibles are driven primarily by age, rarity, condition and the desire created by a particular brand or maker. Obviously, the older the item is, often the greater the rarity, but not always. Also, the older the item, the less important is condition compared to a newer item. In other words, a farming magazine from 1919 is old, not necessarily real rare, but would be more acceptable with some wear and tear than would a common 1954 Hoard's Dairyman.

In the past 30 years, we have seen a revolution in pricing for fine collectibles and antiques, and it is now coming to farm and farming collectibles. Some recent changes include: cast iron seats selling for $5 ten years ago now bring over $100; hit and miss engines bring hundreds, or even thousands, of dollars; good advertising signs commonly reach into three figures; certain antique tractor prices were on an upward spiral in 2003 when I wrote the first edition but have somewhat leveled off now; toy tractors can reach astronomical figures if needed to fill a gap in a collection; and the list continues. The main thing keeping down some prices specifically for farm collectibles is what I stated earlier: the weight and bulk of some desired items makes it hard to move them, limiting their demand and prices. This, too, may change as these items become more difficult to find and other items keep increasing in price.

For specific values, see the sections on different types of farming collectibles in the book itself; however, in general, items have been going up on a 10 to 15 percent per year basis the last few years according to my own observations and those of others. Of course this cannot be guaranteed to continue but will likely continue upward at some scale. Our economy is stronger today than it was when I wrote the first edition in 2003 but still not nearly as strong as it was at the time of record-breaking sales for many items registered in 2001 and 2002. As I write this paragraph (late July 2006), the Dow is still under 11,000 and the world is continually nervous about the Middle East and these two issues alone are likely to have another temporary softening of pricing on some items. The better items seldom lose as much value as average items and sometimes even in a weakened economy they hold their value due to rarity. Sales in 2005 and 2006 at major auction houses certainly confirm this with new record-breaking sales for duck decoys, fishing lures and paintings, for example.

Regarding advice on valuation, I would suggest keeping up with the sales data from auction houses, going to local auction houses and farm auctions, visiting antiques stores, and reading as much as you can find on farm antiques and collectibles. Also, prudent following of online auctions is an excellent test of what people are actually willing to pay for a particular item. As to deciding the best place for an investment, again, only you can decide. However, with that caveat, I think it's important to note that better items retain and increase in value more rapidly than mediocre items. This is true in all antique and collectible areas. But, it is your choice to make, not mine or anyone else's.

❧ Chapter 2 ❧
Farming in Print

This section covers collecting book and non-book print items related to farming such as manuals, pamphlets, magazines, advertisements, calendars, etc. Many of the manuals for tractors and farm equipment have become both highly collectible and highly priced within recent years. Farm books, books dedicated to farming and not advertising for farm items, are only briefly covered due to the enormity of the subject; however, I have listed a few farm books as examples of what is available to collectors.

Reasons for the increased value of some of these items are that they have been the only source of data on the antique items themselves, they are often colorful and full of nice illustrations, and they take up little space and add significantly to the general knowledge base of one's collection.

Manuals and advertising items have always shown up at farm auctions, usually in a boxed lot of other paper items. However, the past 10 years or so, most auctioneers have noted with special interest the operating manuals for the more popular John Deere tractors (A & B), I-H tractors (BN, Cub, C, H, M & Super M) and Allis-Chalmers (B, C, WD, any of the D series). I recall selling one Deere manual online in 1998 for nearly $50 that I picked up at a feed mill auction for a few dollars. At recent farm auctions, manuals sold for $20 to $26 each, depending on the age and product, and the least expensive advertising literature sold for $5 and ranged upward to $40 a piece.

The point is that this area of collectibles has "come of age" and many folks are after these items now and recognize their values. However, it is an area where bargains can still be found at farm auctions and in antiques stores. Online auctions will normally command a higher price as bidders from around the world are normally viewing the same item and will not hesitate to bid up a nice item if needed for their collection. When I still had an antiques booth, I had a paper item priced at $2, but when I put it in an online auction, it brought $28. It was there for the taking for a long time (nearly two years) but when it was offered to a broader audience, it jumped in price accordingly. Not all items do the same, but as a general rule, online auctions will at least net the highest possible viewing of an item.

What should you look for in selecting paper items to collect? This depends if you are considering investment potential or personal interest. Let us cover investment potential first. The most important attribute of paper items is "condition, condition, condition," as we antiques dealers like to say, but with paper items it is doubly true. A soiled paper item is of little value; items that are mildewed, torn, and musty are not wanted in a collection. Not that a super rare piece will not be purchased, it is just that its value is no more than 10 percent of the value of a piece in fine shape—maybe only 1 percent. I have turned down paper items for free because they were so musty or dirty that I was afraid of ultimate damage to other items caused by them. Also, beware that paper items with must and mildew can also cause severe allergic reactions, as I learned by experience with one "find" I made of old sporting magazines that ultimately had to be thrown out due to the mildew causing a reaction.

So, whether for value or reference, only select clean items in fine shape. Now, a tear or bent corner is not going to make an item worthless, as these flaws are far easier to deal with than the areas of mildew and dirt. Some dirt will come off with wallpaper cleaner and other cleaning items on the market, but again this should be done only if an item is needed for research or to fill in a gap in your collection.

What else effects value? With paper items, the most important attribute is "brand recognition" followed by general attractiveness of the layout of the item. In other words, a John Deere item is almost always going to garner more attention than an even older item by a small manufacturer such as Rumely tractors and threshing machines. The Rumely item is likely more rare but that is not as important as the fact that far more of us grew up with John Deere A and B tractors and easily recognize them and want to collect items related to them. So, you will find paper items related to John Deere, Farmall, Case, Allis-Chalmers and Oliver to be the most popular tractor-related items and Surge and DeLaval the most popular milking machine-related items, etc.

As a former college president of an art and design school, I can attest to the importance of the layout of a graphic item as being important for its "attention getting" ability. This is true today, it was true in the past, and it is true for collectible paper items. The area of layout includes the color of the brochure or item, the quality of illustrations used, and the general design of the item and its use of illustrations. It is like the folk story of a blind person attempting to describe an elephant when one cannot see it; one recognizes it is an elephant but it is hard to describe to others. The same is true of good layout designs: they are easy to spot and hard to describe, but I will try anyway. Look for nice strong colors, deep yellows and reds, a pleasing orange, an easily recognized green and yellow combination, etc. Then add nice line drawings and the use of good illustrations or photography. Finally, make sure the print is pleasing and easy to read. If an item has all of these qualities and brand recognition and is in pristine condition, it will command a premium price.

Different demands

One final item of value is demand caused by other factors, including generation, crossover collectors, and general attraction. Generation demand is caused by one generation with a greater interest in an item, a brand, or an era. I have documented this type of demand well in my fishing collectibles books and it means that those of us "baby boomers" are far more interested in the tractors of the 1950s (and 1930s and 1940s) than we are of the first tractors on the scene. This is because we recognize them, remember them, drove them, walked behind them, rode on them with our fathers, mothers, brothers or sisters, and saw them daily.

Crossover collector demand includes competition from collectors of related fields, such as tools. A John Deere or Fordson wrench is of as much interest to the tool collector as it is to the tractor collector. It is also of general interest to all farm collectors. This tends to drive the price of an item up if it is of interest to two or more bodies of collectors. The classic example is a Winchester product: these items are sought by folks in many areas of collecting due to the name alone.

General attraction demand is best illustrated by something I first noticed in fishing lure collectibles called the "cute factor." If an item is just plain attractive—pretty, cute, colorful—its value will increase accordingly because collectors from other fields will also be after it. In fishing lures, there is a lure known as a Heddon Punkinseed that is very "cute" and looks like a little bluegill or sunfish. These lures have gone far beyond their "normal value" as they now attract a large cadre of followers that just like their appearance, even if they are not that interested in lure collecting. I am sure many areas of farm household collectibles would fall into this category as well, such as roosters, lambs, calves, etc.

All of the above covers collecting paper items for the sake of value; however, you cannot discount the intrinsic value of an item either. If you have a WD-45 Diesel tractor, you are far more likely to spend money on its manual than some general A-C collector would. Or, even if you simply had once owned the same WD-45 Diesel (as I did), you would then spend more on the same manual.

If we need something for our own research or to make ourselves feel good about a memory, we tend to buy it, regardless of price. I have developed a mathematical formula as follows: item + quality of memory = price. In other words, the greater the quality of a memory related to a particular item, the greater its price will be.

Only the buyer can determine this intrinsic value and it often will not be recovered in reselling an item unless you find another buyer with similar feelings.

Paper collectibles worth pursuing

What is collectible in terms of paper items? Just about anything that meets the qualifications set forth above, but this list is a guide:

- Tractor manuals and advertising items
- Implement manuals and advertising items
- Milking machine manuals and advertising items
- Brochures and advertising items for tools and hand-held implements
- Advertising for breeds of farm animals
- Manuals and advertising items for farm household items
- Advertising for marketing farm products and goods
- Catalogs for any of the above items
- Early (pre-1950) farm magazines
- Any other paper item related to farming

Where do you find these items? Paper collectors are fortunate in the sense that there are many dealers specializing in paper items. Some of these folks sell online and many offer "lists" or catalogs for their specialty goods. It is my opinion that the online auction is the easiest source for finding a specific item to fill in a collection. However, you can also find these items at every farm auction in America, sometimes only a piece or two, sometimes an entire box full of items. I attended a farm implement and tractor dealership dispersal auction in 2000 at which you could have purchased a veritable warehouse of paper items related to farming, manuals, advertising items, give-away items, catalogs, early magazines, etc. However, even at this auction the items went fairly high as their value had already been realized and many bidders were interested in buying large lots for resale online and elsewhere.

As with all items, the best way to find them is to ask. Ask your friends, relatives, co-workers, at every garage sale attended, local auctioneers, farm dealerships, former milking machine route salesmen, the local veterinarian, cow and horse jockeys (no, not the riders, the traders)—ask anyone you can think of about these items. I have found items in the most unusual places by never being too shy to ask.

To give a range of values is both necessary and difficult for this category since it encompasses such a broad area. However, most paper items start at about $2 retail and can easily go up to a $100 for nice manuals of popular tractors and implements. Rare catalogs from dates earlier than 1940 can easily bring upward of $200. I have purchased 1940s DeLaval manuals for $50 and sold them for $35 to $75 the past few years. Simple eight- to 12-page advertising brochures will often bring $5 to $20 depending on the brand, item and condition. Most tractor manuals are easily worth $10 and more likely $25 as a minimum price if in pristine condition. A manual for a John Deere "G" I sold in early 2006 demonstrates what I said about value: It was in "average" condition in my opinion but still brought an excellent price because of its brand recognition and possibly the buyer needed it for his tractor. It sold for nearly $80 and it was not perfect by any means.

Crate label ends for the cedar fruit and vegetable shipping crates and similar tobacco paper labels usually begin at about $4 each and some can bring up to nearly $200 if rare and/or exceptionally interesting graphics are present. A superb site on the Internet dedicated to paper label collecting is http://www.paperstuff.com. This site has hundreds of labels for sale and gives a nice little history of these labels used primarily between 1920 and 1950 here in America. As the site indicates, color lithograph labels have been used to identify products and their sources since as early as the 1880s and had reached their demise by the mid-1950s due to the use of cardboard boxes as mentioned earlier.

The peak of label use in America seems to be from about the 1920s until the early 1950s. Many labels were found in storage throughout America and these are now for sale to collectors, but make sure you are not buying a reproduction, as its value is limited. The average price for a crate end label is less than $10. Tobacco labels, pins and cigar box labels are similar in use, history and value. The little metal tobacco pins were used to mark tobacco as to the farm sending it to market and these are nice little advertising pins to collect.

The interesting thing about the crate end labels is that you can develop a collection within a collection by concentrating only on labels depicting farms and farming, or fishing, wildlife, just oranges or strawberries, etc. Of course, some of the crossover labels such as fishing and wildlife tend to bring more due to competition among collecting fields. But there is likely not a more colorful area of farming related collectibles covering 70 of our arbitrary 100-year history of farming collectibles.

As a general rule, most post-1950 paper items are not worth a significant amount; however, certain manuals and catalogs still commanded quite a bit up until about 1970. As you go back in time, there is nearly a

Here are two examples of collectible crate labels for Brier Rose Syrup. Crate labels are generally **$10 or less** for most, but refer to the Web site cited in the text for more details.

doubling effect every 10 years. In other words, if a 1940 brochure for a New Idea Spreader is worth $20.50 (one I purchased online), then it is likely worth twice that if from 1930. But then again, you must factor in the generation demand for any particular item as well. I think the most valuable farm paper in the near future will be from about 1930 until 1955 due to the interest of all of the "baby boomer" generation of farm kids and farm collectors. I know personally I would much rather see an advertising piece for something I recognize and may have once used than an obscure tractor or threshing machine I only heard of or saw in an antique farm magazine.

Due to market fluctuation and demand differences, this is a difficult area to give a price for particular items, unless they have recently sold. This is illustrated by a recent request made to a major paper dealer online when I asked him to send me $200 worth of paper items to scan for this book. He replied that he would rather not as he could not properly price it. This is a dealer in paper items declining to sell a certain amount because he was afraid he would price it wrong. He told me he would rather just sell it on an online auction and then he would know the value. He was very polite and understanding; he just did not want to sell an item for $15 that he later would see selling for $25. This is not uncommon among dealers of course; however, it does demonstrate the sensitive area of pricing and estimating prices for these

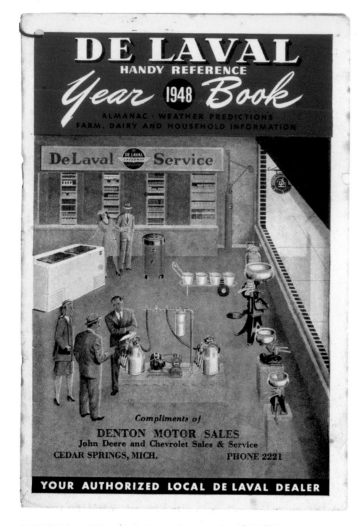

A 1948 *DeLaval Year Book* from a local dealer, **$50-$75**.

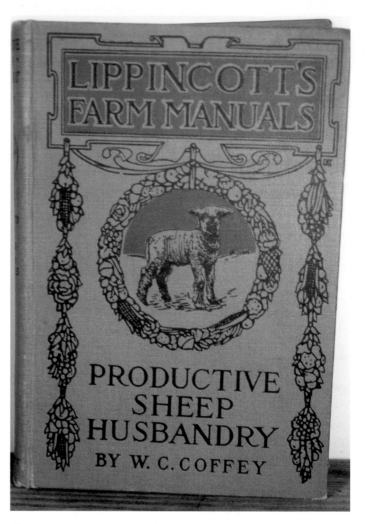

This Lippincott's sheep manual is a wonderful example of farm books that are collectible. There is an entire Lippincott's livestock series, all published in the early 1900s, that would make a nice set for any farm library. This sheep volume is from 1918 and contains many valuable color and black and white prints in addition to valuable data on raising sheep and is in excellent condition, **$23.50**. *Lewis Collection*.

types of items. But my purpose is to give some guidance, which the above information should do, along with the examples documented below.

Antique and collectible farming books seem to be even more volatile in terms of pricing than the paper advertising items. There are numerous value guides available regarding antique and collectible books and one or more of these should be consulted by the serious collector for more information on valuation. However, I have found that books do not seem to have any easy formula in determining value in the field of farm and agricultural collectibles. I have recently purchased books from the middle to late 1800s for less than $20 with superb graphics, lithography and even cutout inserts showing the internal organs and bone structures of farm animals. To me, these all seem like bargains. I hypothesize that there simply is not enough demand by collectors for farming books to be driving the prices to the hundreds of dollars you would see for similar books in hunting, fishing, wildlife, etc.

One general area of interesting books is the *USDA*

Yearbook of Agriculture series published for a number of years by our federal department of agriculture. The research arm of the department of agriculture began in 1865 and many of the early yearbooks of agriculture have important information about early agricultural inventions and techniques of interest to the collector today. These books pick a topic and leading writers cover it in depth and were available from the USDA and/or the Governmental Printing Office. I once owned one with former President Gerald Ford's signature he had used as a text at the University of Michigan. Oh why did I sell that one?! At any rate, these books usually bring from $5 to $30 depending on condition.

The USDA also put out thousands of brochures and pamphlets on farming over the years and some of these have minor collector interest as well. Most of the brochures would only bring a few dollars at best. The reason the brochures are not of as much interest is that they are mainly black and white and are not very compelling in the design category for the most part.

However, earlier ones would command some interest due to line drawings and/or photos of early farm equipment or tools. I sold some of these types related to growing small grains in early 2006 for about $5 each.

Books such as *Silent Spring* by Rachael Carson had a major impact on agriculture as it led to the banning of DDT and many related chemicals. In addition to it being a classic, it is a farm collectible when seen in this light. There were also many books written about soil conservation after the Depression that are collectible, such as the great works by Aldo Leopold and others. A search of any major Internet search engine on agricultural books by topic will generate literally hundreds, if not thousands, of "hits." I suggest using http://www.ask.com or http://www.google.com to begin your online searches.

Some of the how-to books have a following, especially for some of the lost arts such as raising draft horses or the farm orchard. If the book is a first edition, it is almost always more valuable. An example of such a book is from the Lippincott Series on farming from the early 1900s on raising sheep and now that I own it, I want to complete the series on other farm enterprises due to the quality of this book. A very old book may or may not be more valuable depending on how many were printed and circulated. A book with great illustrations is usually more valuable, the addition of the dust jacket usually increases the value, and finally, the signature of someone famous (President Ford) makes the book more valuable.

Regardless, I have included a few examples of what I consider collectible farm books due to their contents or rarity.

This is not a statistical analysis of this field, but simply some items that strike me as important due to information you can glean from them. Any serious collector of rare books is directed to specialty dealers and references on rare books for more detailed information in this area. I have also included some other items that seem to fit best in the "Farming in Print" category below, such as printer's blocks with cow scenes and some other items of interest.

A note about item listings and prices

I researched more than 1,000 online auctions in reviewing pricing for this book. Most listings here and in other chapters represent some of those online auctions. Many of the items from the online auctions are also detailed with photographs in other sales data and/or in Chapter 13 on advertising.

Between the descriptions given and similar items listed elsewhere in the book, you should be able to clearly identify each item described. Also, each online item price was verified by actual auction sale results and/or interviews with experts in the field of farm collectibles and antiques.

Values of some print items

Advertisement, from The Cultivator and Country Gentleman. This is the complete 20-page magazine, clean from a bound volume being purchased $20

Advertisement, for Delco Remy, single-page. This is on a page from a farm magazine showing a beagle, farmers hunting and their "Farmall" type tractor sure to start with its Delco Remy parts in the background $3.50

Advertisement, from *The New York Evening Post*, for Swartwout Farm in Westchester County, NY, found in a formerly bound volume of the newspaper. The price was for the entire newspaper but it was the farm advertisement listed online to attract bidders, and it did attract five active bidders and many more lookers $26

Set of advertisements, from 1954 for Ford, New Idea, Allis, I-H and more. These are simply tear sheets from 1954 magazines $4

Advertising card, postcard size, no date, M & J Rumely Separators. This is a nice advertising piece showing a girl holding a flower and explaining the qualities of the New Rumely Separator. Rumely made early tractors and threshing machines as well and the card shows one of each of them; address is La Porte, Indiana, home to Rumely for years $16

Advertising card, postcard size, no date, mailed in 1914, Lininger Implement Co., Omaha, Neb, published by American Trade Promoting Corp., also of Omaha. This card advertised farm implements, binding twine, wagons, buggies, gas engines and automobiles $12

Almanac, DeLaval, 1946. The low price for this was a surprise, since these often bring $50+, but August often brings lower prices for online auctions . $10.50

Book, hardcover, *1913 Implement Blue Book*, 543 pages, published by Midland Publishing Company, Midland Building, St. Louis, U.S.A., 6" x 8-1/2". This would be great to own, since it's a useful reference for advertising of the era, farm machinery and implements, vehicles, information about makers, and prices $50

Book, hardcover, *Twelfth Annual Report of the Indiana State Board of Agriculture for 1870*, 432 pages, has numerous illustrations of major and minor manufacturers of farm implements, tools, and machinery from throughout the Midwest. Also local agricultural reports by county and state fair results $67

Catalog, *Louden Farm Equipment*, 1919, made available on CD-ROM. This reprint of the 1919-1920 general catalog of Louden Machinery Company is a new item and not a collectible, but it is a valuable research tool. The company is known for its barn equipment and hay unloading tools. Items included early hay carriers, door hangers, dairy barn equipment, litter, feed, merchandise and milk can carriers, hardware specialties and more. The Louden cupola for barns had a weathervane with a cow on it $25

Farm diary, written by a teen-ager describing his jobs around his family farm dating from 1917-1921. This is a most interesting print item and would be a classic piece of research data for early farm life; the price seems low for this type of information $16

Farm diary, 19th century, with line drawings, product of L. Clarke Allison of Alabama and dates from an earlier time period, but I would guess it is the value of the drawings that drove up the price of this .. $140

Farm record book, Funks Seed Corn, 1940. This was for Rob-See-Co, a trade name for J.C. Robinson Seed Company of Waterloo, Neb. I think this is inexpensive for this nice item and the condition is excellent $3

Engraving of an oxen pulling a plow, 1878, inexpensive but beautiful piece of Americana $2

Engraving of a farm scene, Iceland, from 1887 ...... $2

John Deere Tire Pump Operators Manual, five pages, no special graphics, appears to be from the 1950s or 1960s, is Operator's Manual OM-C6-654 .... $15

Matchbooks (matches removed), lot of seven, for implement dealers from Belvidere, Ill, including John Deere, I-H, Ford, New Idea and Oliver. Graphics on covers show some fairly old ones (Oliver with a single walking plow on cover) and newer I-H books $9

Farm implement and tractor magazines and equipment newsletters, 1960s-70s, lot of seven, all trade magazines for dealers, in good shape but quite recent $8

John Deere Farm Wagons for 1950, a nice color brochure on John Deere wagons. I somehow won this online, but lost out on a 1940 New Idea Manure Spreader brochure during the same time period; all the John Deere bidders must have been out in the hay fields that day. Again, this shows the diminishing value of items once they hit that 1950 demarcation point, $7.50. A couple of inside pages of this brochure are on the next page.

WHERE ELSE CAN YOU FIND SO MUCH *Real Value* FOR YOUR WAGON DOLLAR?

(2)

FEATURES:

1. Quality Construction . . . In choosing your new farm wagon, it is important to consider that the modern wagons described in this folder are the product of a factory which has specialized in the manufacture of quality hauling equipment for nearly 90 years. What does this mean to you? It means that whichever "Big 3" Wagon you choose you are getting a wagon that is built to last, a rugged low-down wagon that will handle "pay loads" with safety, a wagon built entirely of new, high-grade material by skilled workmen.

2. Light Weight . . . Yes, a wagon *can* be built to last longer and still be *lighter* than other wagons. John Deere Rubber-Tired Farm Wagons are built with emphasis on quality materials, light-weight, simplicity, and precision, rather than sheer bulk.

3. Light Running . . . Owners report that John Deere Rubber-Tired Farm Wagons are extremely light running. Here again, long experience in wagon construction is your assurance that you are getting a wagon with just the right combination of strength and light-running qualities. You are sure to appreciate the new smoothness of pneumatic-tired wheels running on precision-built Timken tapered-roller bearings.

4. Non-Whipping . . . John Deere Rubber-Tired Farm Wagons are *trailers*—not whippers—even when running at rapid speeds under load. Rigid construction throughout, plus provisions for taking up any looseness that may occur after long hauling service, enable you to keep these wagons running like new.

5. Adjustable Tubular-Steel Reach The John Deere reach is extendable from 83 inches to 131 inches, making it easily adaptable to boxes and beds of various lengths. A means of taking up play in the reach is provided so that any looseness which would encourage whipping is prevented.

6. Demountable Wheels . . . Each of the "Big 3" Wagons is regularly equipped with strong, steel, automotive-type wheels, demountable at the hub.

7. Automatic Brakes . . . Some state laws require 4-wheel brakes if the wagon is to be used on the highway. Others require 2-wheel brakes. Both types of brakes are available with automatic control on the No. 953 Wagon.

(3)

Two inside pages, shown top and bottom, from the *John Deere Farm Wagons* brochure.

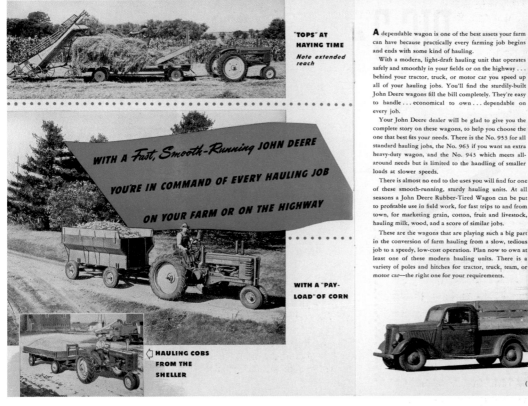

"TOPS" AT HAYING TIME

Note extended reach

WITH A *Fast, Smooth-Running* JOHN DEERE YOU'RE IN COMMAND OF EVERY HAULING JOB ON YOUR FARM OR ON THE HIGHWAY

WITH A "PAY-LOAD" OF CORN

HAULING COBS FROM THE SHELLER

A dependable wagon is one of the best assets your farm can have because practically every farming job begins and ends with some kind of hauling.

With a modern, light-draft hauling unit that operates safely and smoothly in your fields or on the highway . . . behind your tractor, truck, or motor car you speed up all of your hauling jobs. You'll find the sturdily-built John Deere wagons fill the bill completely. They're easy to handle . . . economical to own . . . dependable on every job.

Your John Deere dealer will be glad to give you the complete story on these wagons, to help you choose the one that best fits your needs. There is the No. 953 for all standard hauling jobs, the No. 963 if you want an extra heavy-duty wagon, and the No. 943 which meets all-around needs but is limited to the handling of smaller loads at slower speeds.

There is almost no end to the uses you will find for one of these smooth-running, sturdy hauling units. At all seasons a John Deere Rubber-Tired Wagon can be put to profitable use in field work, for fast trips to and from town, for marketing grain, cotton, fruit and livestock, hauling milk, wood, and a score of similar jobs.

These are the wagons that are playing such a big part in the conversion of farm hauling from a slow, tedious job to a speedy, low-cost operation. Plan now to own at least one of these modern hauling units. There is a variety of poles and hitches for tractor, truck, team, or motor car—the right one for your requirements.

WITH THE HAY CHOPPER

BEHIND THE CORN PICKER

ON THE WAY TO THE COTTON GIN

(5)

Magazines, *The Cultivator and Country Gentleman*, published in Albany, NY, issues contain about 20 pages, are 9-1/2" x 12-1/2", and are clean coming from a bound volume. The interesting advertisements describe particular "farms" for sale and give the details of crops, buildings, fencing, and the farm name .... **$12-18 each**

Magazine, *Farm Journal*, June 1946, cover is quite ragged and this hurt the value. One in fine condition would have brought $10 likely **$2**

New Holland Farm Implement catalogs and a 1914 calendar, lot of five. The catalogs include 1968 combine heads, 1967 combines, 1968 auto bale stackers, 1969 Equipment Buyers Guide, New Holland's own "Our First 100 years 1895-1995 history magazine" **$10**

Paper cover booklet, *A Brief History of Pneumatic Tires for Farm Vehicles*, 18 pages, Goodyear Tire Press, 1938, 5-1/2" x 8". This is a booklet publishing the results of a 1938 essay contest open to FFA members and shows in photographs many pieces of farm implements from the period. The booklet is in good condition, as paper dealers use the term, but collectors would downgrade the "chew" on the edge and normal wear. The item was clearly bought not to collect, as much as for reference, and would be an excellent addition to farm implement references of the period **$22**

Paper cover catalog, 1932-33 Herzler & Zook Catalog, 80 pages, publisher unknown, 1933, 6" x 9". This Belleville, PA, manufacturing company made a variety of items for sawing that attached to Fordson tractors, trucks or hit and miss engines. In addition, 53 pages of the catalog are dedicated to early farm equipment such as anvils, wheelbarrows, concrete mixers, blacksmith tools, drill presses, pulleys, belting, kettles, fencing and supplies, and the Twin City tractor. Again, it has a stain so would not be pristine for paper collectors, but what a great source of data on the 1930s! **$23**

Paper cover catalog, 1906 IRON AGE Farm Implements, 64 pages, color covers, publisher unknown, 1906, 6-3/4" x 8-3/4". According to the sale's pitch, this company was started in 1836 and later purchased by Oliver. This is the complete implement line for garden and horse-drawn farm items and they are shown in the 64 pages illustrated and priced. Implements include Advance Fertilizer Drill, Eureka Corn Knife, Bateman Hoe, various potato diggers, harrows, cultivators, etc. **$26**

Paper cover catalog, 10-1/2" x 24" (folds to 7-3/4" x 10-1/2", color photos, John Deere Hay Making Implements, 1934. This catalog shows four new items in the John Deere line for 1934: No. 4 Mower, Power Mower, Side Delivery Rake and tractor-mounted Side Delivery Rake. This shows the strength of brand in bidding on items, as many of the items already listed have far more useful information, but this item was being purchased for its "collector quality" and not for the data contained within its pages. Also, "Nothing Runs Like a Deere" could be modified in farm collectible circles to "Nothing Runs Prices Up at an Auction Like a Deere" with great accuracy **$38**

Pennsylvania Railroad book, 1911, explains the many wonderful uses of dynamite on the farm. As a lawyer, I found the book of interest telling all the folks how to use something like dynamite that one would be held strictly liable for if harming someone or someone's property. The little 9", 112-page book explains how to increase production, blow up stumps and rocks, use dynamite to dig a well, and many other uses. The book undoubtedly would have done even better if the railroad collectors would have found it in the farm listings **$16**

Photograph of an old farmhouse, black and white, dating from the late 1800s **$10**

A grain mill postcard, from the Chaffee-Miller Milling Co. of Casselman, North Dakota, nice condition **$5**

Two advertisements: The Oliver 70 tractor advertisement, at top, is from the 1937 *Country Home* and the Farmall 12 advertisement is from the 1938 *Country Home* magazine. Even cut out and framed, these advertisements would have collector appeal to a tractor collector or farm enthusiast. See an actual Oliver 70 tractor in Chapter 12.

A Firestone Tractor Tire advertisement shows many vintage tractors. These are from the *Country Home* 1937 or 1938 magazines.

Tractor manuals: *The Allis-Chalmers Model "G" Tractor Manual*, left, **$25+**. *Wheel Horse Lawn and Garden Tractors Owners Manual*, bottom, **$25**. Another Allis-Chalmers manual, for the mower attachment for model B and C tractors (not shown), should start at **$10** and go from there. *Paulsen Collection.*

This plate of a Jersey cow was found inside of a book called the *Biggle Cow Book*, as shown. This plate was removed and sold in an antiques store and we paid a few dollars for it years ago. Again, it's not especially valuable but is a nice addition to a special area of interest and in a form capable of being displayed, **$5-$10**. *Lewis Collection.*

Country Home and *Farm Journal* magazines from the late 1930s and early 1940s, **$10-$20 each**, in clean condition. *Paulsen Collection.*

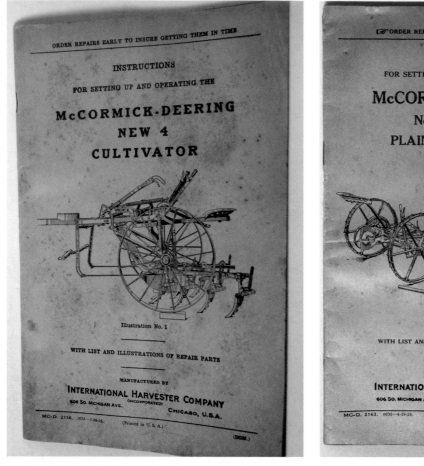

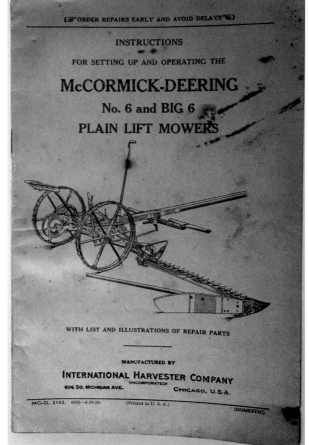

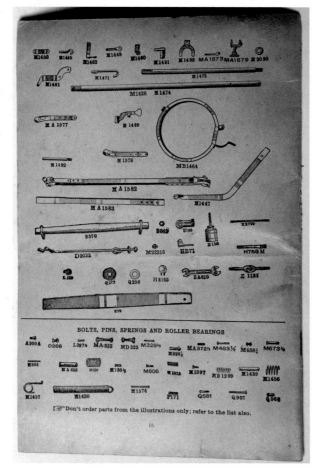

SEAT

The seat is mounted on a hinged seat bar and can be folded over out of the way for adjusting the gangs. The seat can be moved forward or back along the seat bar to properly balance the cultivator for any weight of driver as shown at "A" and "B." Provision is also made ("C") for raising or lowering the seat to three different positions.

(See illustration No. 21.)

DIRT SHIELDS

Dirt shields can be raised or lowered by means of crank "D."

(See illustration No. 21.)

These manuals for McCormick-Deering implements from 1928 would bring a premium price due to their age and collectibility. Shown are the covers and some of the inside details (note the seat style typical of an International, shown above), $50+.

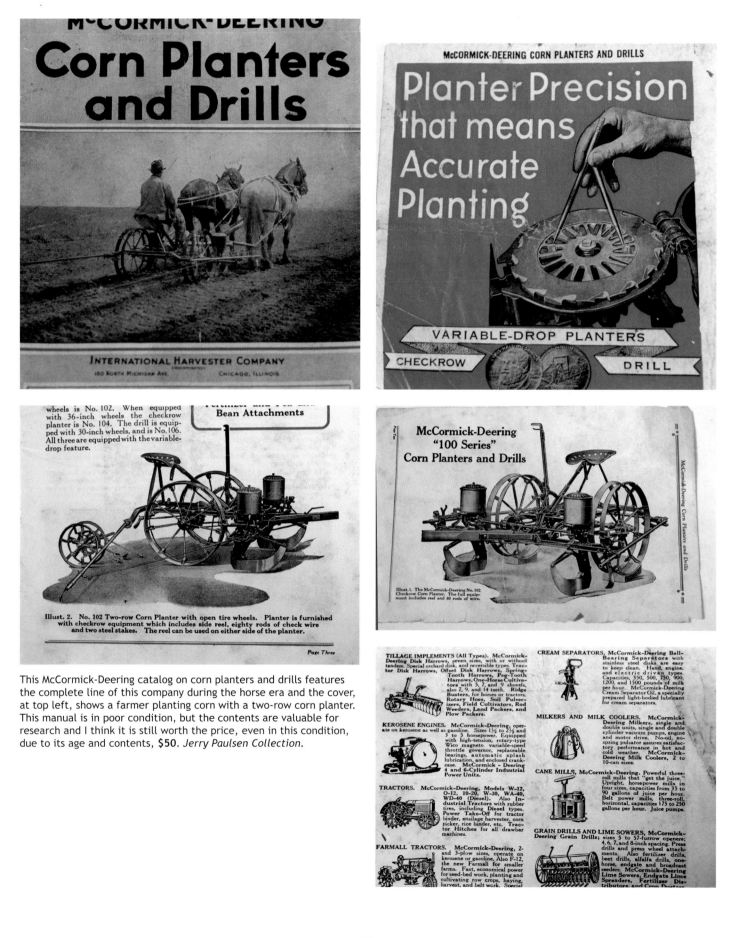

This McCormick-Deering catalog on corn planters and drills features the complete line of this company during the horse era and the cover, at top left, shows a farmer planting corn with a two-row corn planter. This manual is in poor condition, but the contents are valuable for research and I think it is still worth the price, even in this condition, due to its age and contents, $50. *Jerry Paulsen Collection.*

Vibrantly colored crate end labels for fruits and vegetables are becoming highly collectible. Values generally begin at **$4 each** and can go as high as **$200** if the label is rare and/or has exceptionally interesting graphics. This label for Vandalia Brand is in the range of **$5-$15**.

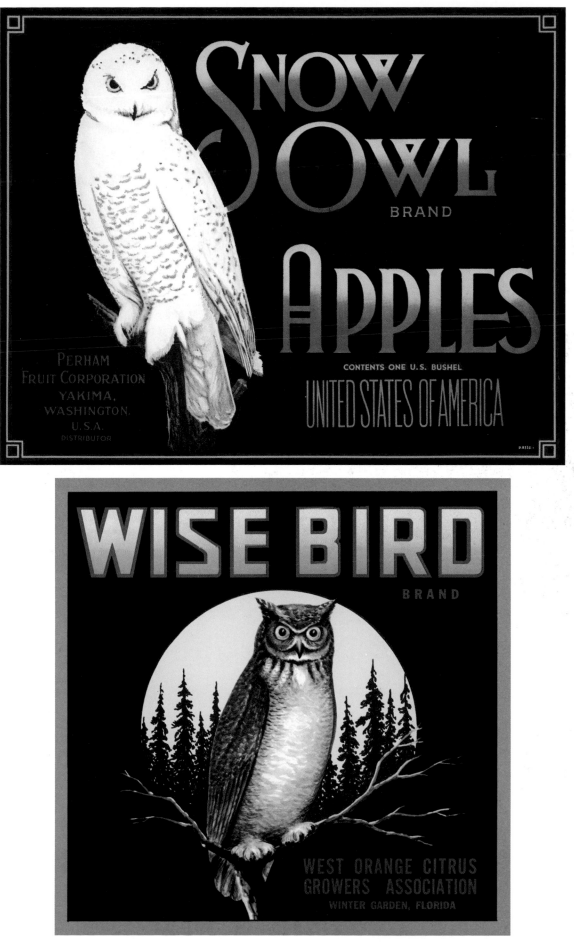

Owl-related crate end labels for Snow Owl Brand apples and Wise Bird Brand, $5-$15.

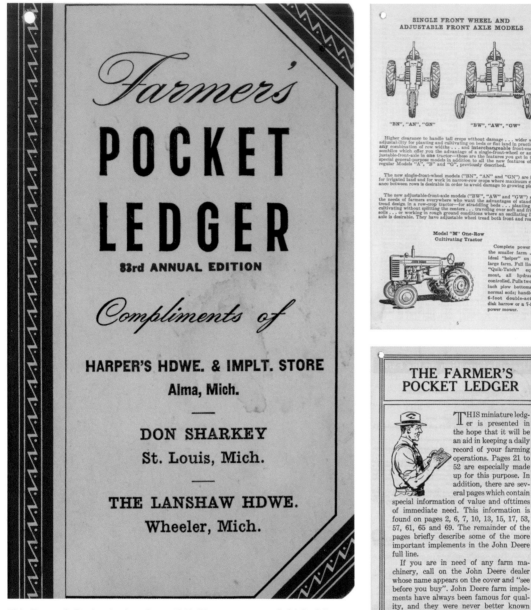

This *Farmer's Pocket Ledger* from 1949-50 was a recent field find from a nearby John Deere dealership, **$50.** I purchased this from a friend for $35, but given the great illustrations of 1949 John Deere tractors and implements, it's worth more. The unique thing is that, although a little dirty on the outside covers, it is in pristine, never-used condition and the inner pages are crisp and clean. The book shows the complete line of 1949 John Deere implements and the A, B, G, and M tractors. It also displays the narrow and wide wheel arrangements available on the A, B and G tractors that then become the AN, BN, GN, AW, BW, and GW tractors by letter designation. This is a great little find for the John Deere collector.

JOHN DEERE COTTON, CORN AND PEANUT PLANTERS

John Deere Cotton and Corn Planters plant cotton, corn, beans, peas, sorghum, and many other seeds with outstanding accuracy. John Deere sawtooth type steel picker wheel for cotton and John Deere natural-drop seed plates for corn and other crops insure accurate, uniform planting under all conditions. Seed plates are available for practically all crops. Variable-drop mechanism gives twelve drilling distances from 5½ to 26 inches without changing plates. Clutch and gears fully enclosed

John Deere No. 536 Cotton and Corn Planter

and operate in bath of oil. No. 536 Two-Row is for drilling only. No. 535 is for checking, hill-dropping, or drilling. Both are adjustable to plant in rows from 32 to 48 inches apart. Automatic marker is regular. Tongue truck and safety fertilizer attachment and tractor hitch are some of the extra equipment available.

JOHN DEERE No. 730 TWO-ROW LISTER

A two-row lister that embodies a field-proved principle of design. In place of full-length beams, the No. 730 has stub beams easily shifted along the tool bar to the desired row-spacing (42 to 54 inches) and locked to position by clamps. Forward wheels carry front of lister and act as gauge wheels. Available with shovel or disk coverers.

ROLLING STALK CUTTER FOR TRACTORS

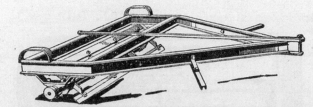

The John Deere Rolling Stalk Cutter is simple, strong (all-steel), cuts more than 3 acres per hour, two rows at a time. For greater capacity, a special hitch can be furnished to make a 4-row hook-up

of two cutters. Knives are of heavy, tough steel. Drawbar extends to rear of frame where an eye is provided for attaching disk harrow, if desired —no strain is put on the cutter frame. Illustration shows the cutter equipped with transport skids, which are regular and gathering rods which are extra. Special stalk straighteners can be furnished and are recommended for best work in corn.

19

Another inside page from the *Farmer's Pocket Ledger* on Page 34.

JOHN DEERE POTATO PLANTERS

Ideal for use with tractors because these latest-type planters with 12-arm picker wheel will plant accurately at rapid tractor speeds. With a new John Deere you can now plant up to 15 acres a day with the 2-row (illustrated); up to 7 acres a day with the 1-row. Simple. Strong. Easy to operate. Light draft. Large hopper. Fertilizer placed in approved band-type method.

LEVEL-BED POTATO DIGGERS

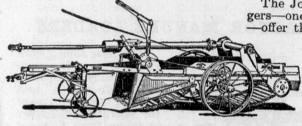

John Deere One-Row Level-Bed Tractor-Drive Digger

The John Deere Level-Bed Diggers—one- and two-row for tractors—offer the very latest features for clean digging with gentle handling. Features include low, level line of travel—no long drops . . . straight-line transmission of power . . . renewable and reversible sprockets . . . safety release clutch . . . steel roller drive chain . . . fully enclosed and automatically-lubricated main drive gears . . . and long-wearing, clean-scouring shovels of forged plow steel. Adaptable to all conditions.

DOUBLE LEVEL-BED DIGGER

This new two-row digger brings all the advantages of regular level-bed diggers (see above). In addition, it is the answer to the trash problem on closely-spaced rows and on loose ground such as muck. Two regular 26-inch elevators run side by side. Shovel is extra strong and runs complete width of digger. There is no place for trash to catch and choke the center of digger. Another new feature is land roller which firms ground to keep potatoes on surface for easier picking.

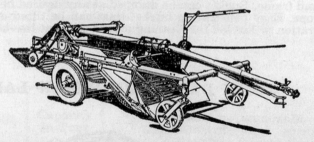

ANGLE-BED POTATO DIGGERS

John Deere Angle-Bed Diggers are "old favorites" for the way they handle tough digging conditions. Available in one- and two-row sizes with wide variety of equipment to meet any special needs. Rear rack is easily convertible from continuous elevator to extension elevator to meet varying digging conditions.

55

Another inside page from the *Farmer's Pocket Ledger* on Page 34.

CALCIUM CHLORIDE FOR RUBBER TIRES

From the following tables, it is easy to figure the exact amount of calcium chloride to be added to water for the more popular sizes of tractor tires. In mixing, do not attempt to pour water onto the calcium chloride as it will cause caking and require a much longer time for the solution to become thoroughly mixed. Instead, pour the calcium chloride into the water. After mixing, allow solution to cool. Keep solution away from ignition, wiring, and clothes.

CONVENTIONAL TRACTOR TIRES

	Water Only		Safe to 20° Below Zero			Safe to 40° Below Zero		
	Lbs.	Gals.	Use This Amount CACL2 Lbs.	Gallons of Water to Use	Total Weight in Tire Lbs.	Use This Amount CACL2 Lbs.	Gallons of Water to Use	Total Weight in Tire Lbs.
4.00 x 15	17	2.04	3.9	2.0	19.3	6.2	1.7	21
5.00 x 15	24	2.88	5.5	2.6	27.1	8.7	2.5	29
5.50 x 16	36	4.33	8.2	4.0	41.5	13.0	3.7	43
6.00 x 12	33	4.00	7.6	3.7	38.0	12.1	3.4	40
6.00 x 16	48	5.76	10.9	5.3	55.0	17.4	4.9	58
6.00 x 22	65	7.8	14.8	7.2	74.0	23.6	6.6	78
6.50 x 16	58	6.95	13.2	6.4	66.0	21.0	5.9	70
7.50 x 10	40	4.8	9.1	4.4	45.7	14.5	4.1	48
7.50 x 16	75	9.0	17.1	8.3	86.1	27.2	7.7	91
7.50 x 18	80	9.6	18.2	8.8	91.4	29.0	8.2	97
7.50 x 22	95	11.4	21.7	10.4	108.0	34.4	9.7	115
7.50 x 24	110	13.2	25.1	12.1	126.0	39.9	11.2	133
7.50 x 36	150	18.0	34.2	16.5	171.0	54.4	15.3	182
7.50 x 40	165	19.8	37.6	18.2	189.0	59.8	16.8	200
8.25 x 36	170	20.4	38.8	18.7	195.0	61.6	17.3	206
8.25 x 40	200	24.0	45.6	22.0	228.0	72.5	20.4	242
9.00 x 10	54	6.5	12.3	5.9	61.5	19.5	5.5	65
9.00 x 24	150	18.0	34.2	16.5	171.0	54.4	15.3	182
9.00 x 28	170	20.4	38.8	18.7	195.0	61.6	17.3	206
9.00 x 36	220	26.4	50.2	24.2	253.0	79.7	22.4	266
9.00 x 40	240	28.8	54.7	26.4	275.0	87.0	24.5	291
10.00 x 28	260	31.2	59.3	28.6	296.0	94.2	26.5	314
10.00 x 36	325	39.0	74.1	35.8	372.0	117.8	33.2	394
10.00 x 44	375	45.0	85.4	41.3	430.0	135.6	38.2	454
11.25 x 24	250	30.0	56.9	27.5	285.0	90.6	25.5	303
11.25 x 28	280	33.6	63.8	30.8	319.0	101.4	28.6	339
11.25 x 36	360	43.3	82.1	39.6	410.0	130.3	35.8	436
11.25 x 42	410	49.3	93.4	45.2	467.0	148.4	41.9	497
12.75 x 24	340	40.8	77.5	37.4	389.0	123.2	34.8	413
12.75 x 28	380	45.7	86.6	41.8	434.0	137.6	38.8	461
12.75 x 32	420	50.4	95.8	46.2	481.0	152.1	42.8	508
13.50 x 24	380	45.7	86.6	41.8	434.0	137.6	38.8	461
13.50 x 28	420	50.4	95.8	46.2	481.0	152.1	42.8	508
13.50 x 32	460	55.2	105.0	50.6	527.0	166.6	46.9	557

WIDE BASE TRACTOR TIRES

	Lbs.	Gals.	CACL2 Lbs.	Water	Total Wt.	CACL2 Lbs.	Water	Total Wt.
7-32	90	10.8	20.5	9.9	103.0	32.6	9.2	109
7-40	135	16.2	30.8	14.8	154.0	48.9	13.8	163
8-24	100	12.0	22.8	11.0	114.0	36.2	10.2	121
8-32	130	15.6	29.6	14.3	148.0	47.0	13.3	157
8-38	145	17.4	33.0	15.9	165.0	52.5	14.8	175
9-24	130	15.6	29.6	14.3	148.0	47.0	13.3	157
9-32	170	20.4	38.7	18.7	194.0	61.5	17.4	206
9-38	205	24.6	45.8	22.5	234.0	74.2	20.9	248
10-28	200	24.0	45.6	22.0	228.0	72.5	20.4	242
10-38	260	31.2	59.3	28.6	298.0	94.2	26.5	315
11-26	260	31.2	59.3	28.6	298.0	94.2	26.5	315
11-38	350	42.0	79.8	38.5	401.0	126.8	35.9	424
12-26	300	36.0	68.4	33.0	342.0	108.6	30.6	363
12-38	460	55.2	104.9	50.6	525.0	166.5	46.9	556
13-26	345	41.4	78.5	37.9	395.0	124.9	35.2	418
13-30	405	48.6	92.1	44.6	465.0	146.4	41.2	490
14-30	510	61.1	106.1	56.0	580.0	184.6	52.0	615

7

JOHN DEERE TRUSS-FRAME TRACTOR PLOWS

Truss-Frame design is a feature of all John Deere Moldboard Plows from the single bottom, integral type to the big capacity, five-bottom, heavy-duty No. 77.

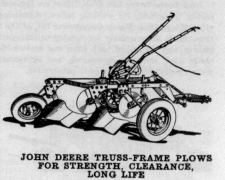

Truss-Frame design, introduced originally in the heavy-duty John Deere Plows built for California's toughest plowing jobs, is field-proved in every plowing condition.

JOHN DEERE TRUSS-FRAME PLOWS FOR STRENGTH, CLEARANCE, LONG LIFE

Strength and clearance are two outstanding features of Truss-Frame Plows. Truss-Frame construction binds all parts into one husky, shock-resisting unit. Shocks of hard work are absorbed by the entire plow rather than by a single bottom. By eliminating the conventional curved beams, greater throat clearance is gained; bottoms are spaced fore-and-aft for maximum clearance; share-point to frame clearance is greater—independent jointers and eighteen-inch coulters, essential in clean plowing where corn borers are a menace, may be used with all John Deere Truss-Frame Plows. All are available with equipment for hydraulic power control.

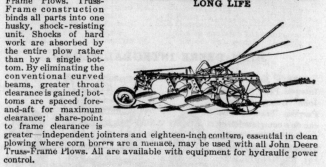

JOHN DEERE TRACTOR DISK PLOWS

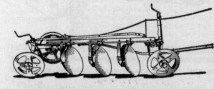

John Deere builds a full line of disk plows with features that offer all 'round satisfaction and full value. The angle steel frame bars with disk standards bolted between, make a rigid, sturdy unit. Roller bearing disk bearings mean lighter draft, longer life. *Heat-treated* steel disks last longer. Width of cut changed by simply angling the frame.

In John Deere Disk Plows ease of correct and lasting adjustment and ability to hold to their work in difficult soil conditions are combined with the strength and clearance you need for lasting satisfaction on the job.

In addition to the full line of drawn disk plows, integral disk plows in two-disk size are built for John Deere General-Purpose Tractors.

11

A couple of additional pages of the *Farmer's Pocket Ledger* on Page 34.

These two little pocket notebooks from 1939 were sent to me by a friend in Oregon, Tony Zazweta, in some of our fishing lure trading deals. My preference is for the Benson, at left, as it shows whiteface sheep similar to the ones we raise, $5-$15 each.

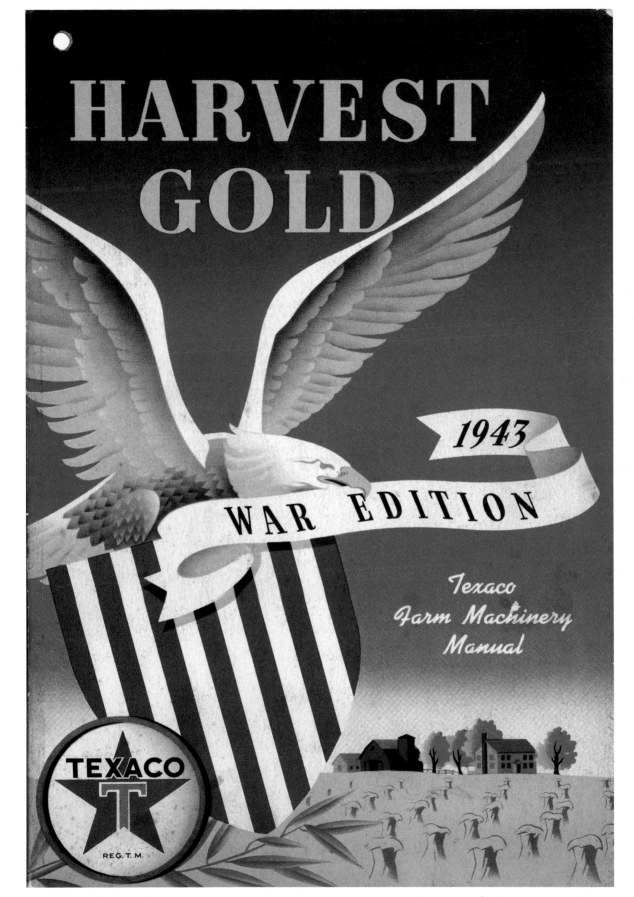

This *Harvest Gold* booklet from 1943 shows the patriotism of the farm community during the war era, **$8**. The contents include a complete listing of all farm tractors and machinery companies in business in 1943 and all major equipment made, as it was needed for the lubrication guide furnished by Texaco. Also, the booklet has many fine line drawings of equipment and photos of the types of oil containers from the era. I purchased three of these Texaco guides from 1941, 1943 and 1947 and paid from $8 to $27.50 for them, all in excellent to mint condition. Again, not only are they colorful in and of themselves, but the data inside is worth a lot to the collector as well.

A Texaco farm manual, *Harvest Gold*, 1947, mint condition, **$17.50**. This example is similar to the one shown from 1943 and again shows many tractors, trucks, oil cans, and data for equipment from 1947. *Lewis Collection*.

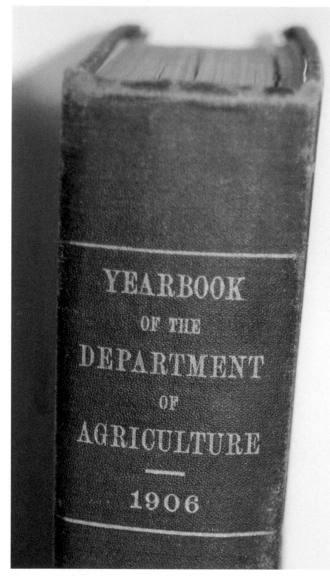

Yearbook of the Department of Agriculture, 1906, **$5**. This was printed in 1907 and followed predecessor publications detailing news and new developments in agriculture in America. A review of the table of contents shows you can learn about everything from modern game wardens to dairy farming. Eventually, the *Yearbook of Agriculture* became dedicated to one topic per year. These are readily available and an excellent source of data on farming and oftentimes on what have become farm collectibles today. My wife purchased this as a gift for me. *Lewis Collection*.

A Grand Rapids National Bank booklet on Michigan laws for farmers, 1922, **$20-$30**.

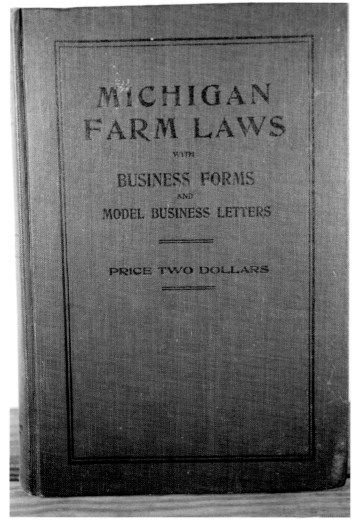

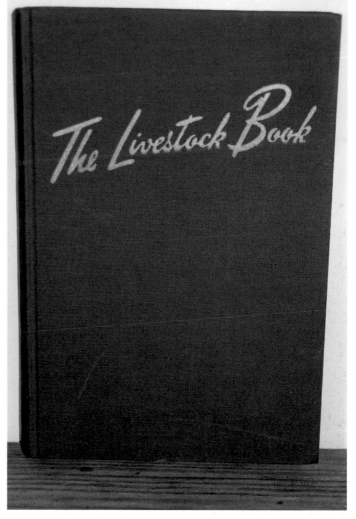

A 1908 first edition on *Michigan Farm Laws*. As a lawyer/farmer, I find this book of special interest and purchased it years ago for a few dollars at an antiques store, **$20-$30**. *Lewis Collection*.

The Livestock Book, 1952, **$35+**. This is a nice book for the farm collector and the inside page also has a personal note from John McKinney, one of the two co-authors, which is a nice touch. *Lewis Collection*.

Two printer's blocks of a Jersey cow, used in advertising layouts for DeLaval and other companies. The large one is about 3 inches and the small one a mere 1 inch; **$15-$25 each**. These have become quite collectible and if it is a recognized "brand," it's even more valuable. I have sold many printer's blocks for $25 to more than $100, if larger and rare.

A printer's block, for King & Sons, Inc. "K-Brand" Seeds, **$35+**. This nice block has a mitten of the Lower Peninsula of Michigan, the large brand Kings and a saying that K-Brand Seeds Are Reliable, and the address of Battle Creek, Mich. This is a great farm collectible with crossover interest, such as Kellogg's collectors, due to the location of Battle Creek.

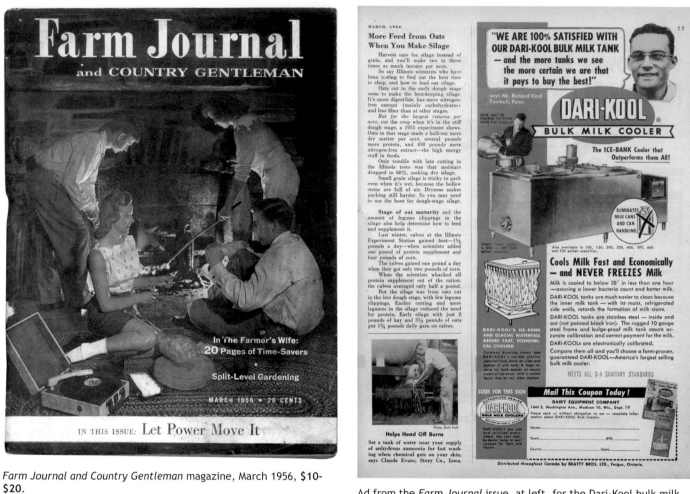

Farm Journal and Country Gentleman magazine, March 1956, $10-$20.

Ad from the *Farm Journal* issue, at left, for the Dari-Kool bulk milk cooler.

A 1947 Fish & Game Law book from New York State, $10+.

A Farmall tractor printer's block in great condition, $40+.

now... drive the tractor triumph of our time ...

The miracle from Massey-Harris

fabulous **MH 50** with *hydramic power*

Row Crop
Twin Front

4 wheel styles ... all designed
for front-mounted cultivation

Row Crop
High Arch

Built to trigger a new tractor age

Hydramic Power! Miracle design! The one system that puts power where you want it...to push, pull, lift, lower, adjust, operate. The miracle-system that pools total mechanical and hydraulic power into a single dynamic force ... instantly at your command to create traction as you need it. And only the Massey-Harris MH50 has it. Massey-Harris, Dept. C-220, Racine, Wis.

*Take the miracle demonstration drive ...
most unusual trial offer in tractor history*

FREE! Schedule an on-the-farm demonstration now. Call your Massey-Harris dealer today. For your promptness he has a special get-acquainted gift for you.

Row Crop
Utility

Row Crop
Single

Always keep your eye on **Massey-Harris**

This ad for the 1956 Massey-Harris MH50 tractor is also in the *Farm Journal* issue on Page 42.

Farm wives needed reading material, too. A *Woman's Day* magazine, February 1945, **$20.**

This 1936 laundry guide printed by the American Washing Machine Manufacturers' Association offers many laundering tips to farm wives and other housewives, **$10-$15.**

❧ Chapter 3 ❧

Farming in Advertising

This is likely one of the hottest areas of farm collectibles and should remain so, given past trends in collecting. This section includes the non-print areas of advertising: tins, signs, give-away items, pencils, pens, and anything else a company could plaster its name onto and get into the general public's view. It also includes many items that manufacturers supplied dealerships with for advertising their products. The most valuable of all of these items is likely the porcelain and tin signs made by the companies for dealers and users of the products. This is also an example of "crossover" demand and "general appearance" demand in collecting. Some of these items I have also placed in other chapters to show particular advertising items.

Tin and porcelain (porcelain generally being older and more valuable) signs are in great demand by collectors in general due to their display value and great colors. My wife and I have collected dairy-related signs for years and there is nothing to spruce up a dull corner more than a colorful DeLaval or Surge sign. These signs have gone from being a mere $5 to $10 auction item to usually starting at $25 and going quickly on up to $100+ if in fine condition. Of course, as always, it is to a large degree brand driven. An obscure company will not usually bring the prices of a commonly known company in farming such as DeLaval, Surge or Deere.

Our favorite buy was an early artificial insemination sign with a Jersey bull illustration that we found on an old barn door at a garage sale. The man wanted to give it to us for free but we insisted he take something for it and finally we negotiated what we thought a fair price and the sign now hangs in our farm kitchen next to the phone.

It is often the finding of items that is more fun than the item itself. The ABS sign well illustrates this point. Value is important, but so is history. It is amazing the things you can find that are "advertising items": barometers, thermometers, tape measures, yard sticks, yard sticks as walking sticks, tin signs in every size and shape imaginable, pens, pencils, patches, hats, knives, can and bottle openers, glasses, kitchen containers, utensils, mirrors, tins, boxes, counter mats, banners, neon signs, calendars, display stands, display racks, salesman's samples, salesman's sample cases, toys, cast iron animals, chalkboards, tools, key chains and watch fobs.

The area of greatest concern to collectors of advertising items is the reproduction and manufacturing of fake items. Many signs have been recently reproduced and it is difficult to tell the reproductions from the originals. This shows the importance of provenance in antique finds. It is far safer to buy such advertising items at an auction with provenance than from an unknown dealer for this one reason. However, even some of the older reproductions—signs and tins reproduced from the 1960s-1980s—are already taking on a collectible nature of their own due to their beauty. But the fake signs and reproduced advertising items are an area of concern that you should know about in this field. This happens whenever a collectible attains a high value: there is always someone in the wings waiting to rip off the unsuspecting buyer! Just be aware of your source, buy from reputable dealers only, buy at a sale where you know the item is original, familiarize yourself with the reproductions on the market, and have fun looking.

Values in this area are from a few dollars to thousands. It would be easy to spend a few hundred dollars on just one or two good signs. A neon sign advertising a local tractor dealership could easily cost more than $1,000. Many small items such as tape measures and measuring cups command only a few dollars, but the bullet pencils given away by dealerships bring from $25 to $75 depending on brand name and location of the dealership. Other items such as display stands used for literature or small products come up for sale so infrequently it is hard to judge their market value; however, the guides given in Chapter 2 on paper collectibles apply to any advertising item, as well as concerning brand names and general appeal to other collectors. I have seen many an urban buyer, who did not have a clue what a milking machine was, let alone a DeLaval brand milker, go after a DeLaval sign just because of its black/yellow color pattern.

This rare and original ABS sign, made of heavy gauge metal, was found on the side of a barn. This sign is not mint condition, but it proudly hangs above our kitchen phone and shows a Jersey bull, $100-$200. *Lewis Collection.*

Items of greatest value in general appear to be those that can be easily displayed in your home. This includes any of the tin or porcelain signs that are smaller than 24 inches by 24 inches. The really large signs are much harder to find display space for in the home. Thermometers and barometers with advertising are also popular as they can still be used and displayed. Next in line would be the small items that can be placed on a shelf to be admired such as any one of the many tins shown in this chapter. An entire book could be written on just dairy-related collectibles (in fact, one has been and is available from Hoard's Dairyman) due to the collector interest in milk bottles, milk cans, cream cans, cream and butter crocks, butter cartons, crocks in general and dairy bottle caps. Most of these items are valued in general collecting books but they are all farm collectibles in every sense. Many of these items have a regional "value-added" to them bringing greater money within their own region than elsewhere. Of course, online sales have had an impact on this aspect but as to antique store and farm auction sales, local bottles will always bring a premium; also, the more colorful the bottle or butter carton, the more value in general.

An antique tin for Mammoth Peanuts is another food-related item with great collector appeal, $50-$75. *Lewis Collection.*

Values of some advertising items

Two crate-end labels, marked "Gay Johnny Fresh Vegetables," shows a Huck Finn-type boy and bucking bronco, vintage 1930s-40s, 5" x 7". Both labels in mint condition (see similar examples in this chapter)... $10

USDA metal sign, from the Federal Crop Insurance Corporation, simple white background with a green leaf design, very good to excellent condition, 14" x 20". This seems a bargain to me, but you wonder about the provenance of the sign, as no details were given $7

A tin sign, has the word "Celery" on both sides, home-made by the farmer selling it, about 16" long $22.50

An ashtray advertising a dairy bar and café in Thorp, Wis., $10. This is another crossover collectible increasing its value a little, due to detailed advertising and demand by tobacco collectors as well. *Lewis Collection.*

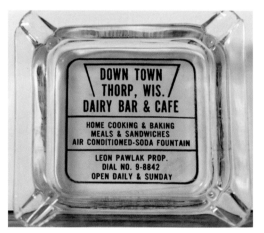

Cast elephants for Crane Co., dated 1905; one is aluminum and two are heavier material. Elephants were often used to advertise stoves and even roofing, shown in the photo at left. Again, this is a great crossover collectible for stoves, household items and elephants. My wife collects small elephants made of cast material and has about 30; $50+ for any advertising elephant.

Elephant ashtray and matchbook holder in cast, Hyatt Jumbo Roofing. This great advertising item would attract collectors from many fields, $100+.

Harris Milling Co. flour bags from the 1950s, **$5-$10 each**. My wife found these bags at a local garage sale owned by a former Harris employee and they are well worth the 25 cents each she paid. *Lewis Collection.*

A Larro Egg Mash feedbag from a General Mills subsidiary in Detroit, $5-$25. Old feedbags make nice advertising items in a collection and this particular bag has the added bonus of being a General Mills subsidiary, increasing its demand due to collectors from two areas. Prices for bags such as this in excellent condition depend on quality, colors, graphics, and locale. *Art Smith Collection.*

A large Kellogg's Linseed Oil Meal bag in near mint condition, $15-$20. *Lewis Collection.*

Sealtest dairy recipe books from the 1940s-'50s, **$2-$5 each**. These are not of great value, but make an interesting addition to dairy collectibles. *Lewis Collection.*

A Badger Brand Red Clover bag with nice graphics, **$10+.** This is one of a number of bags found in an old barn when we purchased our Wisconsin farm in 1997. Most were eaten by mice, but not this fine example. *Lewis Collection.*

Eveready cat bank, plastic with a foil label battery for decoration, **$10.** This is a little too new for the book's timeline at 1981, but it still is a neat little collectible, as what farm does not have at least one cat?

Red Circle Coffee tin bank, **$35-$50.** Banks are great collectibles and this is an example of a kitchen tin turned into a bank by the company for advertising purposes.

DeLaval Year Book, 1949, **$25-$50.** This is an example of the common yearbooks published by many companies and distributed for free to rural route box holders. This one is not mint, as the cover is loose, but it is clean and of special value to us as it is from my hometown and from a classmate's grandfather's (and then father's) business. Also, note it was a John Deere dealership as well. Photos show the front cover, above, and back cover, below. *Lewis Collection.*

A Cities Services 10-gallon can likely used for kerosene is an unusual piece and in fine condition, **$50 to $100.** This item would also have crossover appeal with oil company collectors. *VanAlstine Collection.*

Kent Feeds knit cap from the 1980s, **$5.** This is not an antique, but will gain in value over the years. *Lewis Collection.*

A full Maytag Multi-Motor Oil can in very good condition makes a nice addition to any collection, **$75+**. *Art Smith Collection.*

Hoppe's Oil can, **$40-$75**. This could be in Chapter 10 instead, but I have shown it here as an example of a lead-top can. Most oil cans had lead tops up until the post-war era, but some cans had switched to a plastic top on a lead spout even sooner. But a lead spout with a lead top is an earlier can. Values on oil cans vary by brand and age from a low of about $25 to a high of about $500 for any of the pre-1950s cans. See my book, *Collecting Antique Bird Decoys and Duck Calls*, published by Krause Publications, for a complete history of similar items and photos of many oil cans. *Lewis Collection.*

This John Deere oil can is another rare item, **$50+**. *Art Smith Collection.*

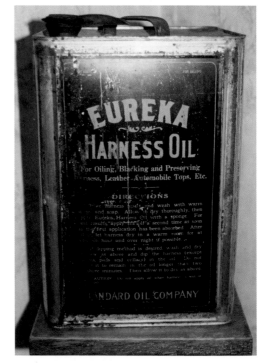

Mobiloil can, **$20**. This was purchased for a few dollars in an antiques store and it has a missing top, but is still worth the money paid for it due to its nice condition and large size. I use it as a little waste can. Again, since my dad was a Mobil dealer, this is a special addition for me. *Lewis Collection.*

A full can of Liquid Gloss furniture polish by Standard Oil Company, with a graphic of a properly dressed Victorian lady using the gloss on fine furniture, **$200**. Art Smith found this very rare can for little money at a farm auction and to also find it full is unusual. *Art Smith Collection.*

A Eureka Harness Oil can made by Standard Oil, **$300**. This is one of our favorite collectibles and is a very rare piece, as it came in its original wooden shipping crate. It is in nice shape and attractive for display purposes. We paid $100 for this in 1995 and would not sell it for $300 today. Since writing the first edition, we have added a second can but without the wooden crate.

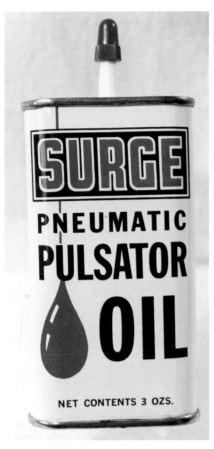

Surge oil can, mint condition, **$15-$25**. This is a newer can, post-1950, as you can tell from the plastic spout. If you milk cows, you need a little oil on the milking machine leathers and this can provided the contents for that purpose. *Lewis Collection.*

Mecca Ointment can, **$10-$15**. Health products for humans and animals alike are nice additions to your collection. *Lewis Collection.*

This hat rack was produced by MoorMan's in the image of its trademarked cow, **$25**. *Lewis Collection.*

MoorMan's Feed egg basket, **$30**. This was once furnished to loyal MoorMan's users for their egg operations and we had a few dozen similar ones to gather and wash our eggs at one time. The rubber coating on the basket protected the eggs in both gathering and placing in the automatic washers we used in the 1950s and 1960s. I traded a copy of the first edition of this book for this egg basket for my wife. *Lewis Collection.*

Butter cartons like the three shown here are a fine addition to any farm collection but fit in especially nice with dairy collectibles, **$20 each**. One thing to do is try to find your favorite cow type (Jersey, etc.) or a local dairy to add to your collection. *Lewis Collection.*

A Smith-Douglass chalkboard-pegboard combination advertising sign, **$200+**. This is a unique piece bought at a dissolution auction for a local grain mill in Ladysmith, Wis. This piece still has the cow drawing on it done by a local schoolgirl as she waited in the warm grain mill office for the bus to come during a cold Wisconsin winter morning. I have left the sign in its original condition because I think it's interesting.

A one-pint ice cream carton for Fair Oaks Dairy from Whitehall, Wis., **$10.**

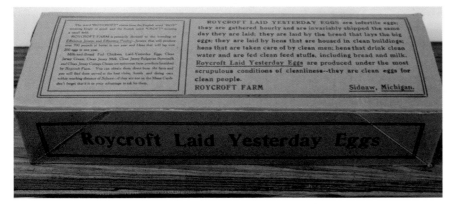

This Roycroft eggs carton is a gift from a good friend and in mint condition, **$20+.** Roycroft Farm is from Sidnaw, Mich., and Sidnaw was on the rail line to Minneapolis and at one time produced thousands of eggs for the city markets in Minnesota, Wisconsin and Michigan. *Lewis Collection.*

Gibas' Dairy carton, shown folded, in mint condition, **$10.** Many collectors have been seeking out bottles for years, but even cartons such as this are a nice addition of more recent packaging. *Lewis Collection.*

DeLaval Oil can, **$50.** DeLaval dairy collectibles have many followers and although not in perfect condition, this can is still a nice enough early example of DeLaval Oil. *Art Smith Collection.*

Master Mix Feed clock, **$25+.** I sold a similar clock at an auction for $35. *Art Smith Collection.*

Pepsi portable cooler, **$100+** even in this poorer condition; mint condition would be close to $500 easily. Collectibles of soda, or pop, as we say in Michigan, are always hot and this cooler is no exception. It is one of many farm and related collectibles on display at Bancroft Farms feed and garden store in Evart, Mich.

Three corn planters, **$30-$40 each**. These are among the items that fall into two or more categories of this book, as they are all clearly small farm implements, but due to the pristine nature of the labels on them all, they could also be kept by someone due to the advertising.

Butter or cream cheese crock, Lansing Dairy Co. "Sunbeam Products," **$50**. This is a great example of a local dairy collectible and was purchased at a farm auction years ago. *Lewis Collection*.

This Richelieu Mince Meat crock is another example of food advertising, **$10**. *Lewis Collection*.

Various crate-end labels still on the crates. One label is older and two are a bit newer to show how these have evolved but are still being used by some producers. Also shown is a local cherry box, below. Although you can buy pristine end labels online, I find the ones on crates of greater interest due to the history of it actually being used and the known provenance of the item, $10-$20 each. *Nerbonne Collection.*

Colorful crate end labels like this one for Polar Bird Brand are becoming more popular with collectors, $5-$15.

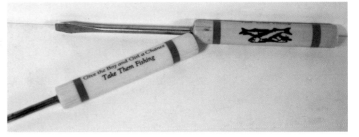

A small pocket diary produced by Weber Wagon Co. of Chicago, $40. My wife's maiden name is Weber, so this is especially fun for us.

Two small screwdrivers from my fishing lure collectibles, $5-$25. These are shown as examples of the types of items also given away by farm implement dealerships. These, along with small tape measures, yard sticks, and rulers, comprise an interesting area of collectibles and bring anywhere from $5 to $25 on most occasions. Again, the brand loyalty and geographical area are important considerations in pricing. Both of the screwdrivers shown are from a bait shop in South Bend, Ind., making them interesting, as it was also the home of a major bait company.

Early Michigan license plates from the 1930s, $50-$75. *Nerbonne Collection.*

An older Ford tractor or truck emblem is a nice addition for a Ford collector, $10. *Lewis Collection.*

A 1938 Michigan license plate, $50, surrounded by two reproduction gasoline signs for Shell and Mobilgas, $20-$25 **each.**

A Jersey paperweight from the Jersey association in Canada, $10-$20. This is a breed loyalty item and was purchased at an antiques store a few years ago. *Lewis Collection.*

A Wayne feed company patch for a jacket or hat, $5. *Lewis Collection.*

Metal postcard advertising the F. Braastad & Company Merchandise store in Ishpeming, Mich., from the turn of the century, $10.

Spear Head plug tobacco pouch, $15-$20. Our tobacco-raising farmers will especially appreciate items such as this, which were given away by the company at one time. This nice old leather pouch was found in a Wisconsin antiques store a few years back. *Lewis Collection.*

Reproduction sign, DeLaval, showing many of the early cream separator advertisements, $20. *Lewis Collection.*

A reproduction tin for Hershey's, $5-$10. This is a necessity for any dairy collection and is not old, but attractive.

Advertising thermometers: Wisconsin Dairies, left, $10; and Dr. LeGear Animal Health Products, $5. The dairy example is in excellent shape, but the animal health example is well worn; both work. *Lewis Collection.*

Various rubber repair kits, shown above and below, **$15-$20**. This is another related advertising collectible found in every farmer's tool crib. Flat tires and hay wagons just seem to go together and when I was younger it was my job to put on the patches and fix the tires. Bicycles also seemed to have flat tires often. These little kits come in a variety of colors and brands and display nicely in a corner of a cabinet. These are all in excellent shape and still have original contents. *Lewis Collection.*

Older tin sign, Nu Icy pop, **$65**. This was purchased at auction four years ago for $35 each (for two of them) and one was sold online two years ago for almost double that. *Lewis Collection.*

Various signs for tractors and implements found at a local dealership are now being collected by the dealership. Shown above is a newer Ritchie waterer sign; bottom left is an older classic red and yellow New Holland sign, and at bottom right is the current New Holland sign in comparison. The older signs are around $100. A very rare neon yellow and red Minneapolis-Moline sign, shown still in its original storage crate in the bottom left photo, is valued at well over $1,000.

This tin butter sign and others like it are much harder to find and command a bit more money than equipment signs, **$100+**. *Lewis Collection.*

The Allis-Chalmers porcelain sign is desirable and easily valued at **$50 to $100**, even in this smaller size.

Various DeLaval and Surge dairy equipment tin signs, **$50-$150 each**. *Lewis Collection.*

A large-sized Shell porcelain sign, **$400+**. This sign is a great example of why you should attend "live auctions" when given an opportunity because it was bought at a dissolution sale of a large hardware wholesaler for only $75, a fraction of its real value. *Art Smith Collection.*

This Moore's Wonderful Rat Destroyer sign is clearly a reproduction, but it's interesting nonetheless, **$20**. *Art Smith Collection.*

I found this half of a Goodyear Tire tin sign at a garage sale and it's only worth a few dollars, but it is still interesting and if intact would be worth $100. *Lewis Collection*.

A Bell System sign, made of porcelain, $75. *Art Smith Collection*.

Dealership sign, Northrup King Dealer, $100+. I bought this sign at a dissolution auction for a local grain mill in Ladysmith, Wis. and although it would not be worth as much elsewhere, it was in high demand by the local farmers due to their association with the mill. *Lewis Collection*.

Another pop-related collectible is this "Open-Closed" wax board sign for Squirt from the 1950s-60s, $25. *Lewis Collection*.

Farm Bureau Member heavy sign, showing Michigan's Upper and Lower peninsulas, has some corrosion but is still a fine addition to farm collectibles, **$50**. *Art Smith Collection.*

A Farm Bureau member paper sign from 1934, **$50**. This was a real steal purchased for only a few dollars and has higher value, even with the water stains, due to its age and fragility. *VanAlstine Collection.*

This Dekalb sign is a newer version of the signs that seed growers place in the field or on the farmstead to show company loyalty, **$25+**. It is made of a Styrofoam-type material and will not weather for dozens of years as tin signs do. This is a gift from a former student and makes a nice addition, especially for someone who won two Dekalb corn-growing awards as I did (see the pins in Chapter 11). *Lewis Collection.*

Pressed board sign, Fred's Tack Repair, **$10**. Even a simple tack shop sign is of some value, as it is one of a kind. *Art Smith Collection.*

An old butter and egg price sign hanging in the butcher shop and showing the day's prices on the two items, **$40-$50**. This is another nice butter item and comes from an antiques store in Wisconsin. I believe it to be an original; however, I also believe these have been reproduced. *Lewis Collection.*

Pet Milk advertising tin sign, **$35-$50**. This is a reproduction (painted on rear side), but is a nice example of a 1921 sign produced by Pet. It is likely about 25 years old, as we have had it for some time but there is no printer information on the sign, other than the original 1921 data. *Lewis Collection.*

Original Keen Kutter Tools tin sign backed with material, **$75+**. *Lewis Collection.*

Grace Agricultural Products sign from the 1950s, made of very heavy metal, **$75+**. *Lewis Collection.*

Loyal Farm Equipment sign, very thin tin, **$25-$40**. This sign, at the edge of our era, was purchased at auction in 1998 for $25. The company went into business in 1956 and this is a fine example of a tin sign similar to the ones by Surge and DeLaval from the 1950s. *Lewis Collection.*

Insect-repellent containers: Lollacapop, **$125+**; Skeeto-Pads (not shown), **$25-$40**. Insects are a constant bane to both farmers and anglers (and hunters to a degree). The Wood's Improved Lollacapop is very rare, in high demand by fishing lure collectors, and expensive.

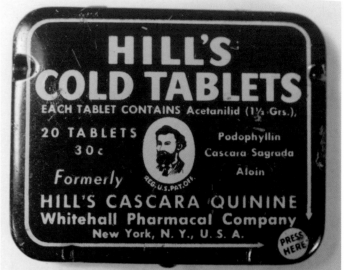

Various health-related tins, **$5-$100+**. Home and animal health created a number of great advertising tins and some, such as Rawleigh's Salve, could be used for both. These tins have many audiences and are true "cross-over" collectibles, which drives up prices. Condition is most important as well and most of these would grade excellent, demanding a premium. Tin values seem to vary greatly from one region of the country to another and of course are cheapest in a "box-lot" at a farm auction. They are fun to look for, colorful, and add to another collection greatly.

Typewriter tins, $5-$15. Typewriter tins are a fun and inexpensive collectible and the great Art Deco example in the center would command at least $30 if in mint condition, but it has a hole in it. *Lewis Collection.*

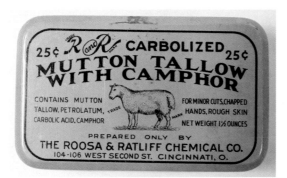

Mutton Tallow with Camphor for bites, sunburn, etc., R and R (Roosa & Ratliff Chemical Co.), has a great sheep illustration showing a longer undocked tail, $40-$75.

Two Dr. David Roberts Udder Balm tins; the small one is still full. The only difference noted is that the small one has "Contains Lanolin or Wool Fat" on the lid and the large one does not, $20+ each.

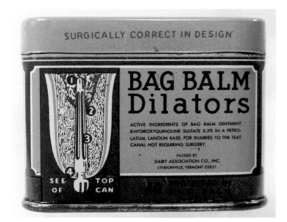

Tin of dilators, Bag Balm brand, a bit newer, $5-$10.

O-H cow salve tin, $40-$75. Animal health is important to anyone on a farm and ointments for cows seem to be the most prevalent, followed by items for horses. This cow salve with a great tin is not perfect, but it's valuable, as it is rare and early. O-H stands for Our Husbands and is a great play on words on animal husbandry.

Bickmore Gall Salve for horses and cattle, free sample tin. This tin is more valuable, as it is an odd size, a free sample, and the front graphics are superb and near perfect with only slight edge wear on the tin, $25-$40.

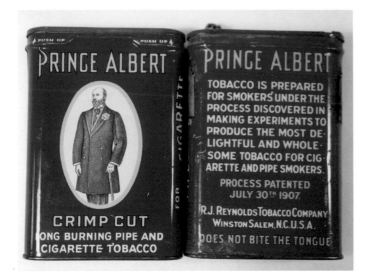

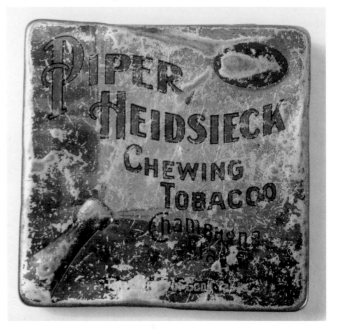

Prince Albert tobacco tins, **$10-$30 each.** Farmers raise tobacco and tobacco items are one of the largest of all crossover collectibles, especially tins. I have collected these tins for years and have a number of them. The first example is also a standard childhood joke: "Do you have Prince Albert in a can?"

Piper Heidsieck tin, rare. This is in rougher shape, but even in this condition, the tin is pricey, **$35+.**

Velvet Tobacco tin, fairly common just like Prince Albert, **$10-$30.**

Dutch Masters Foil Cigar tin and details, **$25+.**

Eisenlohr's Cinco Cigars tin and side detail, **$25+.**

Half and Half tins collapse as tobacco is used, as shown at right, **$25+ each.**

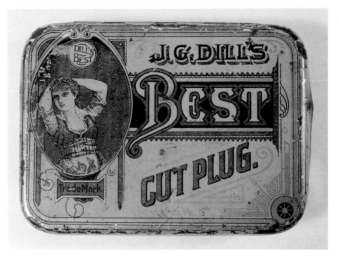

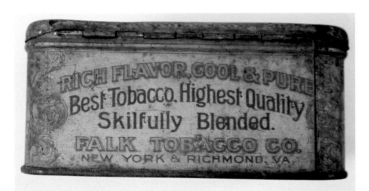

Edgeworth brand tins, $20 for smallest tins to $100+ for star-topped tin. These are the pride of my collection, as turquoise is a favorite color and Edgeworth tins are far less common than many others. The star-topped tin is very rare and the Junior tin is not common, either. The most common is the small rectangular tin. These would all be considered uncommon for tobacco tins, however, compared to Half and Half, Prince Albert and Velvet.

Dill's Best Cut Plug tin is similar to Edgeworth tins in design, $25+.

Falk Tobacco tin. This is uncommon, but it is in poor condition and rough on top, $10.

Uncommon Traveler Cigar canister, $40+.

Maryland Club small tin box for pipe mixture. This was my first tobacco tin ever purchased and it is far from perfect condition, but it is less common than many shown, $25+.

Bugler cigarette case tin with classic World War I "Doughboy" symbol. This is fairly common, but is clean and has a nice design, $20+.

Union Leader Redi Cut tins, older and newer examples. This brand is more common and similar to Prince Albert, but look for variations in tin designs, such as shown here, **$10-$30 each**.

Target Cigarette case with a great bull's-eye symbol. This is a specific crossover with archery and hunting collectibles, **$30+**.

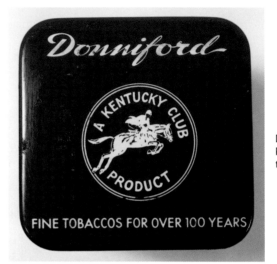

Donniford Pipe Blend tin, **$10-$20**.

Revelation Smoking Mixture pipe blend tin, small trial size, dented. This is a nice series of tins, with rich colors of cream and red and it's fairly uncommon to find the trial size; **$25+** if in excellent condition.

"O-So Beverages" thermometer, **$100-$200**. O-So is my favorite pop from childhood and collectibles of pop, soda or soda pop, depending on locale in the country, are quite popular and can bring thousands of dollars if the piece is rare. I was once fortunate enough to find some rare tin Pepsi signs from the Depression era that each brought more than $1,000 when sold. This is unusual, but people need to realize that some advertising items are some of the most valuable items in many fields of collecting because they display well, are colorful, and, if rare, are of even greater value. *Lewis Collection.*

Lucky Strike tin in mint condition. This was purchased in 1997 or 1998 for $25 and has since increased in value, **$40+**.

This unique fertilizer thermometer is an older item and many antiques dealers wanted it, too, **$240**.

❧ Chapter 4 ❧

Small-Scale Farming and Children's Recreation

This chapter includes the development of farm toys and related items designed for children that have now become collectible. Of course, there are many books already out on toys and even farm toys; however, this chapter will attempt to at least introduce you to the importance of farm toys and related children's items in the field of farm collectibles.

Items which immediately come to mind include: coaster wagons, sleds, farm toys to be ridden, farm animal toys, Milky the Cow, early Fisher-Price farm sets, the Marx farm sets, Ertl tractors and all of the predecessors, Auburn tractors and trucks, Lionel farm-related train cars and accessories (my favorite item was the cattle unloader and stock cars), lunch boxes, cap guns and BB guns, "small scale" tools and tool sets, "small scale" household items, and anything else to occupy the time of a child on the farm.

This chapter is far more selective than others—I have simply illustrated some items that strike me as being farm related. It is recommended that you consult any of the toy books or toy tractor books on the market for a detailed analysis of these fields, but it is hoped that this section reminds you to be on the lookout for these items in your quest to find farm collectibles.

Some good pricing guides include: *Standard Catalog of Farm Toys*, 2nd edition, Krause Publications, 2004; *Dick's Farm Toy Price Guide + Check List* available from http://www.bioptik.com/dicksdesigns and other sources; *International Directory of Model Farm Tractors* by Raymond E. Crilley Sr. and Charles E. Burkholder, published by Schiffer Publishing, 1985—this is somewhat dated, but it's inclusive in its treatment and is a massive work with wonderful photos of toy tractors up through the mid-1980s; and *Toy Farm Tractors*, by Bill Vosler and Andy Kraushaar, published by Voyageur Press, Stillwater, Minn., 1998.

Additional online resources include http://www.toytractortimes.com and http://www.toytractorshows.com for both toy tractor and real tractor history.

One of my all time favorite items, though, of recent 1970s vintage, is "Milky the Cow." Actually, there was a similar cow toy in the 1950s that I recall but do not know the manufacturer. I purchased Milky in the mid-1970s for my children and the toy cow was a marvel that actually gave milk after water and milky-colored tablets were inserted into it. This cow was akin to the crying and wetting dolls, etc.—toys that actually did what the real thing did. One of these cows in its original box would easily garner double its sale price of a few years ago, if not more.

Coaster wagons and sleds are two popular items with all collectors that have a special place in the heart of a farm kid. The coaster wagon allowed us to assist our parents in gardening chores or hauling products like eggs, milk and cream, into the home from the barn.

On our farm, the wagon was a tool and a toy. I would have fun playing with it but also used it to help out. The day the coaster wagon was under the Christmas tree or wrapped as a birthday present with a single bow on the handle is a day well burned into every farm kid's memory. The same is true with the sled, or sleigh as originally called: the first Flexible-Flyer is well remembered by all of us for the joy it would bring in the winter on the local farm hills. But it also served to haul that bale of hay to our pony in the wintertime while doing our own personal chores.

Today, many of these items are purchased to hang in urban lofts, apartments and homes for decoration, or they adorn the walls of a local restaurant. However, you can often find a nice wagon or sled for $25 to $50 at farm auctions or even some antiques stores.

We found a coaster wagon left behind in the dairy barn of our farm when we purchased it five years ago. It had been used to cart things around while doing chores and remained with the farm. It is a good demonstration of the functional use of some "toys."

This die-cast John Deere Model A and driver from about 1952 is in pristine condition, $300-$500. *Art Smith Collection.*

The tractors designed for little folks to peddle instead of plow with are some of the most desirable of all farm collectibles originally made for children. Some of these sell for hundreds of dollars and the nicer the condition and older the item, the more it will bring. I find these items to be similar to Lionel trains—we all wanted one even if our parents could not afford them in the 1950s. I wanted so badly to have a riding John Deere tractor as a kid but I never had one, so when my first son was born I made a trip to the local John Deere dealer to purchase a riding tractor and pull behind wagon. As soon as he could peddle he was placed upon it with pride in suburban Evansville, Indiana, to ride around the suburbs. At age four, we moved him and his tiny brother back to our dairy farm in Michigan and I still recall with great dismay the day one of my farm hands drove our brand new Allis-Chalmers 7000 over Justin's John Deere! It broke all of our hearts, especially Justin's. We replaced it with a riding Allis but it was never quite the same.

As an early parent, I always joked that we should all buy Fisher-Price stock since we all bought the company's

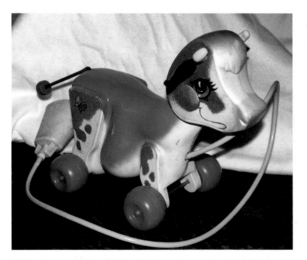

Fisher-Price cow pull toy, $20+. This cow was purchased by me new in 1974-75 for my first son and has been used by both boys and is now a favorite of our nieces and grandnieces. *Lewis Collection.*

toys. I should have listened to my own advice. The Fisher-Price barns and related farm toys have held their value and even increased, if they are the early versions. They are still making this line and have added many things to it but the original little barn in which you placed all the fence and animals has become quite collectible. In addition, the Marx farm sets are of great value, with the Roy Rogers' and Dale Evans' ranch being a closely related item of great value and interest. There were also many other barn and house kits available for farm children and these are all now collectible. In communities in which the Amish live, many handmade crafted barns and farm animal sets show up that are very collectible and desirable. At a recent estate sale, I purchased four cast iron farm animals that were either homemade or simply a small company's efforts to enter the toy market. To simply collect farm animals and barns and related items would be an endless quest.

Toy guns always had a special place for farm kids and the Red Ryder BB gun is famous to all baby boomers. It was a recreational item for the vast spaces of the farm and a pretend hunting weapon, too. Many an hour was filled with target practice sessions to hone hunting skills later needed. Also, many bad guys were disposed of with the Red Ryder and the holstered cap guns also important to the kids of the 1940s-1950s. A Gene Autry cast iron cap gun that cost a few dollars in the 1940s is now worth $300-$500. My former Roy Rogers double holster set would garner well over $100 if I still had it and it was for sale.

There were also special toys marketed to farm kids at a greater rate, such as toy steam engines. All kids liked these but farm kids knew these steam engines were still being used by some "old-timers" to run antique threshing machines and mills. My older brothers spent many hours running their little steam engine and hooking it up with belts to mini-mills and machines.

Also, in our formerly more unabashed sexist past, many marketed small-scale household appliances to farm girls. Tiny little sewing machines, kitchen appliances, and related items were designed to occupy a girl's time and teach her those all-important skills of a homemaker. The little cast iron stoves and utensils are quite valuable and collectible, as are the small Singer sewing machines from the 1950s.

This is just a "remembering" of some of the many items designed for children living on farms, and in many cases elsewhere. It is not by any means all-encompassing but it should serve its purpose to direct our attention to children on the farm when looking for collectibles. I have not even mentioned the special role of games and books for farm children, often far more important than for their urban counterparts due to the isolation of early farms. When your playmates are three miles away, you find games and books far more important to wile the time away than if the playmates live next door or in the same apartment complex.

Values of some small-scale farming items

Auburn Vinyl Farm Implement Set, early 1960s, complete with box, included a tractor, bulldozer, hay lifter, disc, mower, plow and wagon.................... **$115**

Slik Toy (Lansing, Iowa) die-cast aluminum manure spreader, 1960s, about 1/32nd scale. This item has worn edges but is complete and about a 7 on a 1-10 scale.. **$5**

Farm implement, 1/64th trailer hitch **$5.50**

Unidentified Allis-Chalmers-style combine **$6**

Arcade brand two-wheel farm trailer, with one bad wheel (cast iron), 1930s **$20.50**

"Antique 1900s wood barn by Marx." This item was an attempt to trick bidders, as mentioned in Chapter 1. It sold for one bid of $100 and was a good deal at that price, although it was not "antique," nor was it 100 years old as claimed. It was a nice heavy board barn with lithographed sides showing doors, windows, hay/straw, etc., and came with a number of the white plastic farm animals and plastic fence common in the late 1950s. There were also some Hubley implements and an Auburn tractor, really making this a bargain. The funny thing is a listing stressing the quality of the Marx items would have likely brought far more if targeted to the Marx toy collectors properly **$100**

A Hubley manure spreader, metal body, rubber tires, 7"l, did not sell because the hitch was broken...... **$10**

FFA John Deere Model A tractor, 1/16th scale, used to promote the Georgia FFA in 2002, made by Ertl and new in the box **$35**

A John Deere 4400 series Ertl tractor, well used and played with **$10.50**

FFA John Deere NASCAR die-cast car, 1/24th scale, new in the box... **$40**

A nice cast iron road scraper toy, found within the walls of a 1920s home. The seller thought it was a type of plow and listed it as a "farm toy." It appears it may have been an Arcade brand cast iron toy and is in very clean condition with only common wear marks on the paint **$52**

Red Ryder BB gun. This gun is famous to all of us 50 years old or better and sells at farm auctions for $40 to $80 in most cases, if it's in decent condition. The sleeper among the BB guns is the very rare double barrel made to look like a double-barrel shotgun. Also, the silver Daisy pistols from the 1950s are a bit rare ....**$40-$80**

Marx play sets. Too many sets exist to detail here but collectors should be aware of some of the very high values on ones such as the Alamo, Custer's Last Stand, the Roy Rogers/Dale Evans set, etc. Some of the Marx sets sell for thousands of dollars and most sell for hundreds of dollars if complete, new in the box, pristine, etc. Obviously, a set that is common and "play-worn" will only bring a few dollars in comparison. But some of the sets are very rare and I would caution you to do your homework before selling your parent's or grandparent's toys for a few dollars....................**$100+**

An early heavy die-cast Lindy airplane, **$150**. *Lewis Collection.*

Vintage bicycle, **$10-$25**. One of the main items a farm child enjoyed was his/her bike. Most of the older bicycles still sell for a reasonable price and you can often buy them in decent condition for under $25. Of course, some of the early models command far more if a collector is bidding on it. This one is now used for holding flowers. *VanAlstine Collection.*

A very old tricycle, **$50-$100**. *VanAlstine Collection.*

A Boy Scouts canteen holder, **$5-$10**. This is my brother-in-law's canteen and so it has a special family memory, but all Boy Scout items are collectible.

An original Carom board from Ludington, Mich. (also pictured is an old dartboard and a primitive checkerboard), **$35+**. As a Michigan youth, I can assure you that nearly every farm boy and girl owned a Carom board and spent hours playing with it. *VanAlstine Collection.*

This lunch box is a fine example of tin lithography and shows the romantic ideals of farm life around a barn. This is one of my personal favorite farm collectibles, **$50+**.

Various wooden blocks most likely made in Cedar Springs, Mich., in the early 1950s by Blockcraft, **$1-$5 each**. *Lewis Collection.*

A neat little tin lithography duck, West Germany, good condition, **$10-$25**. This is not a specific farm toy per se, but it still may have been found on a farm as a child's toy. *Lewis Collection.*

This doll dress hangs in our guest bedroom today, **$10+**.

These noisemakers sound like a sheep and cow; the sheep version is older, **$10-$20 each**. Young farm children needed to be entertained as well and these toys were sure hits. *Lewis Collection.*

Gene Autry die-cast toy gun and holster, **$400-$500**. This is my own and the value is according to antique shop owners specializing in toy guns.

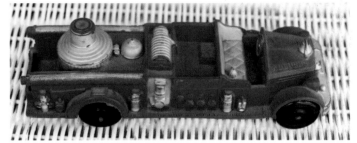

A Fisher-Price Auburn fire truck, above, and a musical "Tiny Teddy," below. The fire truck is near mint, **$50+**; Tiny Teddy is circa 1950 and in excellent condition, **$75+**. Some of the 1950s Fisher-Price characters can bring high values to the right buyers, as is true of the Auburn line.

A .45 caliber Hubley, **$50**.

Barnum's Animals Crackers sand pail, reproduction, **$5-$10**. This is a fun little item and the original of course would be worth quite a bit, but this is still a colorful addition to a child's toy or tin collection and is one of my wife's favorites.

Toy lamb, rubber, made by Rempel Enterprises of Akron, Ohio, **$10-$15**. *Lewis Collection.*

Various stamped steel farm animals, **$10 for the set**. These were a recent find at an estate sale and are unknown to me. They were likely made by a small tool and die operation or in a home shop and are nice folk examples of farm animals. You can build an entire collection on just farm animals from various companies and folk artists. *Lewis Collection.*

Antique and newer farm toy animals, made of pewter and cast iron, **$5-$10+ each**. The front four animals are very old and I played with the cast-iron dogs (right and middle center) as a child at my grandmother's and they were her childhood toys. The center front dog is a glass animal. The animal at left is an older painted Mexican folk cow. The rear row has two cast pewter cows from the 1960s and a newer cast-iron horse.

Older pairs of Nordic skis, for a child and a young teen, **$25-$75**. I have sold many of these skis for up to $75 per pair, depending on factors of condition and rarity. The small pair shown is worth the most due to condition, the presence of the bindings and the unique smaller size.

Old sleds, called sleighs in some parts of America, can easily fetch up to $75 for a Flexible Flyer in great shape. Also, the even older sleds that truly look like a sleigh with the upturned runners will bring even more. Many sleds are sold for only $25 or so at auctions but they are getting harder to find in great condition. At a recent visit to a nearby antiques store, the least expensive sled was $50 and they were priced up to $125 for the older wooden runner models. Small and large toboggans usually do well at auctions too, selling in the same range as sleds, **$25-$125**.

Model railroading toys: a Swift's Premium #6050 Lionel "bank car" from the 1950s-'60s and a tin cattle car from my personal Marx train set from the early 1950s, **$10-$50**. I also had many other cattle cars in my Lionel collection prior to selling it in the early 1990s. You could amass quite a toy train collection just collecting cars related to farming, cattle cars, liquid fertilizer cars, early logging cars, the cattle loading sets and sawmills from Lionel, and many other agricultural and natural resources-related train toys. Prices on toy trains range greatly and many excellent guides, such as *O'Brien's Collecting Toy Trains* and *Standard Catalog of Lionel Trains*, both by Krause Publications, need to be consulted for values. However, at farm sales it is still possible to pick up nice Marx and Lionel items for a few dollars on occasion. At our own 2002 farm sale, we sold some common items bringing decent prices, but the rare pieces brought "book prices" or better.

An exceptional example of colorful tin lithography is the Marx Sparkling Tank, which winds up and sparks while traveling across the floor, **$100+** as it has the box as well. *Lewis Collection.*

Toy train car, **$20**. This is not a farm collectible per se, but it's special if you raise barley or hops for the brewing industry. It was a personal gift more than 35 years ago from my dear German friend, Gerd Dallmann, and has been cherished since.

Arcade motorcycle and rider; the value of these motorcycles depends on the color and model, **$40-$120**. *Art Smith Collection.*

An Allis-Chalmers D21 tractor, early 1980s, **$75-$100**. *Jerry Paulsen Collection.*

A WD 45 Allis-Chalmers tractor made by Precision, **$400-$500**. This was purchased for $100 in the 1980s and is now worth a lot more according to all the trade data. *Jerry Paulsen Collection.*

A nice Farmall C tractor, **$50-$75**. *Jerry Paulsen Collection.*

A Case 600 tractor, **$100**. *Jerry Paulsen Collection.*

An earlier round baler toy, Ertl Allis-Chalmers, **$100**. *Jerry Paulsen Collection.*

Ertl Farmall BN tractor, **$20+**. A recent gift from a friend, this was purchased at a church bazaar for a few dollars, but is worth more; boxes for the tractors also increase the value, as mentioned earlier.

Various tractor models, **$50-$100** for most. According to Jerry Paulsen, most any Ertl or other collectible tractor is valued at $30 minimum and the ones with metal wheels are worth about double that at a minimum. The addition of the original box increases the value twofold again. I know this is true with fishing lure and sporting collectibles, too. Boxes are so often discarded that at times the boxes are worth more than the original items. *Jerry Paulsen Collection.*

A very collectible series of tractors is the FFA Collector Series made for different states and different FFA groups, **$60-$100**. The one shown is the third tractor issued by the Michigan FFA Foundation, issued in 1995 and sold only through Quality Farm and Fleet stores at that time. These toy tractors came in a cardboard box with a certificate of authenticity and markings to authenticate it. Due to the limited production of these tractors and the crossover interest generated by the FFA logo, they have really increased in value. Most sell from about $60, but I have sold many online for up to $100. Of course, the 8N is a very special little tractor in its own right and I know this would sell well. *Lewis Collection.*

John Deere Precision models, **$200+**. Prices start at about $200 and go up from there. *Jerry Paulsen Collection.*

An Auburn farm truck, **$20**. *Lewis Collection.*

Precision model 8N, **$120+**. This cost $120 new and the value keeps increasing. *Jerry Paulsen Collection.*

Small Hubley farm truck, mint condition, **$80**. *Art Smith Collection.*

These are some reproductions of older riding tractors made by Ertl. Farm dealerships are selling these reproductions, such as the Allis-Chalmers and Ford shown, for between $40-$125. The first two photos show two reproduction models and the third photo shows an older 1960s version made for Sears that is not in great shape, but was for sale for only $40. These are not collectible per se, but will likely become so due to limited production runs of the models. A conversation with the local dealer also raised the point that some individuals have reproduced the older riding tractors without disclosing the reproduction status to the buyer, so again: caveat emptor. According to one of my former tool and die clients, reproducing an early riding tractor using the modern CAD/CAM programming would be a simple matter. So, if spending a few hundred dollars on an early John Deere rider, make sure it is real! At a recent farm auction, a fairly nice Murray riding tractor from the early 1960s sold for $75, a Kubota 6950 model brought $105 and a Kubota M9000 brought $125. The M9000 was like new and the earlier Kubota was about 80 percent, as was the Murray. I think these prices are about typical of what you would find at a farm auction but the Murray seemed a little low for the condition.

Mobil tow truck purchased from Mobil a few years ago, **$50 with box**. This item demonstrates the growing interest of toy and oil company collectibles; it currently does not have a great value, but it is the type of item current collectors buy in the hopes of it increasing in value. In my case, I purchased it because my father was a Mobil dealer and I simply liked it. *Lewis Collection*.

This neat little toy truck trailer is missing its wheels and cab, but has nice graphics, **$5**. This came from a box lot at an auction and doesn't have much value, but would be worth more to someone who has the cab.

This Structo 66 gas truck has a friction motor to drive the rear wheels. The Structo brand was a huge manufacturer of toy trucks in the 1950s and most of us that are baby boomers owned at least one. I played with my Structo truck, a cab and a trailer, until it was nearly worn out. This one resembles my father's real truck from the 1950s, **$75+**. *Lewis Collection*.

Arcade tow truck, Model 2201, marked Freeport, Ill., **$250-$500**. This was purchased at an auction in 1997 for $240 and is likely worth about double that price today in its condition. *Lewis Collection*.

Various red wagons, **$10-$100**. The little red wagon is usually present at a farm auction sale and will bring from $10 to $100 depending on the model and the condition. Most sell for around $20 to $25. A few are shown here as examples. An interesting thing to note is that one of the wagons could clearly be dated from the early 1960s due to its name being "Astronaut"—a look at toys from the late 1950s to mid-1960s shows many names and marketing angles related to the space race between America and the USSR of the time period. One example of a more expensive one was from the 1930s with lights on each side that sold for $140 in used condition, but with the original paint still in fine shape; this was one of the earliest of the wagons that I had seen sell recently.

Farm toy collectibles of the future. These tractors, on a shelf at Burnips Equipment in Big Rapids, Mich., are valued at retail price now, but some will make it to the collectibles category without a doubt. Prices vary from **$20 to $40** for most.

❧ Chapter 5 ❧

Farm Implements

This chapter is an introduction to non-tractor implements and their collectibility. Some of the early three-point and two-point hitch implements made for tractors from 1930-1965 are also collectible but are only briefly covered here. A complete and detailed coverage of virtually every important farm implement of the same time period as covered in this book can be found in the *Encyclopedia of American Farm Implements & Antiques* by C. H. Wendel, published by Krause Publications.

However, this chapter covers in more detail how many of these implements are used by collectors and what makes certain items more and less valuable than others.

A manure spreader on steel wheels is showcased at the Bancroft Farms local farm and garden store in Evart, Mich., **$100+.**

Over the past 35-40 years, collectors have purchased cream separators to become garden flower pots, scalding kettles for the same purpose, windmills as decorations, one-row cultivators to set in the yard, scythes to hang on the garage wall, hog scrapers because they looked interesting even though most did not know what they were, wool carders, etc. Most of these functional items are not being purchased to be used but simply to be admired.

Of course, some one-row cultivators get used and some implements are making a comeback as others want to dabble in older agricultural technology. However, most of these things are now collectible due to their age and general difficulty to find in good condition.

What makes a farm implement collectible? Well, like advertising items, ability to display the item is very important. A hog scalding kettle is easy to display in a rural setting by building a two-post mount for it in the front yard, then throw in some potting soil, composted sheep manure in our case, and petunias and you have a nice flower pot. Most urban households do not have the space for a hog scalding pot, though, so they are doomed to be part of rural Americana. But do not buy one online or the shipping will drain your bank account in a hurry.

This leads to two of the biggest downfalls of many farm implement collectibles: weight and bulk. I have been involved in the dairy sector since birth and have always liked cream separators as a collectible since dabbling in antiques and collectibles for the past 30-plus years. However, most of the separators are overlooked at farm auctions due to weight and bulk; people cannot easily haul them home from the sale, it is that simple.

I remember last summer my wife and I found a great fanning mill in nearly perfect shape and almost bought it, but I realized that it could only be displayed in the barn and not the house. This is true of so many farm implements: most are too large, heavy or bulky to display in the home.

It is exactly this reason that keeps the cost on most of these items under $100. I have passed up a lot of $10 separators, not if in perfect condition with all the goodies, but the common DeLaval models with parts or tubs missing.

But people who want larger farm implements are creative and have certainly learned that an antique plow

Horse-drawn implements, such as these spreaders, may be antiques, but they are still sought after in the Amish community for regular use. The I-H sold for **$800** and the New Idea, in the background, sold for **$1,750**.

looks great in the rock garden or that a 1940s manure spreader makes a wonderful flowerbed when dirt is added.

Large crosscut saws adorn the side of many houses or garages. Large equipment simply sets proudly in the lawn with landscaping all around it. My wife and her family totally restored a windmill for a yard decoration mainly for the nostalgic reasons of keeping part of Americana alive, but it's functional, too.

I have included a number of photographs from one great collection, owned by David and Kelley VanAlstine, showing creative decorating with farm implements in many of the following chapters.

Cost of transportation and space for displaying become the overriding concerns for collectors of these items.

As mentioned above and well documented in the book, these implements do not often bring large sums of money but instead remain one of the few bargains in collector circles; but they are only bargains if you have the space to properly display them and keep them from further deterioration.

A recent purchase by Kelley VanAlstine well documents the issue. She was at a local farm auction and purchased the New Idea hay loader shown on Page 95 for only $2, the opening bid. The hay loader actually was in fully restorable condition and nearly usable as purchased; however, there were few people at the auction to purchase implements and it is such a bulky item most could not transport it. Her husband had access to an implement delivery truck not available to most so she purchased it and it now is proudly displayed at their home, which is a veritable museum of farm implements and farm collectibles.

Values of some farm implements

A salesman sample for an "antique hay baler," actually a hay compactor used prior to portable balers, is another unusual item. The seller claimed it to be from a mid-1800s estate and indicated the markings of "SW" were on the item. The winning bid was a lot of money to spend without some further documentation as to provenance and originality, but folks sure liked this item **$2,025**

A seeder box, marked American Harrow Co., Detroit, Michigan, and Windsor, Ontario, patent date of 1876 and 1878. This did not bring any bids with an opening bid of $25 and a reserve, most likely because of shipping costs and display space **$25**

American brand corn planter, made in Burr Oak, Michigan **$17.50**

A single bottom walking plow, salesman sample, 19-3/4" from handles to hitch, with 7-1/2" wooden handles and original paint. This is a most unique item and there are no markings representing any company or any proof of originality; some type of provenance and brand marking would have likely increased bidder interest **$495**

A gorgeous cast iron implement seat, marked "Adriance Buckeye," seat in extra clean condition. I question if these are being reproduced, since the seat simply looked brand new. I recently sold a "forecart" for horse-drawn implements made in the 1990s with very similar seats and that's why I question the age, but the seller claimed it to be a true antique and very old **$100**

A common steel implement seat, with five holes in an "arrow design" and unmarked. Again, the seller claimed it an antique tractor seat and that it may be iron or steel, but it's clearly steel............................$10

A "Dains" farm implement seat, cast iron, 12 pounds, 14" x 14". "Dains" is written on the back of the seat and it has been painted and crudely cast...............$60

A pressed steel seat, for a farm implement, not marked, similar to many I-H seats $11

A seat, claimed to be cast iron but may be pressed steel, marked either 731 or 78, has small crack in the metal...$10

Multiple-hole implement seat, has 26 holes in two roles with a crossroad pattern in the center of the seat, typical for I-H $19.95

Pair of buggy lanterns, kerosene................$27.50/pair

Original Studebaker No. 3 farm wagon, frame also included a nice grain box with sideboard extensions, nice condition and ready to hitch.....................$1,225

A steel wheel, 26", with eight spokes $15.50

Two steel wheels, four feet in diameter, both rusted $25

Pair of steel wheels, 43"...$15

Two large steel wheels, from "an Amish farm," 25" high, double-spoke design, 12 spokes each with a 5" tread $70

Another pair of steel wheels, 44"...........................$15

A single steel wheel, 26-1/2"..................................$13

This nicely restored McCormick (IHC) corn binder was the highest-selling item at the Yoder semi-annual farm sale, **$950**.

An Ontario drill sold first at a huge antique implement auction, **$10**. It brought the low bid of only $10 "as the first item sold," which often happens at farm sales. This was the Yoder semi-annual farm sale that always includes dozens of horse-drawn items and attracts hundreds of buyers, Amish and non-Amish, to compete for them. All items from this point on are from this sale, unless noted otherwise. The two-day sale was in Mt. Pleasant, Mich.

A nice older John Deere corn binder has not been restored, but is still in working order, **$350**.

An Oliver Drill, **$25**.

A Superior grain drill, **$35**.

This drill, Van Brunt on steel, was a favorite at the sale, **$220**.

Dump rake, **$55**.

Assorted eveners, **$5-$32**, and the neck yokes, **$5-$15**. The tongue with eveners only sold for $10 and I sold one for more than $100 at my own farm auction.

An old bobsled and one-horse fills, **$120**; and a John Deere Van Brunt steel grain drill, in the background, **$75**.

A very old bobsled, **$250**.

Another bobsled, with two tongues, **$90**.

A Papec silo filler, $65.

A red/gray bobsled with fills, $140.

A Papec silo filler, top photo, with some close-up data, middle and bottom photos, $100.

This red Eagle silor filler could be driven with a power take-off shaft or pulley drive, $195.

Some details of the Eagle silo filler.

A riding cultivator in decent condition, **$65**.

A small two-section drag and the old spring tooth drag, **$60** and **$10**, respectively.

The red cutter box in the background, **$225**; New Idea corn shredder, **$120**; John Deere two-row planter with missing parts, **$55**; hand corn sheller, **$45**. Shellers always sell well, as collectors like them for home display.

A Mohr walking plow from a Greenville, Mich., manufacturer, **$125**; and a spike tooth drag, **$40**.

An Oliver sulky plow, with detail at right, in nice original condition, **$125**. Most of the time these fetch a far better price and $300 to $500 is not uncommon, so this may have been the "steal" of the day.

A John Deere sulky plow, **$425**.

A small two-gang disk seen behind the Oliver plow, **$75**.

A nice restored John Deere Sulky plow, **$600**. The owner paid $450 for it a few years ago and it has increased in value.

A nice riding McCormick (IHC) disk, **$180**.

A walking furrower and beater cultivator, **$15** and **$10**, respectively.

A primitive spike tooth cultivator, **$10**; and a primitive furrower to match, with broken handles, **$5**. These two items were well aged and likely on their way to a garden spot.

This small Conestoga manure spreader is new but still interesting, $1,600; a steel forecart, $15; in the background is part of a Conestoga wagon on a John Deere steel gear on rubber, $600.

A beautiful old hay tedder and cast iron seat, $85. The tedder has a flat left tire but is in otherwise excellent working condition, and the seat alone is worth the price.

A primitive forecart for horse hitch items, $20.

New Idea spreader, two wheels, with original paint and good wood, $410.

New Idea ground driven spreader on two wheels, with original paint in goodcondition, $150.

New Idea Model #8 manure spreader, fully restored and in working order, was the gem of the show, **$1,750**; and a repainted Case in nice shape, **$120**.

A Rosenthal corn husker/shredder, model 40, serial number 22285, made in Milwaukee, Wis. by the Rosenthal Corn Husker Co., **$450**. Of all the original-condition items, this was the finest waiting to be restored and I thought it should have been the high selling item, but again the price stayed down due to its size and weight and the fact most people cannot move such an item easily.

A spreader on four steel wheels, **$100**.

A McCormick (IHC) New Ideal mower in very rough condition, **$7.50**.

This McCormick (IHC) riding cultivator had many competitive bids, **$435**.

International Harvester, four-wheel Model 200, prized by many buyers, **$800**.

A David Brown four-wheeler on rubber, **$325**.

An early grading scoop for use with horses, **$100**.

A McCormick #7 silage cutter in great condition, **$800**.

This John Deere No. 4 mower received a bid of $675, but was a no sale, **$600**.

Various items: large set of wheels, **$55**; small set of wheels, **$35**; cultivator, **$8**; and grinding stone, shown below, **$45**.

A cast iron implement seat marked #147 with no other marks, **$100+**. *Art Smith Collection.*

A windmill without a fan is on a farmstead near our farm. Since working on this book, I have noticed more than 20 windmills in the 19-mile drive from our farm to my office. Most of them blend into the landscape similar to this one, or the fans are gone, they have been built around, or trees have taken them over, etc., **$2,000**.

A tractor-mounted International mower on the Nerbonne farm, **$25**. This item is not really too collectible, unlike the riding mowers. Of course, if it was needed to fill a collection, it would be a real find for someone who might be willing to pay more for it.

A nice riding cultipacker on the Terry Nerbonne farm, **$75**. The seat alone is worth at least **$25**.

This is the seeding chart of the walk-behind seeder shown below.

This walk-behind seeder is one of the finest farm implements I've found and is on the Nerbonne farm. Terry Nerbonne bought it at a farm auction for only **$25-$35** a few years ago and its value has greatly increased. The close-up at right shows the cog mechanism. It works just fine and I would think it would be better pulled by a horse, but there is no place in front of the wheel to hook it up. I guess an enterprising farmer would be able to use an evener and hook it to the frame of the stand but this seems awkward to me, **$100+**.

An International-Harvester wood wheel grain drill is still used by Terry Nerbonne and pulled with his John Deere 60. I have shown the drill and some close-ups of details. According to sales data given earlier in this chapter, value would be from a few dollars to a few hundred brought at a good consignment auction of horse equipment, **$300**.

A four-wheeled manure spreader, on steel wheels, is used as a lawn decoration on a neighboring farm, **$50+**.

An abandoned hay loader is parked along US 10 near Evart, Mich., **$100+**.

The implement photos here and on Pages 95-98 are all from the David and Kelley VanAlstine collection, except where noted. See the listings in this chapter for example values, as well as information in the chapter, An Interview with "the Expert(s)," for additional values.

A John Deere two-row corn planter hides among the willows at the VanAlstine farm, **$25**.

A repainted furrower, **$20-$30**.

A John Deere Van Brunt grain drill is used as part of the VanAlstine landscaping, **$200-$300**.

This is a New Idea hay loader that Kelley VanAlstine recently purchased near Evart, Mich., for only $2, as no one came to buy implements at a general farm auction that day. This was actually in working order when parked in the yard, **$200-$300**.

This is believed to be an Oliver two-bottom plow, $75-$100.

A four-wheel New Idea spreader on steel, owned by David VanAlstine's grandfather, $75. The John Deere B in the background is shown in Chapter 12.

A John Deere dump rake, $50-$75.

Potato digger, Champion brand, $100.

A nice old Massey-Harris side delivery rake, formerly owned by Kelley VanAlstine's grandfather, Hugh Strey of Remus, Mich., **$150-$200**.

Wheels from a horse-drawn corn planter, John Deere Model 290.

A Wolverine Deluxe hand-powered walking cultivator, made by Fuller Mfg. Co. of Swartz Creek, Minn., **$100+** in this fine condition.

An old pump head, **$10-$15** in this condition.

❧ Chapter 6 ❧
Farm Tools

This chapter concentrates on the smaller tools of the farming trade, such as wrenches, hammers, shovels, rakes, hoes, etc. Again, there are books dealing with some of these items on the market, including the *Encyclopedia of Antique Tools & Machinery* by C. H. Wendel, published by Krause Publications. This book details many of the tools included in this section and is recommended background reading for the novice collector.

However, there is no book that deals specifically about farming tools and some of the special wrenches and items needed to repair farm implements, such as the items needed to repair chains and sickle bars and specialty items including hay knives and hay hooks.

Early advertising illustrations are often the only source of information about these tools and there are a number of them in Chapter 13 to show many of the possible finds in the tool category.

Wrenches that have the brand name John Deere, Ford, Fordson or DeLaval all bring a premium price to collectors of farm items, but are also in demand by collectors of tools and hardware items in general. This is a driving force in the pricing of tools: there is competition with other collectors for the same item. Add to that the brand value of an item and the cost goes up even more. It is not unusual to find simple wrenches or pliers going for five to ten times the normal value due to the presence of a brand name or trademark on the item, e.g. Winchester.

On the other hand, many tools are so uniquely suited only to the farm that most collectors do not recognize them or know what they were really used for and that in turn keeps the values down.

For instance, in researching this book, I was shocked to see the general utility fencing tool that I still use being invented in the late 1800s and looking almost identical. Yet, most urbanites would not know this is a fence tool or its history.

Actually, many of the tools we still use on the farm came into being in the late 1800s or early 1900s and have been modified rather little the past century. Fence-stretching tools are another interesting sideline to collect; early stretchers have been around for more than 100 years commercially and most of these would be passed over at auctions.

One item I was thinking about was the common grease gun. Oil cans and oilers are a common collectible and really gaining interest in many fields, and I paid $10 each for a collection of about 30 oilers for fishing reels; however, I do not know of any collectors going after early grease guns yet.

How do you display them? Well, for those of us still farming with a huge pole barn, an old grease gun on each post would be interesting to say the least. The grease gun is such an important tool to the farmer—what implement does not need grease?– and a good one has saved many a repair bill by properly lubricating the equipment or implement. Also, some tractors came with a specific grease gun, such as the Farmall Cub, making it of interest to collectors.

Another item that is unique to farming, and only from the past 50 years or so, is the bulk tank wrench. Each bulk tank for milk had to have a wrench to couple and uncouple the bulk milk truck's hose for emptying the product of the dairy. I have had about five bulk tanks and all the wrenches were different. I am sure this would make an interesting "modern" collectible and would be an item most people would overlook as it is a rather bizarre looking large wrench unknown to all but dairy farmers or milk haulers.

Marked items are of greater value than unmarked ones as a general rule. Many functional items also carried the brand name for the tool's intended use and this adds greatly to collector value today.

I have owned stainless steel buckets that say DeLaval, wrenches that say Fordson, pliers that say Winchester, Keen Kutter axes, Stanley planes, New Idea tools, etc. Any of these brand names increase the item's value greatly.

A common early box-end wrench, showing details of markings, $5.

This bulk tank wrench, a Dari-Kool brand, was found in our old milk house, **$10-$20**. *Lewis Collection.*

Many of the mentioned tools are listed in general collector price guides and some have even had complete books dedicated to them. The history of Winchester, John Deere or Keen Kutter can fill many books. Please consult any of the general references for a general guide to tools and then do the "value-added" for the brand names desired, usually doubling the value of an item if not adding even more value.

There are also unusual farm-related items gaining interest in more than one collecting field, such as early chain saws. Crosscut and buck saws have been collected for some time now, but folks are starting to collect early chain power saws and related items. The chain saw became a permanent fixture on every farm when it was invented and should indeed be seen as a farm tool.

As with many tools, this one is sought after by more than one group, but it is not real popular yet as a collectible so the costs are still down on most items. Old saws themselves often go for a mere $5 to $10 at farm auctions. Bargains can be had for sure if you keep a watch for these items.

As a matter of fact, I had written the above paragraph not knowing that I would find the David VanAlstine collection of chain saws. It turns out that a neighbor has collected saws for some time now and a few of his saws are shown in this section. He informed me that even though the saws were invented in the 1920s, with even earlier models being made, the idea of power saws did not become popular in west Michigan until the 1940s and early 1950s

Thus, you will not find the earliest saws in all regions due to different adoption rates of the technology by the buying public. However, his collection of chain saws and the way they have been displayed shows that indeed some have already started a very serious collection of power saws and related items, such as the early weed whacker.

Also, not long after writing this chapter, I viewed an hour-long special on the History Channel about early power lawn and garden tools that had an excellent segment on power saws and weed whips.

The special also covered the growing interest in older equipment to a small degree, but it did a great job of covering the invention of all types of this common farmstead and suburban equipment.

I would highly recommend viewing this segment if interested in older lawn and garden equipment and the history of power saw development.

Tools and implements designed for barn use is another category to keep an eye open for if you have a place to display the items. This includes everything from the common wheelbarrow to the feed cart used for delivering grain or silage to farm animals in the barn. Also the stanchions used to hold in the animals are collectible, especially if made of all wood construction. Early watering devices, oiling devices and cooling devices are also collectible. The problem again is space for display. I have shown some of these items here and also in Chapter 7, Horse Hardware and Stable Items.

Various early chain saws displayed on the beams of the VanAlstine garage, with some dating from the 1940s. Trading of chain saws is fairly recent so there is not any real solid pricing information on them; however, the days of the $5 chain saw on the "jewelry wagon" at the farm auction are likely over for good.

Other items related to tools due to functional use involve oils, greases and sprays. As already mentioned, oilers are collectible, grease guns may become so, and early sprayers are also in demand. The actual oil cans, grease tubes and spray containers are in demand if the graphics are good and the container is clean. Pricing also depends on brand demand to a large extent, with Mobil and Standard Oil products in great demand.

One thing to be aware of are laws related to selling and transporting cans with any liquids still in them, and of course the proper disposal of any contents. Most auctioneers will no longer sell these items due to federal and state laws regarding insecticides and pesticides.

However, a fine old DDT container (empty) from 1940 produced by Standard Oil makes a novel addition to any farm collection. An oil can will bring anywhere from $5 to $50 or more depending on age, rarity and condition.

Going back in history a notch, most of the major oil companies also produced harness oil for the horse trade. We own a fine example of a Standard Oil Eureka Harness Oil can and shipping crate, shown in Chapter 3, Page 50. I paid $100 for this item in an antiques store in rural Michigan in 1997. I am sure it is worth at least three times that amount today. There were also little saddle soap cans and harness soap cans that make a nice addition to a farm collectibles collection, which also crosses over into Chapter 7, Horse Hardware and Stable Items.

Values of farm tools

A **"foot adz,"** an adz shaped like a foot on a 31" handle. These are still available and you cannot date anything like this without an examination of the item, and this may or may not have been "primitive" as claimed **$8**

Cow bell, 6" x 4", common steel type. An interesting trick of the seller was to tie an old piece of baler twine to the bell to make it look older, but the twine clearly did not go "with the bell" as it was merely some frayed twine added for "color" (see photo of similar bells in Chapter 7) $15.50

A **small steel calf/goat bell**, 3-1/2" x 3-1/2", was listed as a horse or wagon bell but horses normally do not wear bells, unless mounted on collars............... **$5.50**

A **bull ring bull-towing device**, shaped like a gun with a trigger on one end and two metal grasping claws on the opposite end....................................$21.50

An **old calf/goat collar**, 3-1/2" x 2-1/2" x 4", appears to be steel **$5**

Farm cream carrier, four quarts, 11-1/2" high, made of steel (not stainless), has one small dent. The handle is marked "Liquid 4 Qt." **$23**

A **bull lead cane**, James Manufacturing Company, 60" with an end loop that was used to lead bulls safely. This is a more unusual item dating from the early 1900s **$20**

Tail-docking device for sheep, wooden handles, and a cutting/cauterizing unit. The seller did not know what the item was and listed it only as an unknown primitive farm tool..**$2**

Three corn dryers, early steel models for drying full ears of seed corn, hold 10 ears of corn.............**$23.50**

Five corn dryers, of a wire construction, hold 24 ears of corn.. **$27**

Corn husker, made of metal and leather................**$7**

"Scrimshaw" whalebone corn husker. This is a most unusual item and does appear to be a tool identical to manufactured corn huskers made out of bone with a leather thong to hold the implement, even with adjustment holes. My guess is that it was not a corn husker but a knotting device for net making, similar to many I have in my own collection, and it came from Long Island, an area not known for its corn growing. I also am certain the bone which was rounded somewhat would have simply slid off the ear of corn and not grabbed the kernels as the wood/metal huskers do **$50**

Hand flail, made of a wooden handle and the flail piece of wood for dried beans, beautiful item with nice patina on both the wooden handle and the wooden flail piece
.... **$9**

Wooden flail, two pieces, long handled, hinged, well worn but nice patina **$6**

A very old hay hook is hand-forged and long handled, $25+.
Narbonne Collection.

Antique grain measure, made of wood with metal strapping, 14-1/2" across the top, 44" girth, and 7" deep. According to the seller, this is from the 1870s, but the 1870 date on the side is likely a patent date, although it still gives some idea of vintage........**$50+**

Two hay hooks: a common red-handled one and a blacksmith version of an all-metal hook. Again, the listing seller called them primitive, which they are not; however, they may be from the 1940s or 1950s.........**$6**

A nice older hay hook, appears to be cast iron **$15**

Primitive hay knife.................................**$10.50**

A common hay saw or hay knife, 37" long and 2-1/2" wide, has two wooden handles (one on the end, one on side), still has original paint on the handles . **$15.50**

Pair of hand-wrought hinges, cast iron, over 24", from

a farm with the markings UB Co. cast into the hinge in small raised letters......................................**$22.50**

A farm lot of items, including two hog scrapers, a bull nose ring, assorted hog nose rings and a hand-held corn husker **$7.50**

Pair of horse clippers, by Coates, with a patent date of 1897..**$5**

Set of ice tongs, cast iron................................ **$10**

An early pair of steel ice tongs, 12" x 24"........... **$4.25**

An oversized oak nail keg, 19" high, 13" diameter and 46" center girth, in nice condition **$20**

Three 3-foot levels, mainly newer ones.................... **$8**

A seamed Babson Bros. Surge milker unit, without cover, seller mentioned it would make a nice planter..........**$50**

Dairy milking stool, three legs, made of steel, 12" high, new old stock **$20**

Two vintage milk stools, wooden, homemade **$22**

Milk stool, three legs, steel, in fairly rough shape, not bent but worn... **$29**

Three farm tools: a small steel frying pan; A pair of blackened sheep shears made in England and marked "27 England"; and a hay hook with A wooden handle
.... **$30**

A galvanized pail, 2-1/2 gallons, has dents on the rim and bottom. These pails are common at farm auctions and I was surprised it even sold................ **$3**

Two metal and wood pulleys, excellent shape, fairly early examples of the type of pulleys used on hay slings
.... **$6 each**

Two hay rope pulleys, wood and metal, excellent condition...**$11.50**

Milk-stripping pump, unmarked, sold with DeLaval items. This is a glass unit that was placed directly on the cow's teat and the metal pump on the other end would strip the teat of milk for testing for cream content, etc. **$5**

A two-man crosscut saw $30

Pressed steel seat, with round holes, unmarked $11

"Primitive dairy separator." This was another attempt at duping the public because this item is actually a simple, low quality dairy strainer. This strainer is made of steel, not stainless, and is placed on top of the dairy can or milk tank opening to strain out hair, dirt, etc. and not to separate cream $5

Another seat, marked 731 or 781 on the bottom. Again, shipping costs really keep prices of implement seats down for online auctions unless the seat is very rare and clearly identified $10

The Cyclone seeder I mentioned that the seller claimed was Amish. This was not Amish, nor was it necessarily old, as they are still available throughout the farm lands of the Midwest for grass seeding and spreading fall pasture mix, clover, and other grass crops $24

Pair of iron sheep shears, 12". The seller claimed them to be an antique over 100 years old and made of cast iron, but they were common steel shears. Actually, these same shears sell for a little more at many farm auctions $5.50

An old scythe anvil and hammer, made by a blacksmith known as Dengelstock. These two items were used to sharpen early scythes by driving the anvil into a stump or log and then placing the scythe blade upon it for sharpening with the special hammer. The seller was complete in the listing and helpful in explaining the history behind these unique tools. Also, he had owned them for 40 years, giving them some nice provenance $46

Common hand scythe or sickle, 12" blade, wooden handle, marked "Little Giant, North Wayne Tool Co., Oakland, ME USA." $11.50

Scythe, nice condition $6

"Antique Amish farm wagon hub." This is another example of exaggerated listings; the hub had actually been turned into a lamp, which is something the Old Order Amish certainly would not be using. It was a common wooden hub, likely fairly old but not Amish, and the type found on covered wagons, stage coaches, and common farm wagons until the advent of steel hubs and running gears $30

Seven glass waterers, for chicks. These waterers have become collectibles the past 20 years and were used to water baby chickens in the 1940s-1960s and look like a giant "juicers" $13

Two nice wool carders, marked "The Only Genuine Old Whittemore Patent Improved No. 8 Wool L.S. Watson & Co., Leicester, Mass" $25

Rathbone's Farm Implement Wrench Book, one of the leading sources for information on early wrenches and a "must-have" item if you are trading significantly in wrenches .... $45-$60

A dozen nice old wrenches, but not properly described other than one I-H wrench $10.50

Wrench, marked D and the #ED51, open end, one end angled $26

Farm implement clevis wrench, three openings, manufacturer unknown $25

Vulcan Plow Company Clevis wrench, No. 101 .... $22.50

J8 Frost & Wood implement wrench $8

I-H F354 implement wrench $4

No. 5 S implement wrench $3

Implement wrench, Frost & Woods (Smith Falls, Canada), #378 .... $13

MM E13 implement wrench $10

I-H R319R implement wrench $15

A Vulcan implement wrench $8

Deering implement wrench $8

Unidentified wrench $8

Four wrenches $7

Six wrenches $5

Chain-repair tool, made by Albert Lea Foundry in Albert Lea, Minn. This tool was once found on nearly every farm and is another reminder of how farmers had specialty tools to repair conveyers, manure spreader chains, and other similar items, $10.

Foot adz and closeup details, $25+. *VanAlstine Collection.*

Old pickaxe, $25+. *VanAlstine Collection.*

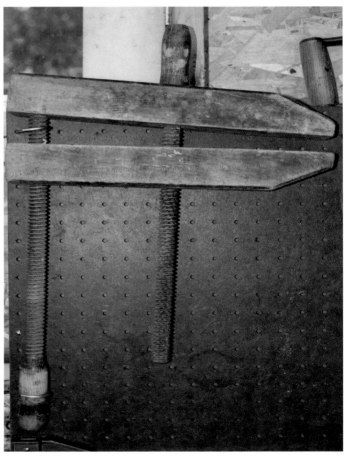

Set of woodworking clamps, $50+. *Jerry Paulsen Collection.*

A chain lever device, $15-$25. *Nerbonne Collection.*

Corn-husking gloves and picks; the glove with all of the studs is the most unusual one, **$5-$20**. These items are selling for these prices on average and some of the more unusual ones may command a bit more. *Art Smith Collection.*

In the top two photos is a barrel-mounted "Black Beauty" corn sheller, **$25+**. This device offered an easier way to shell ear corn than the hand method. *Art Smith Collection.*

A hand-made creeper used for auto, truck and tractor repair on the farm is a unique item, **$20**. *Art Smith Collection.*

A hay knife, left, **$10-$30**, and an American Standard corn planter, **$25**, lean against a milk can at the Art Smith farm. The painted milk can is only worth a few dollars.

This old post-hole digger has heavy pipe construction and a tooled handle, **$25-$35**. *Nerbonne Collection*.

A beautiful old egg crate with original paint, **$25-$35**. *Nerbonne Collection*.

Two very old eveners from the Nerbonne barn. Nice aging and patina would make these in demand to a collector; also much older hand-wrought hardware makes them attractive, **$20 each**.

A walking one-row horse-drawn cultivator in good condition, **$35-$60**. *VanAlstine Collection*.

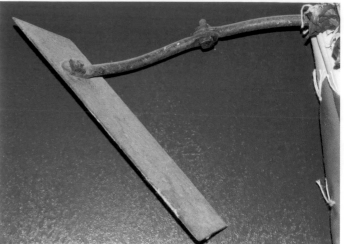

An early metal cement float was used for flat work, **$10-$20**. *VanAlstine Collection.*

A three-tine hay fork, right, has metal reinforcement on the bottom of the handle. This type of tool is older than the ones with a straight insert into the tool tip, **$15-$20**. Also pictured is an old fork with a handmade handle, far right, **$35+**. Both items are from the *Nerbonne Collection.*

Prices for fanning mills, such as the one shown in the top two photos, usually depend on the location and condition, **$50-$200**.

Another interesting early fence-stretching tool, **$10-$20**. *Art Smith Collection.*

An early fence-stretching tool, **$20**. *Art Smith Collection.*

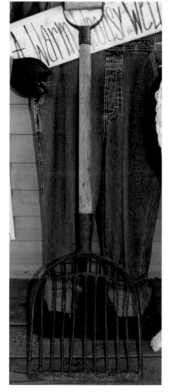

Is this a silage fork? This unusual farm fork has a metal band at the fork ends for scraping on cement and my guess is that it was designed to clean up silage in a cement manger, although it's smaller than any silage fork I've ever used. It would be ideal today for handling bark by landscaping personnel, **$25**. *VanAlstine Collection*.

This fork is the reinforced type older than the straight-line insert type, **$15-$20**. The details of the handle are shown at right.

A primitive furrower, **$35**.

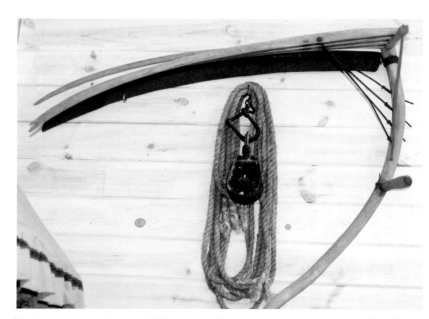

Antique grain cradle, circa 1880, shown with a rope, tractor clevis and pulley. The scythe part is fairly common but seldom do you find intact grain cradles today, especially in such pristine condition, **$150-$200**. *Bancroft Farms Collection*.

A hay grapple in nice condition, Myers brand. This was used to grab the loose hay from a stack on a hay wagon and lift it up into the barn. This was in the Nerbonne barn when he purchased it years ago. Although these are unique and harder to find now, their value is not high as there is not a good way to display one for most buyers, **$50-$100**.

Another type of hay grapple also from the Nerbonne barn, **$25-$50**.

A cant hook, made by the Leach Co., Oshkosh, Wis., **$30+**. *VanAlstine Collection*.

This cant hook is an older tool in like-new condition, made in Evart, Mich., by a logging tool company when still in business. This is not real old but the company was local and is now out of business so it makes a nice "local collectible" for someone interested in logging, **$25**. *VanAlstine Collection*.

A fairly old cant hook, **$25-$35**. *Nerbonne Collection*.

Various tools: an old hatchet, **$20-$30**; a barn beam drill used to drill holes for the pegs in post and beam construction, **$20-$35**; and a primitive hand-forged hay hook, **$10-$20**. *VanAlstine Collection*.

These two very old hand-held hay hooks are hand forged, have hand-carved wooden handles and are heavy duty, **$25+**. *Nerbonne Collection*.

Large pair of ice tongs made of wrought iron, **$35**. *Art Smith Collection*.

Antique buggy jack, **$30+**. *Bancroft Farms Collection*.

An old Model T jack, **$20**. *Art Smith Collection*.

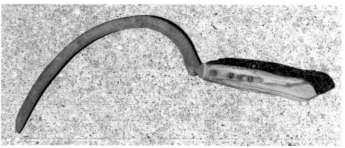

Hand corn knife, small size, **$10-$15**. *Art Smith Collection*.

Nice older corn knife, **$20-$25**. *Nerbonne Collection.*

A collection of old screw jacks, **$20 each**. Many of these have interesting details and stampings to increase the beauty of old functional items and make for yet another interesting sideline in collecting. *Art Smith Collection.*

An even older corn knife with stamping details, **$30-$35**. *Nerbonne Collection.*

A hay knife, **$15-$25**. *Nerbonne Collection.*

A screw jack from our farm. I use it for its original purpose and also as a weight to hold open the chicken coop door during the daylight hours, **$20**.

An old machete, **$5-$10**. *Art Smith Collection.*

Line level, unmarked, ornate design and nice casting, **$10+**. *Lewis Collection.*

Older and newer hoof picks; large version is older, **$5-$10 each**. *Art Smith Collection.*

This grain bag/milk can mover, made by the Lansing Company, Lansing, Mich., was used for moving cans and grain bags in the barn, **$35+**. *VanAlstine Collection.*

A feedbag cart, **$12**.

A milk can, **$10-$30**.

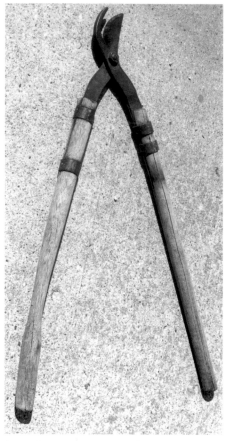

Pair of woodworking planes, **$25 each**.
Planes sell for anywhere from $10 to well
over $100, depending on brand, style,
model, etc. *Paulsen Collection*.

A set of primitive pruners, **$25**.
Art Smith Collection.

This marked pulley has brass trimming, which
adds to the value, **$25+**. *Art Smith Collection*.

A potato planter, **$20-$30**. *Paulsen Collection*.

Wooden pulley in excellent condition, **$10-$20**.

Pulley mechanism from the top of the barn for hay loading into the mows. This mechanism ran on a rail (upside down from the way it was photographed) and would lift the grapple hooks full of hay and then release them into the mows for stacking. Again, this has little market value but is of great historical value, **$25-$50**. *Nerbonne Collection.*

Old cast well water pulley with ornate design, **$20+**.
Art Smith Collection.

Three nicely aged pulleys found hanging in an old barn, **$5-$15 each**.
Nerbonne Collection.

A primitive rake with wood dowels as teeth is reinforced with light wire braces, **$50+**. *Nerbonne Collection.*

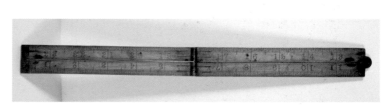

A folding ruler in nice condition was purchased years ago in a "box lot" at a farm auction, **$20**.

A primitive wooden rake in nice condition, **$50-$75**.
VanAlstine Collection.

This bucksaw still has its original paint and is in nice condition, $35+. *Paulsen Collection.*

This "Guild Sander," an early electronic tool made in Syracuse, New York, is at least 40 years old and a nice addition to a set of woodworking tools, **$50**. *Paulson Collection.*

Bucksaw with nice patina, **$25**. *Nerbonne Collection.*

Two examples of bucksaws, **$10-$25 each**. *Art Smith Collection.*

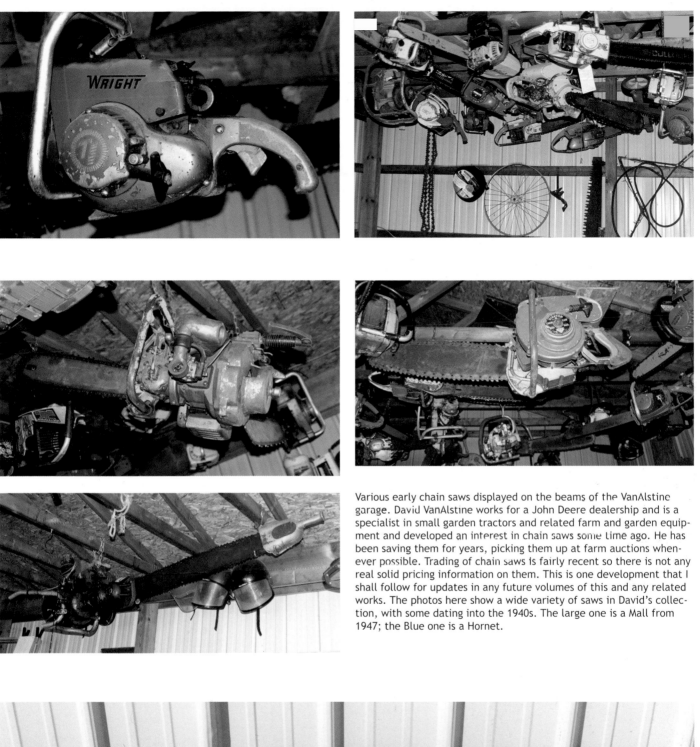

Various early chain saws displayed on the beams of the VanAlstine garage. David VanAlstine works for a John Deere dealership and is a specialist in small garden tractors and related farm and garden equipment and developed an interest in chain saws some time ago. He has been saving them for years, picking them up at farm auctions whenever possible. Trading of chain saws is fairly recent so there is not any real solid pricing information on them. This is one development that I shall follow for updates in any future volumes of this and any related works. The photos here show a wide variety of saws in David's collection, with some dating into the 1940s. The large one is a Mall from 1947; the Blue one is a Hornet.

One-man crosscut saw, large size, **$25-$35**. *Art Smith Collection.*

Saw set tools, **$10+ each tool**. *Art Smith Collection*.

Is this a handmade grain scoop and/or dustpan? Whatever it is, it's a nice primitive piece, **$10**. *VanAlstine Collection*.

Scythe, **$10-$25**.

A primitive barn scraper made by Terry Nerbonne's dad a number of years ago, **$15-$20**. *Nerbonne Collection*.

A barn shovel in nice condition is not as old as the pure wooden handled one, **$20**. *Nerbonne Collection*.

An older shovel, **$25+**. *Nerbonne Collection*.

This older shovel has a complete wooden handle and is rare, **$25+**. All-wooden handles clearly predate the more common wood-on-steel handles on most shovels found today. I even have one with a solid wooden handle without the finger hole carved in it. *VanAlstine Collection*.

A Conneaut #3 shovel and details, **$25+**. *Lewis Collection*.

A newer long handle shovel and spade, **$10-$15**. *VanAlstine Collection*.

This old shovel has an all-wooden top and is without a hand-hole in the handle. This is likely a primitive handmade replacement for the original, **$35-$50**. *Lewis Collection*.

A spokeshave with nice wooden handles, **$10-$20**. *Art Smith Collection*.

A primitive sprayer for livestock insecticide, and a can to add fluids to an engine, **$5 each**. *Nerbonne Collection*.

An old draw shave without its wooden handle, hand wrought, **$20+**. *Nerbonne Collection*.

A combination walking and measuring stick, with great advertising on it for "Michigan State Industries" and all of the products made at Jackson State Prison in Jackson, Mich. This is likely from the 1940s or earlier, when the prison system provided many market products, not just stamped license plates, **$25-$35**. *Paulsen Collection*.

This yardstick advertises Jamesway Barn Equipment in Vassar, Mich. The nice part is that my wife's maiden name is Weber, so this is special to us, and an example of the type of items that are collectible but even better when local or tied into a person's history somehow, $10+. *Lewis Collection.*

Sears garden tractor, Series 38, Model 50B, #19951, 5 horsepower, from the 1930s, **$300+.** This was made for Sears and called the "Handyman" tractor, and had a 12" plow and cultivators. This is something I nearly bought myself but could not carry it home in our Mustang convertible. I think it should have brought at least $600, but buyers were not after it, as they could not haul it easily. The buyer told me he was prepared to bid it up to $800, but he got lucky and owned it when the gavel went down at only $300. This is the type of collectible that will likely increase in the future as more collectors are developing interests in garden and lawn tractors.

This primitive wheelbarrow has a metal wheel and was used for moving grain shocks, **$50+**. *VanAlstine Collection.*

Wagon frame on steel, **$85**.

Another early lawn tool is this electronic "weed-whacker," **$10-$20**, shown with a 1950s chicken waterer, **$10**. *VanAlstine Collection.*

Various wheels, top and bottom photos, **$25-$35 each**.

Wheelbarrow, used to carry shocks of grain or corn, **$50+**. *VanAlstine Collection.*

A beautiful workbench over 100 years old, **$100+**. This was purchased by Jerry Paulsen at a farm auction for less than $100 and is a nice addition to his workroom.

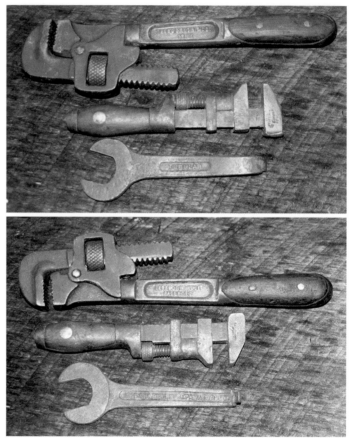

A complete set of wrenches by Walden Worcester, **$5 each**. I recently purchased these from a collector friend for this amount and they should be worth that or even a little more each if sold as a complete set. It is unusual to find such a complete set of wrenches from one company.

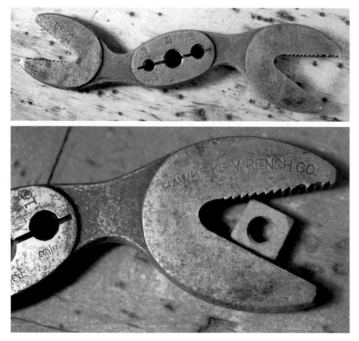

This Hawkeye Wrench Co. wrench, top and bottom photos, fits any square nut or bolt head, **$10+**. *Paulsen Collection.*

Three other various wrenches, shown front and back sides. The top wrench is from The R.O. Smith & Co.; the middle wrench is from the Coe's Wrench Company of Worcester, Mass. and has the 1800 L. Coe's Patent; the wrench on the bottom is from "The Sharples Separator Co." and is for a cream separator, **up to $50 each**. Again, the existence of a brand name such as Ford, John Deere, International, Case, etc. increases the values greatly, often commanding up to $50 for certain wrenches. Only a thorough examination of current books on tools will give you a complete understanding of this complex area of farm collectibles.

This smaller sized open-end wrench has the number 25 on one side, **$5+**. *Paulsen Collection.*

This open-end wrench has number 677 on one side and an H in a diamond on the other side, **$10+**. *Paulsen Collection.*

A number 10 adjustable "Merit" wrench by Stillson Wrench, **$25**. *Paulsen Collection.*

Wrench, marked "Reverse Gear Wrench," **$10+**. *Paulsen Collection.*

An old Fordson adjustable wrench in fine working condition, **$20+**. I use this on the farm today and the curved handle allows me to reach many odd angles.

This unusual set of small pocket open-end wrenches are not real functional, but are handy to have in an emergency, **$5-$10**.

Texaco Home Lubricant can in excellent shape, **$75+**. These brand name oilers sell for $50 to $500 depending on name and condition. Texaco has the advantage to the seller of being a crossover collectible, making buyers pay a premium for the item in most cases.

Unknown tool. *Nerbonne Collection*. This appears to be designed to clean a small trough, gutter or eave. It may also be a cement tool. If anyone has information about it, please let me know.

Nokorode Soldering Paste tin (full), by M. W. Dunton Co., **$10+**. All of us taking "farm shop" learned to solder and weld and I made a grain scoop used on our farm for years in farm shop class. Water tanks develop leaks and soldering is a handy art to know.

Grease stick in a tube, Cities Service Door-Ease, **$35+**. Again, oil collectibles would drive prices up on this nice advertising tin, but it also was used on a farm.

Chapter 7 ⤖

Horse Hardware and Stable Items

Of all my favorite terms related to farming, "horse hardware" has to be tops on the list. Most folks would not have a clue what this means, but it includes old collars, hames, ivory rings, bells, buckles, decorative brass, tugs, and complete sets of harnesses, as well as antique tongues for farm equipment made by a particular company, such as Deere or International Harvester, and tools to care for horses such as picks, combs, halters, brushes, tack boxes, etc.

This chapter covers the growing popularity of collecting horse hardware and I have also included stable items related to other farm animals.

Any animal used for draft purposes on a farm or in delivery of farm goods has to be harnessed to the equipment in some fashion and the various techniques used have not changed much in thousands of years. For the horse, it means the dressing with a collar kept in place by a set of hames, to which is attached the back bands and bellybands and the surcingle around the middle to hold it all in place. Then, a set of tugs would be attached directly to the hames (often these were permanently attached) for the actual pulling. The tugs would then be hooked up to the eveners or wagon poles or whatever was being hauled. Of course, a long set of "lines" replaced the reins to control the horse and these were attached to the bridle in the same way as a set of reins.

For the oxen, usually castrated male bovines so called for their draft use and not their potential beef use as steers, the main necessity was a wooden yoke to which was hooked the necessary tugs. Harnessing a bovine was not nearly as complex, as all of the weight of the implement was directly on the front shoulders of the strong animals transferred there by the yoke.

However, in some regions, folks did actually harness cattle in outfits similar to a horse harness, but for the most part, you will find single- and double-oxen yokes in most farm country where cattle were used for draft purposes. A whip was also often used to get the attention of the cattle and to control their direction.

The most obvious and likely first item in this field to be collected historically was the sleigh bell. These are colorful, well made, and sound nice, too; also, everyone seems to know what they are.

At one time, each family with a horse and sleigh had some decorative or functional bells for the equine part of the equation. Early brass bells that were hand cast sell for $10 each and complete sets can command up to $250 if in good condition. Sleigh bells are popular with many collectors, as they can be so easily recognized and displayed. This should keep the values increasing in years to come.

The next area of popularity has been the horse collar and a set of hames that mounted the harness to the collar of a horse. As mentioned earlier, the hames often frame a mirror set within the collar, which is a nice way to display a functional piece of horse hardware in a modern home. The nicest and most valuable set of hames is a wooden set, or a set made of wood and metal with nice knobs on top of the framework.

Metal hames in nice shape and with good paint are collectible, but not in the same quality category as wooden hames with a nice brass knob ball on top. The collars do not make much difference, as people are buying them simply as a carrier for the mirror, but condition is important: no one wants a collar that has had a mouse nest in the stuffing or been chewed on by mice. A collar with fancy double or triple stitching will bring more than one with simple single stitching. Also, deep solid black leather will bring more than a collar that has aged or has sunburned leather.

Ivory rings (actually these are Bakelite) found on "spreaders" are likely the next category of interest because they hang fine from the hames around the mirror. The ivory rings for harness were designed for a dual purpose of decoration and to carry the lines (the leather reins from the bridle to the driver's hands) and keep them out of harm's way (the horse's hooves).

Some farmers started adding ivory rings to decorate the harness even more. These rings have become quite popular with collectors due to their beauty and uniqueness.

A few years ago these were nearly free at an auction and now command anywhere from $1 to $10 per ring, depending on material, condition, and competition at the sale. A nice set of spreaders sold for $5 at the large Yoder consignment sale, which is inexpensive for the condition the set was in, but it was a huge sale with hundreds of horse harness items for sale.

Closely related to the rings is the category of rosettes and brass trim. Many farmers spending 10 hours a day behind a team of horses or mules decided to have a more aesthetic experience by decorating the harness with small rosettes or other brass hardware additions. They did not serve any functional purpose; they were simply to make the harness pretty. These rosettes and brass mini-horseshoes and floral designs first appeared on the horse's bridle and then spread back to the harness itself. The decorations were often a status symbol indicating the wealth of the farmer. The driving harness used to go to town was often decorated more than the "work harness"; however, some work harnesses had many ounces of brass added simply for decoration.

Related to the rosettes and decorations are all of the functional buckles and contraptions needed to make a set

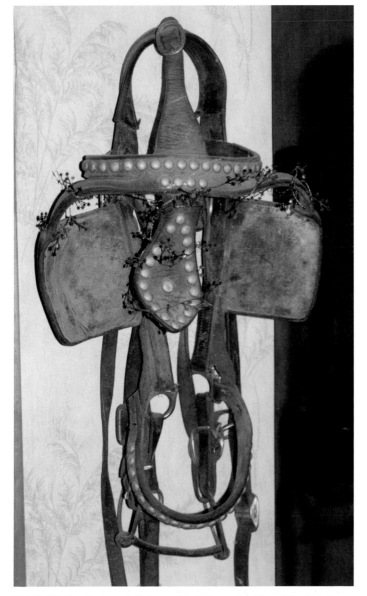

This bridle is priceless. It belonged to Prince, the king of the Percherons we owned for years. It hangs in his memory in a corner of our dining room, decorated for Christmas.

of harnesses work properly. Many of these older brass items are now selling for $1 to $10 each if in pristine condition and of vintage age.

Finally, whole sets of harnesses are sometimes bought to hang on the wall of a restaurant or family room. It is difficult to assign a collector value to sets of harnesses, as they also retain a "user value" regardless of age. I have bought and sold many sets of harnesses for as little as $25 to $800 a set, depending on condition, trim and age of the leather, and completeness of the set.

Very old sets of harnesses found hanging in a barn that have not been oiled have little value other than to a collector, as the leather is "dead" because it had not been properly oiled and cannot usually be brought back to life.

Implement tongues are actively sought by collectors of farm collectibles and include all of the major names in farm machinery manufacture. At a recent auction we sold a beautiful John Deere wagon tongue with original paint, and a toolbox, for more than $100. The tongue was found in the hayloft of our Upper Michigan farm when purchased in 1999. This demonstrates that these items are still out there waiting to be found. The tongue was in perfect condition and stored out of harm's way for at least 70 years. Any tongue with a name on it will bring more than just a functional implement tongue.

Seats from early implements and tractors are also highly desired by collectors and some of the early cast-iron seats garner hundreds of dollars. These seats are used for everything from bar stools to implement restoration, which drives up the prices. Again, brand recognition is important to values. The pressed-steel seats are not worth nearly as much as cast-iron versions, so if you buy one over the Internet, make sure you know the seat material before shelling out a lot of money. Also, I know of some factory reproductions of cast-iron seats, so again beware if not buying directly from the original owner.

Cow hardware is also important and fits in here as well as anywhere else. We sold a nice single-ox yoke seven years ago for $75 and a nice set of yokes today could bring up to $500. Driving whips for oxen or horses are also collectible. Dairy cows also had their own special devices for training, including cow kickers and little devices that transmitted a shock to the cow's back if she hunched too much while using her latrine facilities (cow trainers).

There are also the surcingles that hung over the cow's back to place a Surge brand milking machine in mid-air while the cow was being milked, and three-legged milk stools that bring $10 to $50 at farm auctions.

Horse and cow care also included many specialized brushes and pieces of equipment, including tack boxes. Horses also had to have extensive foot care products and many of the early hand-forged devices are gaining value.

Veterinary products and home remedies related to horse and cow care also make nice additional items to one's collection.

Many of these products came in colorful tins and jars that are desired by collectors in general, which drives the prices up some.

Again, some of these items contain their original contents that could be dangerous and you will need to dispose of these contents only according to the law and recommended procedures.

Last, but not least, is the ultimate horse or oxen related item: carriages, carts and other implements of this nature. About the only high demand I ever see for horse-drawn (which includes oxen-drawn) equipment is by people with horses or oxen—not the general collector crowd. The only exception is the person who wants an item for a lawn decoration.

Horse-drawn implements and conveyance devices have really shot up in value the past 20 or so years.

When I bought my first team of horses in 1978 (Star and Stripe, three-fourths Belgian, one-fourth Quarter horse), it was not uncommon to find an old buggy or sleigh for $50 at a farm auction. The last two buggies I have sold brought more than $500 each and the last sleigh (it was a dandy) brought about the same price and I cannot buy it back for $1,000 (I have tried). Old horse-drawn hay mowers were $10 twenty years ago and now fetch a good price if still functional. Horse-drawn manure spreaders are the same story.

You could easily spend $5,000 for a decent carriage, sleigh, mowing machine, forecart, manure spreader and riding plow. Of course, it would depend on brand names, age, attributes of the carriage and sleigh, and condition. But no one is going to walk away from a sale with a few bucks invested and get these items any longer.

A buggy seat in good condition, $50-$100.

Values of some horse and stable items

Dakota farmstead cast iron hook, found in the barn for hanging harnesses.. $10

Broken hames pieces, likely being purchased for the two brass knobs thrown in the deal. The hames themselves were broken and cracked and not worth much; however, one was the older wooden version.. **$3.25**

Harness hanging hook, cast iron $10

A horse farm mirror, the type hung in a stable or mounted on carriages... $53

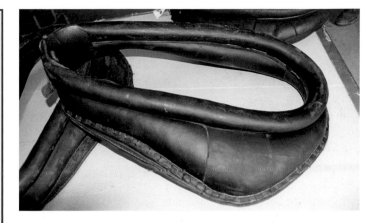

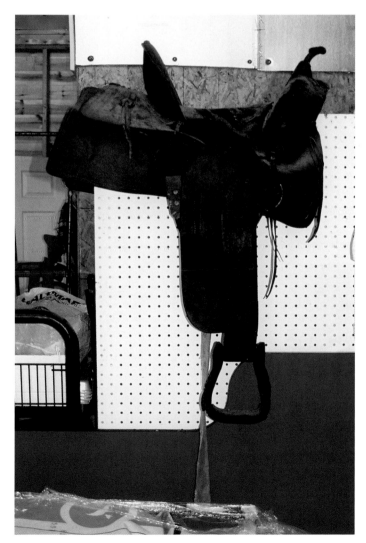

Antique saddle, military style, **$400+**. *Bancroft Farms Collection.*

Various horse collars shown in these three photos. Thousands of items related to horses and draft equipment are sold in a two-day period at the semi-annual Yoder consignment sale in Michigan. At a recent sale, collars sold as follows: a fancy 27", **$61**, and 25", **$55**; a 25" in nice condition, **$47.50**; a newer 24", **$70**; an older 23" in nice condition, **$40**; an old/dirty 22", **$22**; a plain 19", **$24**, and another plain one, **$40**; a plain 18" driving collar, **$26**; and many others sold in the $30-$35 range if usable. Small driving collars, 15" or 16", only fetched $5 each and some of the old work collars, even with pads, only sold for $10-$15.

Set of hames and horse collar, has original brass knobs and is in good condition, **$25+ for the set**. Many people take a set like this and insert a mirror in the collar to make a functional piece for their home. *Art Smith Collection*.

Various harnesses, **$5-$25**. At a recent Yoder sale, these sold between a few dollars to hundreds of dollars for quality working or driving harnesses. The values on harnesses at most farm auctions is quite low, as often the harness was not stored properly and the leather is really "dead" and cannot be revived. I have purchased some examples for $5-$25 that when taken to my local Amish harness maker were saved by a good soaking in his oil tank. But buying harnesses to use is risky business and unless you have a lot of experience with it, I would advise buying something known to be complete and in good shape if you are wanting to use it.

An old "horse muzzle" or cribbing control device, **$10**. *VanAlstine Collection*.

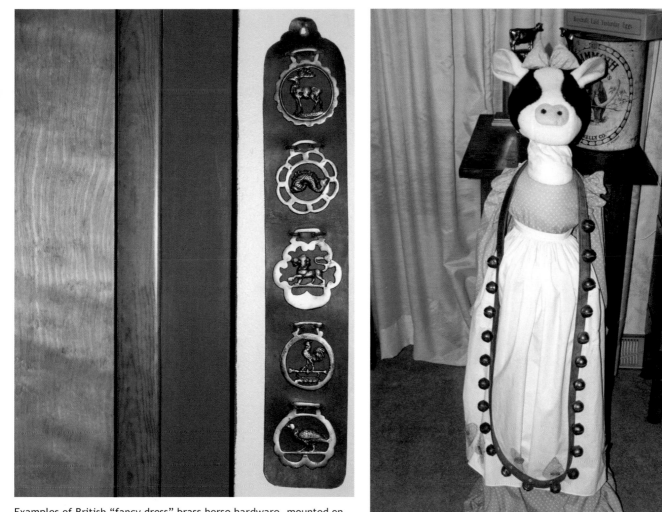

Examples of British "fancy dress" brass horse hardware, mounted on a leather strap and hanging on display in our living room, **$50-$75**. *Lewis Collection*.

The set of sleigh bells featured below hangs around our maid Bossy.

This is a set of sleigh bells an Amish harness-making friend installed on new leather for me. The set has 25 bells, **$250**. *Lewis Collection*.

The ultimate horse- or oxen-related items in this collectible field are carriages, carts, buggies and other implements of this nature. The carriages and buggies here were among those offered at a recent sale. Most will sell for **$500-$800** at a minimum, with many bringing four figures.

The items in these two photos were all sold at a recent Yoder sale and included an old doctor's buggy, some nice old cutters, some Amish-made buggies, and some newer models made by a Canadian firm. Prices ranged from a few hundred to a few thousand dollars depending on models. In general, old doctor's buggies do well, as do cutters and sleighs, stagecoaches, delivery wagons with markings and any other unusual item on four wheels. With some good shopping, buggies can usually be found in this range: **$500-$800.**

Horse buggy seat, **$50-$100**. Art Smith has this in his entryway to sit on while putting on boots and shoes, which is an interesting adaptation of a horse item to a household.

A small cowbell, **$25**. *Lewis Collection.*

A large simple cowbell made of steel hangs from a tree, **$10-$15**. *VanAlstine Collection.*

Older brass bell, larger size, **$25**. *Lewis Collection*.

Cow number tag, Hasco brand, made of brass, **$5-$15**. This number would hang from a chain around the cow's neck to identify her to a farmer or farm help. I still have the number tags from a few "great cows" that are very special memories to me and they also make neat collectibles. Value depends on materials used to make the tag.

This unique calf trainer was used to wean a calf from nursing; the little points went into the calf's nose and hurt when it tried to suckle its mother, **$10-$25**. *VanAlstine Collection*.

Dairy barn drinking cups, **$6-$10 each**. The older cast iron versions, as shown in our own dairy barn in the photo at right, should bring more money, as they are in more demand.

Stainless steel milking machines, **$10-$20**. The machines, mainly Surge but also a Chore Boy and some De Laval, had parts missing, broken handles, or something wrong with them to be used (seams, welds, brazes, etc.), but would end up as someone's planter in the yard or on the farm house front porch.

This cow stanchion was built right into the barn and is the oldest known style. These are **$50 each** if removed from the barn as a set. *Nerbonne Collection.*

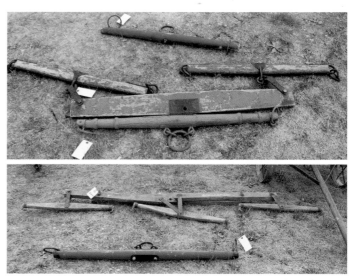

Various eveners and neck yokes, **$5-$40.**

Cow stanchion, made of cast iron and used as a mirror frame, **$10-$50.** This was made by Art Smith after his wife Kim had seen a similar one in an antique store for more than $100. Again, this is a nice use of a farm collectible and the stanchion by itself is worth between $10 and $25; wooden ones could command double that easily.

Wooden stanchion in nice condition. Wooden stanchions are in far more demand than the cast iron or steel varieties, **$50+.** *VanAlstine Collection.*

Steel eveners, for a three-horse hitch, with a modern Farm Bureau clock mounted on the center horse evener (a future collectible?), **$35-$50**.

A neck yoke and single evener, **$5-$10 each**. *Bancroft Farms Collection.*

Three neck yokes with nice aging and patina, **$10 each**. *Nerbonne Collection.*

Two eveners and a neck yoke (bottom left), **$5 to $15 each**.

This primitive milk stool has four legs and is nice condition, $25-$50. *Nerbonne Collection.*

Primitive hog trough in nice condition, $10+. *Nerbonne Collection.*

Barn lamp, repainted, $10. Marked original lamps are worth much more and some more than $100.

A barn light, made of copper, **$300**. This came from a dairy barn near Coopersville, Mich., and I have owned it and a mate to it for more than 30 years. I paid at least $50 for them then and they have increased in value. *Lewis Collection*.

Two old fire extinguishers from the Nerbonne barn, **$25-$40 each**.

An old cream can, **$15-$25**. *Nerbonne Collection*.

This old keg was at one time full of doughnuts or dough for doughnuts, **$25**. *Nerbonne Collection*.

A hay spear made by Myers of Ashland, **$25-$50**. This is from our dairy barn in Wisconsin that we took with us for a memory of the farm. *Lewis Collection.*

A Red Comet fire extinguisher made of brass, **$50-$75**. Barns and stables should always have these in them.

This set of "fly chasers" is an exceptional find, as these certainly do not trade often and are rare, **$300+**. *Nerbonne Collection.*

Original ropes and pulley; ropes are in fine condition; pulley, **$10-$20**; ropes, **$50**. *Nerbonne Collection.*

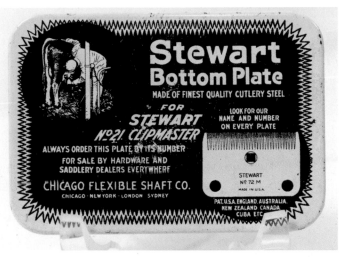

An advertising tin for Stewart Bottom Plate for the Stewart Clipmaster, used to clean hair from udders and also for shearing, **$25-$40**. Also see bag balm tins and others in Chapter 3.

This pulley hangs in the Bancroft Farms store, **$10+**.

Old tack box in nice condition, **$40-$50**. *Nerbonne Collection.*

Livestock sprayer shown with two oil cans; sprayer, **$5**; oil cans, **$5-$10**. *Nerbonne Collection.*

This large metal bolus administrator is shown primarily to help identify it for people. They appear in online sales quite often as an "unknown" tool. This one is about 20-30 years old and worth the cost of a new one, **$10**. *Lewis Collection.*

We end this chapter with a mystery item. Is it MOM or WOW? This cast iron piece hangs by two lags and has room for items to slide into and room for a center bucket or lid. Two guesses are an inflation shell holder and lid holder for a milker, prior to stainless steel laws being in place, or an old branding iron holder with a place for the cooling water to be held in a center bucket, **$50+**. *Bancroft Farms Collection*.

❧ Chapter 8 ❧
The Farm Kitchen/Household

This chapter briefly covers items related to the preparation and preservation of food that were not unique to farms but of special importance to farm kitchens, given their isolation from "store bought" food in many cases. Also, most farms had an extensive farm garden for family use (see Chapter 9), making the preservation of goods even more important.

There are many fine books on the market covering kitchen collectibles, including *Spiffy Kitchen Collectibles* by Brian S. Alexander and published by Krause Publications, but this chapter will be an overview of important items to the farm family including canning items, pie safes, Hoosiers, early refrigerators, small utensils, etc.; and other items of interest around the household and farmstead.

Many of the items in this chapter can be found in early advertising pieces touting the laborsaving qualities of the item. Things that immediately come to mind are the old apple corers and cherry pitters used in preservation of those fruits. Related items include the famous blue Ball jars and early tops and jars for preserving food.

Kitchen utensils with wooden painted handles are highly collectible and important to farm households and collectors. Also, cookie jars, bread boxes and all the other odd and sundry items found in a kitchen are important to farm kitchen collectors.

When I think of farm kitchen collectibles, I cannot help but think of all of the miniature renditions of farm animals that adorn the kitchens of hundreds of thousands of Americans, farmers and urbanites alike. What kitchen does not have a rooster, hen, cow, pig, sheep, or some farm animal as a towel decoration, cookie jar, sugar bowl, candy dish, or something else? So again, the items related to the farm have spread everywhere due to the "general attractiveness" of the item. This increases demand and value.

On a larger note, early iceboxes are quite collectible and valued at $300-$1,000, if in great condition and made of oak. In our last kitchen, we had an antique wood cook stove, a Junger from Milwaukee, Wis., valued at about $1,500.

Pie safes are a nice addition representing the importance of preserving fruit in pies and a traditional piece usually fetches at least $300.

Hoosiers are great kitchen cabinets that were designed to store flour, spices and needed cooking items and today are valued at $300 to more than $1,000, depending on condition, brand name, color and completeness.

The giant butcher blocks, once found in many farmstead butchering centers, are worth $300 or more and are being reproduced across America.

In addition, there is the related area of kitchen and food preparation cutlery. This now brings in collectors of knives and Americana in general, increasing the value of good knives such as a Case (see Chapter 10).

Some items such as kitchen steels are still inexpensive, as little as $2 each, but many items of cutlery are worth more than $30 and some more than $100 each.

An antique bread box from England, **$100+**. *VanAlstine Collection.*

Now, if you add flour sifters, egg baskets, porcelain funnels, specialty kitchen tools, early bowls, butter churns, crocks, egg scales, cutting boards, cast iron pots and pans, early kitchen appliances, dishes, bowls, cups, saucers, plates, sugars, creamers, ice cream scoops, salt and pepper shakers and spice sets to the items already mentioned, then you have a glimpse of the farm kitchen.

It is the same kitchen as elsewhere, except with a few more items usually added.

Finally, there are items unique to a farm, such as extremely large tables and benches used for the threshing meals necessary to feed a hungry crew.

I have also included a sampling of things that simply strike me as either country or farm related that you would likely find on a farm in the past, and often still today.

"Old" wire canning jar tote scam

One of the biggest "trick listings" I've seen online was for an old wire canning tote, which the seller claimed over and over again was a "farm find" and sold many of them for between $9.99 to $14.99.

These were actually canning bath liners that held seven-quart jars and can still be purchased today and quickly weathered outside with a little exposure. They are simple galvanized steel and pick up the "aged look" quite easily, even by simple use canning.

I still can tomatoes every year and mine looks just like the ones sold as "old" and is only a few years "new." These can be purchased wherever canning supplies are located.

Maybe the seller did not know they were newer and really thought them to be a "find," but I simply know this does not look right when the same photo is used over and over again to sell an item such as this. The value is $10 or less.

Farm families could find a wealth of information on the preparation and preservation of food, including uses for the apple crops, in the various magazines geared toward life on the farm. Issues of vintage magazines such as this *Farm Journal* are generally **$10-$15 each**.

This is a nice display of mixed collectibles, priced elsewhere in the chapter.

Here is a another nice display of mixed collectibles and a creative use of wooden apple crates from our nearby orchards. The photo shows an old grate from a gravity feed heating system, **$30**; the apple crates, **$20**; some nice crockery pieces, **$25-$35**; and an Amish bentwood rocker, **$300+**. *VanAlstine Collection.*

Some values of home collectibles

Split oak gathering basket, excellent shape and from an early estate in Philadelphia. This is a fine example of early Americana $210

Woven basket, likely a reproduction given some newer screws in the handle noted by the seller. The basket has older elements also, two cast-iron rivets and an iron hook; however, the newer screws were a problem for buyers. This basket was also not unlike many made in the 1980s when basket-making classes were "in vogue".......................................$17.50

A butter mold, with a daisy pattern for the mold, nice patina, used from 1920 to 1970 on the seller's family farm in North Carolina. It had been cracked in the center and glued to restore it............................$20.50

Screen door and matching porch door, from an old farmhouse, including hardware, nice condition. This was a nice set of doors but they were a "pick-up" only item (e.g. no shipping), likely keeping down the bidding.. **$8.50**

Antique farm dinner bell, #2, 16". These are common at online auctions and most are reproductions, but an honest seller offered this one and included all kinds of data and even a site on old bells found at http://www.americanbell.org/belltalk/ so prospective buyers could learn more about the bells. What I really liked about the listing was the openness of the seller to share information..$51

A wire egg basket, good example of a nice collectible. The seller juiced up the description by claiming it was an "Amish" egg basket and maybe it is, but it is a common rubber-covered wire basket used to wash eggs in automatic egg washers during the 1950s........$13.75

An egg carton, with lithography scene of a rooster and hen, 1940s, nice condition. This is definitely from the war era since it has references to turning the carton into money for the defense effort $12

Set of three antique gaslights, from an old farmhouse in South Dakota, excellent condition. This is one of the few true household antiques I've found online....... **$105**

Wooden egg crate, wooden top missing. These 12" cubical crates were common up until the late 1950s and made to stack egg cartons for shipping and/or were provided with cardboard dividers to place the eggs directly into this crate. We had literally thousands of laying hens in the 1950s and we used these crates to ship eggs directly from the farm to the wholesaler where they were then placed into cardboard cartons of one dozen each. The wooden top slid into the crate and had a wooden or metal handle for lifting the crates. See the one shown in detail in Chapter 6 .... **$10+**

An interesting "auctioneer's cane," claimed to be from the 1930s but I do not think it was that old. A common type of livestock cane still used today is likely why it had little bidder activity. Although not a kitchen item per se, general household items are included in this chapter as well.............................. **$5**

Wooden carrier, for a milkman to use, marked "Lakeview Farm" on one side and "Farm Fresh" on the other, also has a picture of a cow. This is likely a reproduction or an item made to look old, but without physically examining the item I could not be sure; however, it did not appear old by the construction of the sides to the ends (there was no dovetail work)...... **$10.50**

Foot scraper, cast iron, has prongs to place it into the dirt outside of the back door, nice condition.... **$20.50**

"Kraut slicer," used to prepare cabbage for kraut processing. This is a popular item at farm auctions. A smaller version with a serrated edge and made of wood was also sold for preparing fancy vegetables ....**$10-$25**

Lightning rod ball. This is one of everyone's favorite household items and is actually a barn item in most cases, but some were also found on houses and carriage houses. These have been hot collectibles for at least 40 years and the cobalt blue ones easily reach $100. The lightning rod ball is always a good item to have to sell, as collector interest is high, has been high, and will likely continue as these are beautiful items that are limited in number and fragile..... **$100+**

A "firkin" is a pail, made of wood, often painted, and found in the northeastern part of the United States. A specific firkin painted green was sold from a Maine farmhouse and measured 11-1/4" in diameter at the top, 12-3/8" at the bottom and was 11-5/8" high ...**$90**

Less valuable crockery and tins adorn the front porch of David and Kelley VanAlstine's home and show a nice decorative touch near the garden with the crockery holding flowers. Each piece is **$5-$20**.

Various collectibles: a crock with blue trim, holding quilts, **$35**; a large kraut cutter, **$50+**; and an antique candle mold, **$65+**. *VanAlstine Collection.*

Farm print, depicts a thatched grass roof house and barn, a Percheron team, a Terrier and a man and woman; gilded 47" x 33-1/2" frame, European design. This is a common print found in the 1930s-40s in many homes...**$50**

Four 19th century reprints of pigs and sheep, two prints of each. They were clearly marked reproductions and I've included them only to show the interest in farm related items and prints...........**$12**

Watercolor, depicts a snow-covered farm landscape, signed by Herbert Jacob Gute of New York (1907-1977), 13" x 18". The bidding reached $100, but it did not sell due to a reserve price .... **$100+**

A Scandinavian Lefse grooved rolling pin, wooden, from the Dakotas, turned from a solid piece of maple, 21" l...**$43**

Vintage farm rocking chair, 1930s or earlier. This item shows the problem of shipping for online auctions of large items, as shipping was from $90 to $200 depending on location. The item sold for $35, but the shipping would deplete the savings of many. It only received one bid and was likely by a local who could pick up the item **$35**

An old Crane apron front sink, cast iron/porcelain, has a couple of minor chips to the porcelain, 42" w, 20-1/2" deep and 14" h splashboard **$290**

Single-bowl kitchen sink, 30", cast iron and porcelain, small chips, Columbia, 30-1/2" wide, 19-1/2" deep **$150**

A simple old stool, used in the kitchen to reach items, dating from roughly 1900, painted orange **$42**

A kitchen table is an important item in any farm and many are for sale online. A nice walnut 61" x 38" table circa 1860 reached a bid of $86, but did not sell due to a reserve price; however, some online table sales reach four figures and many are in the $250 to $500 range .... **$100-$500**

Primitive gate-leg table, nice condition, covered with layers of paint, 38" round. This did not meet reserve and ended at $81 with six bids; again shipping, which was only $45, most likely deterred bidders ....**$80+**

Enamel-top four-legged table, used for bread and noodle making or canning preparation, is common at farm auctions. Many are painted and/or repainted**$32**
Weather vane, cast iron, arrow, heart and knot design, found on an Iowa farmhouse, 13"................. **$35-$50**

Old six-pane windows. These types if windows were found in every farm home in America in the early 1900s until the remodeling craze of the 1960s removed so many in favor of double hung windows. I sadly left a number of these behind over the years and now wish I had them to sell............. **$30-$50 each**

Stained glass window, from a New York farmhouse, nice condition, 19" w x 52" l.................................**$50**

Beautiful stained glass window, square shape, 28" x 32-3/4" **$135**

A No. 2 bell, cast in 1938, C. S. Bell & Co. from Hillsboro, Ohio, **$100+**. Of increasing value to collectors is the variety of bells found on old farmsteads, but you need to beware of reproductions of cast iron products such as bells and seats.

Wooden berry basket holder, **$20-$30**. This is filled with *Farm Journal* and *Woman's Day* magazines from the 1940s, **$5-$10 each**. *VanAlstine Collection.*

An old threshing bench in nice condition, shown in front of our farm home. We bought this for only $5 at a farm auction, but more realistically, I would value it at **$25-$50**.

Nesting kitchen bowls with a nice farm garden motif, marked Bake Oven on the bottom, **$50-$100 for set of four.**

Butler Paper box, oak, two drawers, with original labels, **$300-$400**.

A pair of German shepherd bookends made of copper, **$80+**.

Butter churn, Daizy brand, **$100+**. *Art Smith Collection*.

This is my favorite pattern on a syrup pitcher. We also have the nesting bowls including the largest one ever made, which is far too large to display anywhere. This is a very popular collectible USA-made pattern and the items sell high. The bottom is stamped simply 1414; pitcher, **$75+**; bowls with this pattern, **$50-$250 each**.

A Scottish Highlander bull, hand-sculpted from California Redwood. This household decoration was modeled after some photos of ones I had shown the artist and then combined with the Texas Longhorns he had seen in the California foothills near Laguna Beach. This has no known market value, as it is one of a kind and not for sale, but it is a neat little farm item made for me when I was away from the farm and living in Laguna Beach.

This butter churn, made by the Union Mfg. Co. of Toledo, Ohio, is still in extremely nice condition, **$300+**. *VanAlstine Collection.*

A smaller butter churn, **$200-$300**. *VanAlstine Collection.*

This is a more detailed view of the manufacturing mark on the butter churn at top left.

These colorful sets of Ransburg canisters, in the top photos and below right, were made in Indianapolis, Ind., in the 1940s-50s and are in fine condition and complete, **$100+**. Ransburg pieces are noted by their distinctive artist palette trademark on the bottom. Ransburg items sell well and my wife and I collect them, and a number of interesting pieces are shown. Prices for most cookie jars begin at $50 and usually only go to $125, depending on condition. Smaller pieces may even bring more if rare, but common salt and pepper shaker sets sell for a few dollars to usually $30. *Lewis Collection*.

A candle holder in the form of a dairy cow, **$5+**. This is not an antique, but a neat little item.

Roosters in the house! Many farm homes are full of collectible porcelain farm animals and we seem to have more chickens and roosters than any other type, even though we are former dairy farmers and currently raise sheep commercially. The rooster cookie jar, above, is a rare Ransburg piece, **$200+**. Some of the old glass roosters and hens, left, were inherited from my wife's grandmother and have been in the family for many years; other items were picked up here and there until we had a flock, **$10-$100+**. *Lewis Collection*.

This little chick is a family heirloom given to my wife from my mom, as are the geese in a row, **$25+**.

This hen dish is another family heirloom recently given to my wife from my mother, **$75+**.

My favorite cookie jar, a hen and her chick, has a beautiful patina in the glazing and is mint condition. This was purchased for my wife in 1998 from an antiques store and is simply as country as you can find, **$235**. *Lewis Collection*.

A miniature glass nesting hen, $15+.

Turkey is for Thanksgiving, as is this set of salt and pepper shakers used to make up a glass "turkey," $25-$50. We also have a set with red heads.

This Native American pottery quail from the Southwest was purchased in the early 1970s from the Acoma region, $25+.

A general shot showing our Krispy tin from Grand Rapids as seen in the VanAlstine collection as well, **$10-$20**; more Ransburg pitchers, **$75-$125 each**; and a neat three-frog planter, **$75-$100**.

West Bend wind-up clock, 1940s-50s, still works fine, **$25-$50**.

This decorative crock has beautiful light blue glaze going to white in the center and shows two cows, one standing, and in another field is some shocked corn, has two small chips. This is an heirloom kitchen piece that has been in the Lewis family for at least 100 years and came with the farm my father purchased from my great uncle in 1946, **$100+**. *Lewis Collection*.

Graniteware colander in nice condition, **$10+**. This was purchased at a farm auction some years ago for a few dollars, but it's now worth more, although some chipping hurts its true collector value. *Lewis Collection.*

Various crocks, **$25-$50+**. *VanAlstine Collection*.

Pie safe in nice condition, showing the crocks in the photo above, **$250**. Also pictured is a large clothing basket with a country quilt draped over it, **$50-$100**. *VanAlstine Collection*.

A nice detailed crock, with extra graphics, **$50**. The star also pictured was one of the original city of Big Rapids Christmas decorations. *VanAlstine Collection.*

Some nice crockery jugs and USA Ware, **$50+**. *VanAlstine Collection.*

Adorning the VanAlstine cupboards are more crockery pieces and other various items: a Maid-Rite scrub board, a graniteware strainer, a New Era potato chip container, two other wash boards, a Gold Medal tin tea box, and an old Quaker Oats container, **$25-$100**.

Two crocks, each in nice condition. Brown and white crock on the left, **$35-$50**; white crock with No. 4, **$75+**. *VanAlstine Collection.*

A crock full of brass door knobs, a nice heater grate, a milk case and a beautiful crock with flow blue designs, most are of significant value, along with a gorgeous pair of lady's shoes. Milk case, **$20**; rest of the items, **up to $100+**. *VanAlstine Collection.*

Glass items of interest include an early 1950s O-So grape bottle, left, to match thermometer shown in Chapter 3; a Milk of Magnesia bottle; and a very old bottle on the right made in Ladysmith, Wis., **$10-30 each.**

A crockery jug, **$25**, along with a nice advertising pail, **$25**, and two pairs of wooden skis, **$25-$50 a pair**. *VanAlstine Collection.*

Dairy collectibles are covered in detail in the *Hoard's Dairyman* book cited earlier, but here are a few examples, above and at left, of what is collected by those interested. Caps normally sell for **$1-$5 each** and bottles vary greatly by region and company name but bring **$2-$25 each** on average.

This die-cast Black Americana dish holds fruits, candies or other kitchen items, **$75+**. *Art Smith Collection.*

An end of a three-tier store display rack from the 1950s for McCormick Gourmet Spices, **$25+**.

A typical 1950s egg basket, **$25+**, if in good condition. These were made to serve two purposes: carrying the eggs and also to place them in the automatic washing devices developed in the 1950s to make egg processing easier. We had about 30 of them on our farm for egg gathering and washing, and the metal wires were covered by a thick rubberized/plasticized material to protect the eggs during washing. These have become very collectible and are used today for everything from magazine holders to laundry baskets. *Art Smith Collection.*

An evener used to hold an American flag, **$10**. *VanAlstine Collection.*

This crankshaft from a John Deere 4020 now supports the mailbox at the VanAlstine farm. This item isn't old, but it's neat, **$10+**.

A wooden darning ball was a necessity needed to sew the socks on a farm, **$10+**. *Lewis Collection.*

Graniteware and a country sign, along with a neat little pair of children's boots, show a warm welcome to the VanAlstine country home. None of this graniteware is of great value due to condition, but it shows a great way to display your graniteware with a chip or two, **$5+ each**.

This Hoosier has been adapted to modern function as an entertainment center in the VanAlstine home, **$500+**.

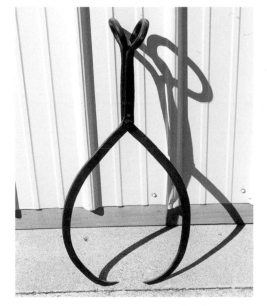

Set of ice tongs, large size and made of cast iron, **$35**. *Art Smith Collection*.

A neat ice cream scoop given to us by a dear friend is not a vintage item, but it's too cute to exclude. When the head is turned it "moos," reminding one not to dish up too much (like that would ever happen), **$15+**.

Old sad iron in nice condition, **$10-$20**. These used to sell for much more and the rare ones still do. *Art Smith Collection.*

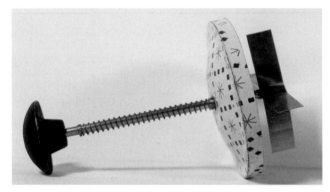

This jar top churn or mixer appears to be from the 1950s and was found at a local estate sale, **$1.50**. This can be placed upon a jar for an instant blending of ingredients. *Lewis Collection.*

A steel lawn chair from 1950s with much of its original paint missing, **$5-$10**.

A beautiful old wooden ironing board, **$35-$75**. *VanAlstine Collection.*

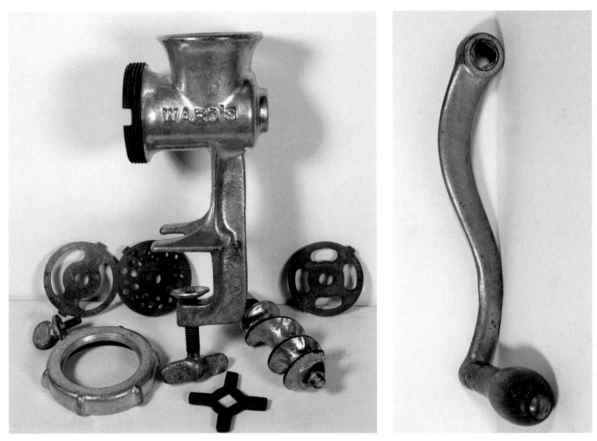

Meat grinders were used to prepare meats for sandwiches and other purposes in every farm kitchen across America. This one, a Ward's brand, is ours purchased at a farm auction and used to make ground bologna sandwich meat, **$35.**

Three-legged milk stool, about 50 years old, **$25-$50.**
Art Smith Collection.

A Clipper Fanning Mill is now used as a coffee table in the living room, **$200 at least.** *VanAlstine Collection.*

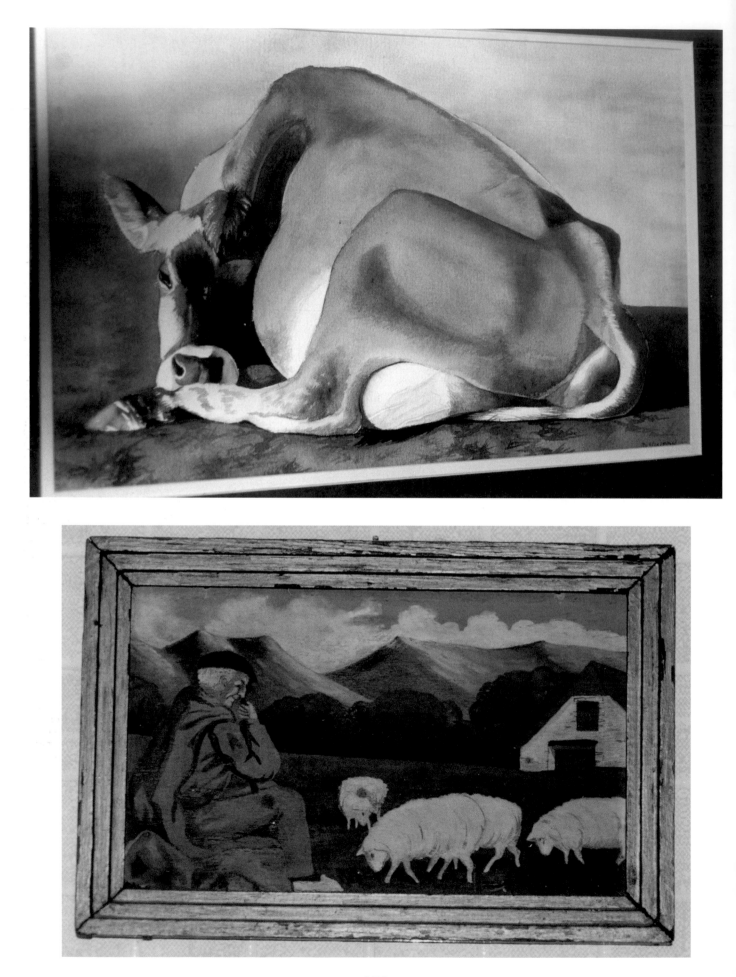

Various farm paintings from our own home, above and on Page 168, **$50-$300**. Some of these are valuable, being worth a few hundred dollars each, and some are fairly common prints. The reason they are shown is just to make collectors aware of yet another area to look for in farm items. We like prints and paintings with farm animals in them so we have bought a number over the years. Though of recent origin (less than 20 years old), original illustrations will increase in value and make great additions to a country home. One is an original painting of our former Jersey named Star as she was napping in the sun that day, shown at the top of Page 168; it was painted by Doris Vinton, former National Society of Illustrators award winner, and a good friend. The others are paintings and lithographs we simply enjoy. *Lewis Collection.*

More farm artwork from our home: the small painting, at the top, is about 6" long and has slight damage; the larger one is about 12" long and shows Oxford sheep, one of the three breeds we raise, **$50-$150 each.**

This is more original artwork by Doris Vinton. As it has for many artists, the peacefulness and serenity of farm life has inspired works of art for Doris. She paints many other things as well, but farm scenes seem to dominate her work. Full-panel paintings shown include a Michigan round barn; an abandoned truck; and a serene winter scene on a Michigan farm. Full-panel paintings sell for **$500**, half-panel for **$300-$350** and quarter-panel for **$200-$250 each**.

This is more original artwork by Doris Vinton. The full-panel painting of an old McCormick-Deering (I-H) tractor and sunflowers was found not far from my original home which I purchased from Doris. The strawberries piece is a quarter-panel and rooster is a half-panel. Full-panel paintings sell for **$500**, half-panel for **$300-$350** and quarter-panel for **$200-$250 each**.

Pole insulators were once a popular farm collectible, but have gone out of favor and the value has dropped accordingly, but they are colorful and can usually be found at every farm auction, **$2-$5 each**. Rare ones are still valuable, the same as rare canning jars, but common ones are not that valuable. *Paulsen Collection.*

Egg scale, Jiffy-Way, sold by Sears and Wards, **$25+**. Many of these types of scales show up at farm auctions today and I weighed many a thousand eggs on a similar scale as a child when we had a few thousand laying hens on hand; a related collectible would be the old egg candling machines consisting of a simple light in a wooden box to check for impurities in the egg. *Lewis Collection.*

Star Gazers, Star the Jersey and a common lithograph of a border collie and a lamb found in many farm households and given to me by my dear mother-in-law because the dog looked so much like our dog Bandit. The antique table, a gift from my wife's aunt and uncle, has some Star Gazers raised by Wendy and two copper elephant bookends surrounding an antique booklet series of little leather bound classics given to me by an aunt when I was a child (about 60 books in set). The Jersey is by Doris Vinton and is a half-panel original watercolor of our own cow Star, **$350+**. Dog/lamb print, **$75**; Star Gazers, priceless; antique table, **$200-$250**; bookends, **$50**; and Little Leather Books, **$5+ each**.

Butcher roly poly, reproduction from Chien, 1980, **$25-$50**. *Lewis Collection.*

A pump and handle serve as a modern mailbox post on a nearby homestead. Many hours were spent pumping water from a similar pump at our one-room country schoolhouse. Thank goodness we had running water on the farm even in the 1940s when I was young. These pump heads and assemblies sell for upward of $25 at auctions as collectibles and for even more if still operable, as many Amish farms still use them, **$10-$25**.

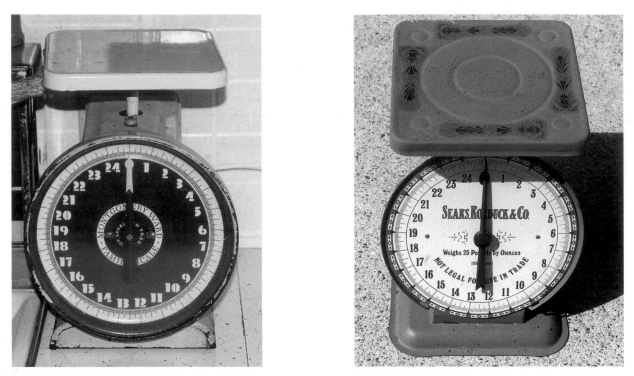

Set of scales; the one made for Wards is from our kitchen, and the one made for Sears, Roebuck & Co. is owned by Art Smith, **$25-$50**. At one time, I had about 10 sets of scales, as I found them colorful and interesting.

A cast-iron sink from a dairy milk house, sold at the Yoder consignment auction for a bargain, given prices received online for the same type of item, **$35**.

A beautiful Detroit Jewel stove, **$1,500**. *VanAlstine Collection.*

Details of the egg crate, seen on top of the Jewel stove in photo on Page 174. This is made of aluminum and holds three dozen eggs in the little holders, **$35-$50**. *VanAlstine Collection.*

A lard and a shortening tin, **$25 each**. We use a Farmer's Peet lard tin for our wastebasket in the bathroom. *VanAlstine Collection.*

A Vail & Crane Cracker Co. tin from Detroit, Mich., **$75-$125**. *VanAlstine Collection.*

This Sunshine Krispy Crackers tin is colorful but not in perfect condition; **$25**, even in less than mint condition. This is of special local appeal, as the crackers were made in nearby Grand Rapids, Mich. *VanAlstine Collection.*

A reproduction Shredded Wheat recipe tin box, from the early 1970s, $5; and an original pair of green-checkered glass stove top shakers, $30. *Lewis Collection.*

Watkins Cocoa tin and details, free trial size, rare, $30+. The Watkins brand was a major competitor on early farms with Rawleigh products and I remember both representatives visiting our farmstead in the early 1950s.

Yellow Creek Shortening tin, Elkhart, Ind., **$20+.**

Various older spice tins, including Durkee's and Defiance shown at the top, and Premier and Sudan brands shown above, and containers are popular household collectibles and range in price depending on brands, colors, age, etc. but are always popular and dress up a farm kitchen nicely, **$10-$30 for most.**

This cardboard container of Ivripic brand toothpicks has a nice paper label showing an elephant. This is in poor condition, but it's fairly rare, $10+.

Bowers Cocoanut Nut Crisps tin, $15+.

An antique trunk in a Bancroft Farms display, with two original shipping labels remaining from the Railway Express Agency, $100+.

A washboard by the National Washboard Co., No. 862, has a hen on the reverse side, nice condition, **$25+**. *Lewis Collection.*

This wringer/washing machine from the 1950s is on display at Bancroft Farms, **$25+**.

An early wringing device on an old washtub shows wash day on the farm was never fun. It was made by The American Wringer Co. of New York and is its Horse Brand Clothes Wringer (trademark is a horse in a lucky horseshoe), **$25-$50**. *VanAlstine Collection.*

A water boiler sitting on an old table, **$30**, and advertising boxes underneath, **$10-$20 each**. *VanAlstine Collection*.

An old washing machine, **$50**.

This water bath, originally used for cooling milk cans, now holds a Petunia plant, **$25**. *VanAlstine Collection*.

An old water boiler in poor condition, **$10-$15**. *Nerbonne Collection*.

Water jug, a ribbed-glass version of the same type of jug at right, **$20**. *Lewis Collection*.

Glass water jug, clear green, **$10**. This glass jug is one of many types and colors that make an interesting collecting sideline for kitchen or household collectibles. I have seen one display of these water jugs covering an entire wall of a home and it was most impressive. *Lewis Collection*.

Earlier water jugs: a Hercules in a wooden box, at left, **at least $50**; and a newer Shay Spring Water jug in a metal frame, above, **$25-$35**. They are both unusual, but the Hercules is a little more in demand due to the wooden crate. *VanAlstine Collection.*

Beautiful cast iron weather vane and glass globe, $150+.
Art Smith Collection.

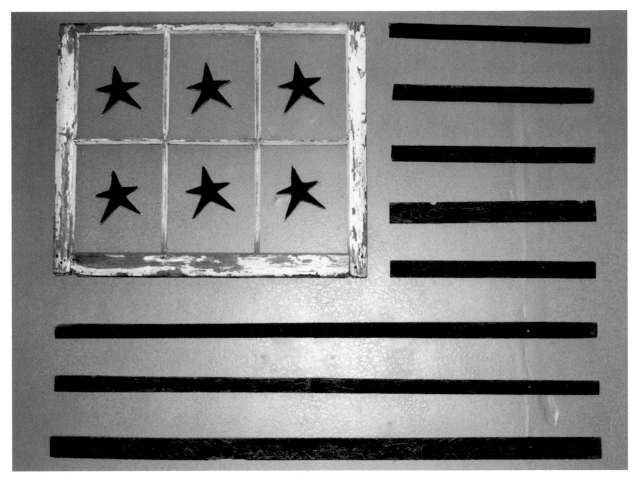

This six-pane window has an unusual use designed by Kelley VanAlstine, **$20+.**

Multi-pane windows removed from the cabinet they once adorned, **$50 each**. As noted earlier, these windows are now collectible and used for farm home restoration projects as well. *Art Smith Collection*.

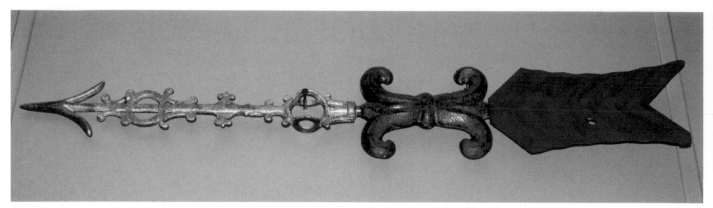

This weather vane is made of heavy cast iron and beautifully detailed, but is repainted. This is from the original VanAlstine family barn, **$50+**.

Wool carders, **$25**. They are on a Hagar ashtray, **$20-$30**, and in front of a nice McCoy planter, **$50**. *Lewis Collection*.

Chapter 9

The Farm Garden

This chapter covers the one field still lasting into today's economy in large scale—the garden companies and their seeds, and the family garden. Each winter morning, many people sit in anticipation of the seed catalog coming in the afternoon mail, bringing with it hopes of spring and abundance in the garden.

There are many items of interest in this field: advertising specifically related to seeds and gardening, early gardening tools, seed packages, catalogs, and the comeback of "heritage or antique seed varieties" in recent years. Seed display units from old hardware stores are in demand, as are calendars and "give-away" items from seed companies.

No chapter in the book likely means more to me personally. I truly became a farmer with the assistance of a farm garden. In anticipation of joining the Future Farmers of America in the ninth grade, my father allowed me to have one and one-quarter acres for a garden to raise some money to buy my first animals for an agricultural production project.

With that piece of land, at age 11, I grew one acre of sweet corn and a variety of other produce and sold it all wholesale to a man with a stand on the main highway 2-1/2 miles from our farm. I grossed about $756 for my efforts and with the money purchased three bred gilts that each gave me 14 or 16 piglets. I then raised and sold them and purchased a dozen Holstein heifers and, as they say, the rest is history.

At age 15, I talked my dad into buying a dairy farm with me; we already owned a small one but this one was bigger with cows included, and off we went a few miles down the road with my 12 heifers and 25 cows already in place. By the end of high school, we milked 120 head and I became Michigan's Outstanding Dairy Farmer in the FFA for 1965. The proudest moment of my farming life all started due to a farm garden.

Actually, we raised more than 20 acres of pickling cucumbers for Heinz when I was real young. When I was 4 and my brothers were 13 and 14, my dad told us we could have all the money from all the cucumbers we could pick to buy a television set, which was the first in our rural neighborhood in 1951. So this is a big garden, but 20 acres of pickles is just a garden.

Today, we all still anticipate the first cucumber of the season, that first vine ripened tomato, the early potatoes that taste so good from your own earth, those fall crops as they mature and the parsnips we leave in the ground to sweeten with age.

There is something about hope lasting eternal when you garden and the seed companies know this all too well. Also, they must hire illustrators from the Planet Unbelievable to design the covers and illustrations of the plants you get from their seeds, and only their seeds.

We all know it is not going to happen on our land, yet we buy the seeds in anticipation of giant fruits and vegetables appearing shortly after planting and full-size Sequoias growing within one year. The original carnival barkers have nothing on seed salesmen.

Many of the items in the seeds and gardening category are paper items. This includes such items as early seed catalogs, seed bags and boxes, advertisements for seeds, cloth seed bags for the farm trade, and crate labels of fruits and vegetables. Any of these items increase in value greatly if in pristine condition.

As with most common catalogs, seed catalogs also get tossed, making early seed catalogs collectible and valuable. Anything from the 1940s or earlier is going to bring at least $20, if in fine condition, just for the value of illustrations alone; add to that the demand by a particular company collector and it will quickly double in value. For instance, Funk's Seed Corn has been in existence since the 1800s and if you collected Funk's signs and memorabilia, you would pay more for a 1930 brochure than someone just interested in illustrations of seed corn. Now, if you were given an award by Funk's, collected Funk's, and had a shot at the same item, you would likely pay even more. That is how the "value-added" approach works with antiques and collectibles—the more personal an item gets, the more we will pay for it.

Tin signs are also important in this area of collecting. All of the farm seed companies and many garden seed companies produced tin signs for the farmer to place in the field by the roadside for passing motorists to see the brand and type of corn, barley or alfalfa. These signs are a thing of the past, as seed companies now provide a sign made of composition board or material that is not going to last the test of time (see one shown in Chapter 3, Page 62). However, some of the early seed company signs bring the same price as early tin dairy signs, $50 on up, depending on age and condition.

Often these signs do not even come onto the market until a farm is sold and even then may not be sold, as they are often a part of the landscape and not found in the barn or house.

Early seed corn was shipped in wooden boxes and one of these boxes with the labels still intact would be worth well over $100, as they are rare. Seed corn companies eventually started shelling their corn and shipping it in the more common cloth bags that became popular with collectors starting about 30 years ago. These bags are far more common but condition is still often an issue and

nice ones with colorful graphics can still bring a decent price, but many can be found for a few dollars at auctions.

As with the seed corn, early garden seeds came in wooden crates and boxes and then in both cloth bags and cardboard boxes.

Some of the early cardboard boxes were colorful items with great illustrations of the fruits and vegetables you could expect from the enclosed seeds. These items are all collectible and some are still found at auctions for reasonable prices.

This little flower garden, shown near the end of the season, adorns our farmstead and is lovingly crafted and tended by my wife, who gets me to weed once in a while, too.

Little Gerry, our prized pet rooster, amongst some garden plants. His value is priceless.

A farm garden decorative windmill is a common lawn ornament today and this one is covered with vines and also showing some traffic signs collected by their owner. Windmill, $50+; signs, $20+.

My wife's garden shed, a former carriage house/early garage, a threshing bench and some "rock sculpture" on an iron chair. I take credit for the climbing roses that were likely planted about the time of my birth by the Peters family.

The early seed companies also spent a lot of money on nice wooden display units for the hardware and feed stores. Many of these stands had outstanding graphic displays and beautiful lettering on them and were well constructed. Though common at one time, with modernization of hardware and feed stores, many have been permanently destroyed and tossed out. A few make their way to market and the prices vary widely and wildly from a few dollars to a few hundred depending on location and demand. It is far more likely that you will find one of the more common metal display units for sale; these still bring up to $50, as they are usually adorned on top with nice tin lithography signs and illustrations of fruits and vegetables.

Some groups, such as the Shakers, were shipping seeds early in the 1800s and any of their items would be doubly valuable as a farm collectible and piece of Americana. Items from the early communal societies such as the Shakers, the Oneida or the Amana colonies, would bring a premium due to the wide appeal of these groups.

Fruit and vegetable shipping crates and labels have taken on a real interest with collectors the past 30 years and demand is only growing.

The labels used on the ends of these crates are little works of art in most cases and have become in great demand for framing and display. Again, watch for fakes, but most still sell for only a few dollars so they are not being reproduced at the same rate as porcelain and tin signs.

In addition, there have been ingenious and common garden tools around for more than 100 years that are worth collecting and include: old wooden-handled (e.g. no metal on handle at all) shovels and forks, early one-row cultivators for gardens, old hoes and spades, early row markers for planting, step potato planters, potato diggers, mulching devices, scarecrow devices, and special decoys of owls to scare away birds and pests.

Values of some farm garden items

A seed identification display, made by Wendell Hester of Manilla, Ind., shows 24 common weeds found in Indiana, including wild lettuce, ragweed, fox tail, etc. This consists of a 5" x 7-1/4" unit with two panes of glass, bordered with a handmade galvanized metal frame **$26**

Wooden berry baskets, lot of 33, consisting of new old 1940s stock **$18**

Carrier for six berry boxes, including the six boxes. The carrier is 18-1/2" long x 12-1/2" wide and large enough to hold six of the 6" berry boxes **$10**

Vintage farm garden ornamental rooster (called a chicken), 1930s-1940s, 19" high. This was likely not as old as claimed, but it's a nice lawn-type ornament with some age **$25**

Hive smoking set, made by the Walter T. Kelley, Co., in good working order and fine condition **$6**

Simplex typewriter, a give-away item from the Lancaster County Seed Co., Paradise, Pa. This is one of the most unique items I've found online. The Simplex was introduced in 1892 and this typewriter was an early model. This was a neat little item is in its original shipping box and marked as a Seed Premium on the box ....**$50+**

Louden's Cut-Out Form, for High Curb Mangers. This is a neat adaptation of a tool to the garden and was a turned into a garden planter. The item was actually used to make curbs for one's dairy barn...**$20**

Hand corn planters, used normally to either inter-plant corn that did not come up in the field or as garden... **$10-$25 each**

Seed corn bags, above and in the photo at the top, are for field corn, but similar smaller bags were used for sweet corn in the 1950s-60s, yet and I bought mine in similar bags in the 1950s; **$10+ for most.**

Gardens make me think of a nice relaxing picnic and here are two collectible types of baskets: a 1950s Asian theme tin with handles, in the top photo, is a family heirloom belonging to my wife, Wendy, **$50+**; the nice splint basket, below, has a hinged lid and complete contents for a picnic, e.g. service for six, **$25-$50+**.

Boilers, such as the three here, are often used as garden decorations. Most copper boilers sell for $25-$50, sometimes higher at certain auctions, and the tin versions for about $12-$25. *VanAlstine Collection.*

This antique buggy is on the back porch of David and Kelley VanAlstine's home. The funny thing about this beautiful stroller is that they found it at a home while visiting; the people were using it to cart wood into the house. I never thought I would see a nice antique being used as a wood cart but "one person's treasures..." It is well used and weathered, $25-$35.

A corn planter hangs on the wall at Bancroft Farms, $25+.

A child's high chair and a galvanized bucket are on this corner of a small garden house on the VanAlstine property, $5-$75.

Two metal chairs found in the VanAlstine gardens, $5-$10 each.

Not much is left of this garden cultivator, but it makes a nice addition to this focal point in the VanAlstine garden, $5-$15.

These two cards by artist Doris Vinton show the beauty flower gardens inspire. Each card is original artwork and hand painted, and one also shows a vintage watering can, itself a collectible; **$5+ each card.** Used by permission of the artist.

Flowers need planters in the home and these two decorative planters have a farm motif and the little lamb is used to store our pens/scissors next to the kitchen phone (yes it is a "land-line" and a "dial" phone), **$10-$25 each**; the goat is a gift from a dear friend.

These two pump heads have a decent value because they are both in working order, **$50+**.

A hand pump, still in the ground but not functioning, on the Nerbonne farm, **$100+**.

Garden crops as salt and pepper shakers. These are actually a household collectible, but this nice set of shakers is so typical of a Midwestern garden I included it here, **$10-$15 a set**.

This Planet Jr. garden seeder is in nice condition and all lettering is still visible, **$15**. This was a real bargain at a recent Yoder consignment auction.

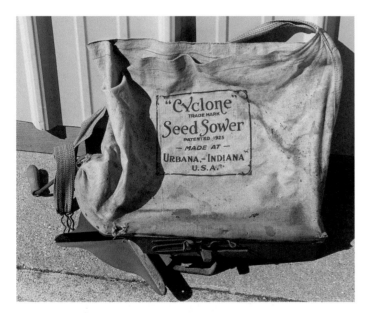

Reproduction tin signs shown for sale at Bancroft Farms. Original signs are worth hundreds of dollars, but most reproduction signs made since 1980 are **$10-$20 each**.

The "Cyclone" seed sower, described in Chapter 1, Page 13, shows the patent date and the original paper label on the bottom of the seeder, **$25**. These are common and plentiful throughout the Midwest and were used to inter-seed crops and plant the garden. *Art Smith Collection.*

These white pine stumps are more than 100 years old. Purchased for landscaping, these were originally used for fencing, **$20+ each**.

Carter's Ideal typewriter ribbon tin with a garden scene. Tins have become hot collectibles, **$5-$15 for most**. See Chapter 3 for more examples.

Tubs also make nice additions to the garden. The washtub with the three holes in it, top right, was done for some sorting purpose to fit around a three-legged table; another washtub, at left, sits on its original stand. Galvanized washtubs are not high priced and usually only **$5-$20**, depending on size, age, type and condition. *VanAlstine Collection.*

A nice use for a square washtub is this large flowerpot at another focal point in the VanAlstine garden, $10.

Another wooden hub wagon wheel sitting in a hog trough decorates the VanAlstine home. Both pieces are in nice condition and really break up the harsh lines of a foundation and add character to the entire homestead. Wagon wheel, $35-$50; trough, $5-$10.

A vintage red wagon holds flowers and is displayed next to a neat roll of barbed wire at the VanAlstine farm, $25-$50.

Wooden hub wagon wheel used as a centerpiece in a neighbor's garden to set off a new tree planting, $20+.

Windmills, used to water animals in the fields, draw water for the home and barn and to water gardens, are in great demand by collectors and restorers. This windmill still is on Art Smith's garage. Windmills can command up to $2,000 if in decent condition.

A large wooden wheel adorns the VanAlstine garden. The origin of this wheel is unknown, but I am guessing it is a counter-weight from a mill or pump, $50+.

The VanAlstines use a variety of farm collectibles and primitives to set off their beautiful gardens. The photos here show their use of implement wheels, kegs, a bobsled, a buggy tire, a primitive tool carrier and a pump head in the gardens. The gardens were toward the end of the season but still beautiful as can be seen. Values were previously given for items.

Some additional VanAlstine garden photos showing a tin water or grain tub, some barbed wire, a wooden handled shovel, at left, and a nice steel child's lawn chair, $5-$25.

Various decorative items, from left: a nail keg used as a flowerpot, a graniteware dish, a silage shovel, and a child's "necessary" chair holding a flower pot; **$20 each** in the condition shown. This is a nice way to use these items for display. *VanAlstine Collection*.

A primitive tool carrier, a graniteware frying pan and an old wooden chair set off this garden scene at the VanAlstine home. None of the pieces are worth more than **$10**, but it makes a nice scene on the porch of this little garden house.

Two collectible crate-end labels, **$5-$15**.

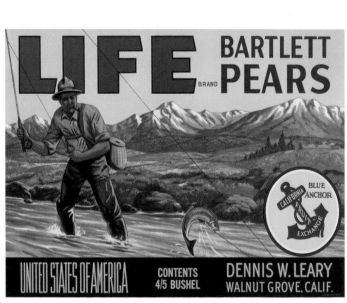

A collectible crate-end label, $5-$15.

❧ Chapter 10 ❧

Farm Recreation

Hunting and fishing were often necessary for farmers to provide needed food and were usually not seen as recreational activities in our earlier history; it was simply an extension of food production.

With this in mind, many companies marketed items to farmers in a different manner, including selling crow and owl decoys to deter the crows as pests from the farm and garden, and the marketing of predator calls to eliminate those "bad" animals from the farm.

I've covered hunting and fishing collectibles extensively in more than a dozen of my books on fishing collectibles and my books on duck decoys and related sporting collectibles. However, I think it's worth noting that some of these items had a special niche on the farm long before they were seen as recreational.

Chapter 13 shows some special advertising to induce the farmer to buy a particular product that is now seen as recreational in nature. Also, there were games and recreational activities specifically marketed to farm families that are covered here and in advertisements in Chapter 13 as well. Clearly, many of these items are now in the field of general collector interest, but it is important to show their relationship to farming and farm family life.

Advertising items are valued according to the same guidelines in Chapters 1 and 3. However, some of them are far more valuable, due to the high demand of sporting collectibles at this time. Any of the actual calls, decoys, rods, reels and lures are worth anywhere from a few dollars to a few thousand and it all depends on age, quality, rarity and demand—the same factors for all collectibles. But for the most part, many sporting-related collectibles are available within a price range of $20 to $50.

Other farm recreational activities of interest include the outdoor activities of sliding (sledding in some parts of the country), horse riding, things related to the showing of animals and the county fair, the role of baseball in agrarian America and the numerous games and parlor activities developed to wile away the time prior to the advent of television and radio.

Of course, many of these could be covered under children's games and toys also, but I have placed them here if more oriented to the entire family.

Values of some farm recreational items

The best source for sales data on these items is to review any of the books available, including any of mine. Also, current values can be tracked online at http://www.ebay.com and other online auction services.

For an excellent overview of the importance of bird decoys in collecting, I would recommend starting with *Collecting Antique Bird Decoys and Game Calls*, 3rd edition, by Carl F. Luckey and Russell E. Lewis, Krause Publications, 2003. In it, I show a number of crow decoys and crow calls, in addition to hundreds of duck decoys; also, I discuss the importance of predator calls to farming and show examples. It is also an excellent source to examine quality photographs of related collectibles such as oil cans, shot-shell boxes, knives, and advertising items.

As to fishing lure collectibles, I suggest either of my books as good starting general references: *Classic Fishing Lures* and *Fishing Collectibles*, published by Krause Publications. For the more advanced collector, refer to any of the five volumes in *Modern Fishing Lure Collectibles* also by me and published by Collector Books. All of these books have been published from 2002 to 2006 and are current in their pricing. Also look for my newest book, *Warman's Sporting Collectibles*, to be published by Krause Publications in late 2007.

Besides hunting and fishing items, additional collectibles to look for in this field include other farm recreational items, many of which are mentioned earlier in the book, such as: croquet sets, badminton sets, Jarts, Carom boards, dart boards, BB guns, large farm play sets that may have been homemade (e.g., barns, fencing, even wooden animals made on band saws), outdoor play equipment, riding toys (horses, tractors, bicycles, etc.), toy wagons, sleds, toboggans, archery items, baseball and softball equipment, books on parlor games for children and families, etc.

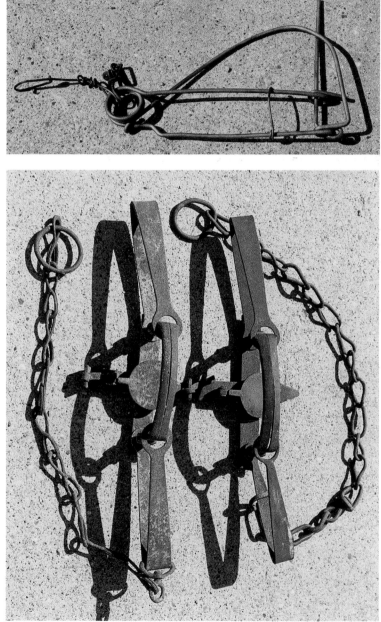

Additional collectibles of interest related to this chapter are items related to trapping, as it was part recreational and part economic for many farmers. Traps have increased in value recently, as have items related to trapping, such as trap identification and license tags, and scents for trapping. Three examples of collectible traps are shown here; see the comments of Art Smith in "An Interview with the Experts" also regarding trap values. Traps sell for $5-$500 or more each, depending on type, age, brand, size, etc. *Art Smith Collection and Lewis Collection.*

Crow, duck, goose, turkey and other game calls are popular collectibles. Farmers also used fox and coyote predator calls. The turkey call shown above is **$75+**. Calls are often found at auctions for a few dollars and are usually a good buy, as many can sell for $25 to a few hundred dollars depending on the age, maker, type, rarity, etc. Also, many calls are unmarked, making it difficult for the uninitiated to tell the value. One simple guideline to keep in mind is that most metal reed calls are usually older than plastic reed calls; of course, older calls usually command more money. Also, packaging is important and really increases the value of the call. Again, readers are directed to my book on the subject for a complete value guide. *Lewis Collection.*

Baseball is America's pastime in many ways. We all played it as children, rural schools had baseball tournaments, we watched it as we grew up and most rural communities had teams. Softball was also a big rural pastime and most communities still have leagues. Of course, baseball cards were a part of our youth and we all yearn for those Mickey Mantle and Al Kaline cards we used in our bicycle spokes to make the bicycle sound like an engine. In addition, you could spend a lot of time seeking out older items such as the "Official Clincher" giant softball from the 1880s shown here, **$20+**.
Lewis Collection.

Not only are baseball cards, baseballs, football helmets and other items collectible, so are the advertising items teams have licensed such as this "Hockeytown" ashtray for the Detroit (Hockeytown) Red Wings, **$25+**. This is a gift from my friend Ron Kommer of Pennsylvania.

Although covered earlier, bicycles, wagons, skis and sleds were certainly farm recreational items for many of us. Additional related items would be skates, early snow coasters, etc. Sleds and wagons like those shown above and in the three photos at left each sell for **$25-$50.**

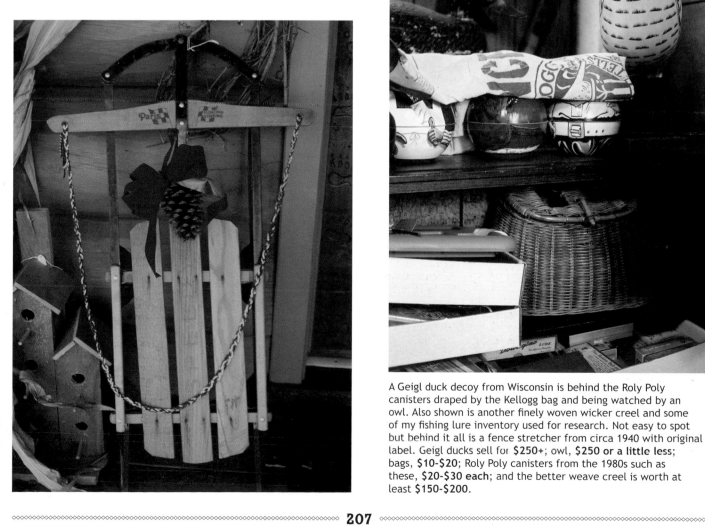

A Geigl duck decoy from Wisconsin is behind the Roly Poly canisters draped by the Kellogg bag and being watched by an owl. Also shown is another finely woven wicker creel and some of my fishing lure inventory used for research. Not easy to spot but behind it all is a fence stretcher from circa 1940 with original label. Geigl ducks sell for **$250+;** owl, **$250 or a little less;** bags, **$10-$20;** Roly Poly canisters from the 1980s such as these, **$20-$30 each;** and the better weave creel is worth at least **$150-$200.**

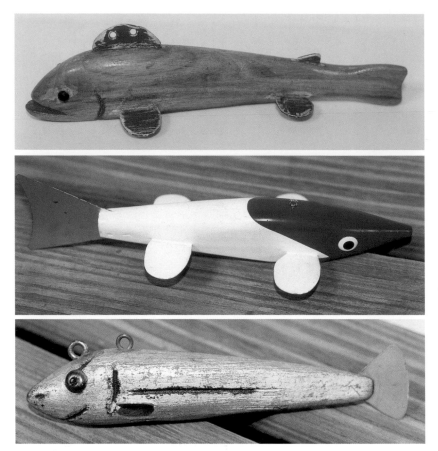

Shell boxes have become a popular collectible and values vary widely, but often you can buy them for very little at farm auctions, unless the auctions are well advertised ahead of time to attract buyers. This example is popular with collectors, **$25-$50.**

A small decoy believed to be an Oscar Petersen is shown at top, **$500+**; as well as a typical Minnesota decoy, middle, **$25**; and an unknown Michigan decoy, **$50+**. *Lewis Collection*. Spearing for fish was a winter pastime in the North, from New York through Minnesota primarily, and collectibles related to spearing include both the fish decoys and the spears themselves. You need a lot of guidance in this field to determine the value, but collectors should be aware of these little fish as being valuable, ranging from a minimum of $25 to thousands for rare Oscar Petersens from Michigan and some of the very old New York decoys. Often a spear sells for only $10 at a farm auction and would be a good buy at that price.

Gun manual, **$10-$20.**

Various recreational collectibles: a rare "sleeper" Canada goose decoy circa 1940s made by C. C. Roberts and J. Rheinschmidt of Wisconsin, **$500+**; an extremely rare Canadian goose decoy by Ben Schmidt, a known Michigan carver, **$3,000-$4,000**; and a modern fish decoy, **$50-$75.**

A glass target ball for early trap and skeet shooting, **$100+**.

A dram measure, to go with shell loading equipment shown at left, **$25+**.

Reloading shotgun shells was common in earlier times and these re-loading tools are very collectible. The old reloading tool shown should bring at least **$100**. *Lewis Collection*. These tools are often over-looked or unidentified at farm auctions but some command a decent price on the collectible market.

Advertising items are very valuable and this 1938 *Shakespeare Catalog* is no exception. Due to its early date and mint condition in its mailing envelope, this is worth about $300. I have also shown a color chart for the famous Shakespeare mouse lure as an example of one lure to collect. *Lewis Collection.*

Here are a few lures and a neat old scale received when I purchased the fly-fishing company archives of Weber of Stevens Point, Wis. The scale was previously used by the company in its mailing operations. The lures include some rare colored CCBC plunkers, a nice rainbow Pikie, some rainbow Heddon River Runts, and some more common Bombers in rainbow. There is also a nice little Heddon Crab Wiggler. These lures range in value from **$10** for the little red/white L & S lure hanging on the scale to more than **$300** for the plunker in the box because of its rare color. The scale is **$75+**. *Lewis Collection.*

This Hollowhead lure has an interesting history. It was manufactured from about 1946-1949 in Grand Rapids, Mich., using scraps of mahogany wood. A friend is a nephew of the maker and I was fortunate enough to buy all of the remaining stock of the company that had been stored in the maker's garage for nearly 45 years. I have sold many of these all new in box for between **$35-$65**. *Lewis Collection.*

South Bend is one of the "big five" lure companies and this nice three-hook minnow with glass eyes in a crackleback paint pattern is a nice addition to any collection, **$150-$200**. *Lewis Collection.*

Creek Chub Bait Company of Indiana was famous for its Silver Flash color, as seen here on a highly collectible Dingbat lure in fine condition, **$40-$75**. The lure can have a higher value for other colors. *Lewis Collection.*

Bud Stewart, a famous maker of fish decoys, also made lures and sold them nationally by advertising in sporting magazines. The Crippled Mouse and Chub lures here are not mint, but still excellent lures to find, **$30+ each**; if mint, **up to $100**. *Lewis Collection.*

A jointed Musky Sucker Minnow from the 1950s is one of many rubber Musky baits offered in Wisconsin, **$30**. *Lewis Collection.*

Mark Brunning Brown Trout ice spearing decoy, 12" long, **$175-$200**.

B&M frog spear #1, West Point, Miss., but made in Japan, mid-1950s, **$20+**.

Even empty boxes are valuable if in clean condition. Here is an early 1950s Wood's box, **$20**. *Lewis Collection.*

These little advertising screwdrivers are nice to add to a fishing lure collection, **$10 each**. *Lewis Collection.*

Split willow creel circa 1940s, with fish leather closure, **$125**. Split willow, splint and wicker creels are always popular at farm auctions and most sell for $75 minimum, and a good Lawrence or Turtle brand creel will easily break into four figures.

Wooden line spools are very collectible and this one with a rooster is a great crossover item, **$25+**. Many fun collectibles can be found with farm motifs on items not related at all to farming.

Unknown Virginia decoys, **$150-$250**.

An advertising piece is this Lazy Ike Catfish Bait tin (full), **$10-$20**.

German-made boating whistle, **$50+**.

Hong Kong-made copy of a Marble's brand match safe, **$25**. A Marble's can is **$75+**.

Wax Vestas advertising tin from Australia, nice condition, **$25+**.

The Case XX pocket knife I use, **$20.** It would be worth more, but the blade is well used and worn. Values vary so much depending on quality of blades, condition and the numbers of Xs on the shaft. I use many of my antiques and collectibles to give them personal added value, as I think an item deserves to be admired not only on a shelf but sometimes also in your pocket.

General shot of my photo studio area showing collectible items detailed elsewhere in this volume and some collectible lures, too. Most of the lures shown are circa 1950-1970. Value: lures shown range from $5-$10 each for Atlantic lures and Japanese copies hanging on sign, Radtke Pikies (blue) are about $75 each and the Le Lure green lure hanging by the rod is valued at about $200. Other items are priced in the text elsewhere.

These various fishing and farm collectibles are in my den: A girl with a goat statue, two cow candles, numerous antique and collectible fishing items, an antique scale once used by Weber Fly Fishing Co., a splint woven picnic/fish basket, a collectible wooden display unit from the Montague Rod and Reel Co., a rare book, a printer's block, and the Mobil and Arcade trucks shown earlier. Most items shown are in the **$50-$250 range**, but one Meek reel would top **$1,000**. Many of the reels shown are rare Meek and Vom Hofe and range from **$500-$800 for most**. The picnic/fish basket is valued at about **$200**, as is the display case. The scales are worth **$75+** and the statue and cows worth about **$25 each**.

friendship and joy, you cannot know one without the other

may wisdom be bountiful this holiday season

More artistic inspiration from decoys and fishing is seen here in Doris Vinton's artwork. After growing up on a private lake on our farm, it is hard for me not to have gushing feelings when I see the boy on a dock or for me to remember the great Christmas of 1958 when my dad brought home my puppy Mittens for me. Cards are **$5+ each**. Used by permission of the artist.

❧ Chapter 11 ❧

Farm Organizations

This chapter includes collectible items from organizations such as The Grange, 4-H and Future Farmers of America. Most American farmers have been a member of some form of organization or cooperative and each of these groups in turn has produced items that have become collectible by their scarcity or design, such as the toy tractors endorsed by the FFA in Chapter 4.

At this time, many of these items have little known market value, but as our demand increases for farm memorabilia, it is anticipated that we shall see an increase in the trading of pins, awards and certificates in much the same way as similar fraternal society and military items have increased in value over recent years.

This chapter is the most speculative of them all due to the little data we have on many of these items and the fact that many of them are very personal by design. In other words, someone's blue ribbon from the state fair is valuable, but how do you place a dollar value on it?

Only time will tell which items become most collectible, but if an examination of fraternal and military items has any bearing, and I think it does, the pins, medals and awards will become increasingly valuable as fewer and fewer people are actively involved in agricultural production.

I have included a number of my own awards as examples of what to look for and how these would be valued as to rarity. Clearly, a pin that is given to one of 22,000 people is worth more than a pin given to each chapter member of the FFA.

This is a beginning way to value such items and will help collectors be more knowledgeable at farm auctions if they are for sale. I also give some online sales data prices and show some of Art Smith's own FFA memorabilia as well.

Some farm granges used tin or porcelain signs to mark their location, as found in other areas of collecting, and these would be of similar values. Again, values are still being developed but this is another area that should not be overlooked.

Also closely related are such cooperatives as the Farm Bureau and the hundreds of local co-ops that produce electricity and provide fuel for farmers. These co-ops gave away pens, pencils, clocks, thermometers, water gauges, calendars, etc., and many of these items have advertising value as discussed in Chapters 1 and 3. Eventually, this area will be better known and patterns more developed for these important personal pieces of farming history. In the meantime, I hope this is a guide for you.

Values of some organization collectibles

Older FFA officer indicator for the president. This was the desk sign that we always placed out in front of the appropriate officer at chapter meetings, in this case the president. As more and more chapters cease to exist, look for items like this being offered for sale by local school systems **$51**

Two FFA jackets, officer's pins still on them, both in great condition. These were a real bargain, since the pins alone are worth even more **$12.50**

Another FFA jacket, without pins **$8.25**

Another FFA jacket, without pins, from Missouri **$13**

A Schrade Commemorative single-blade knife, model SCH-LB8, Papa Bear, 5" closed locking clip blade with brass bolsters and Staglon handles, with the FFA insignia on the blade **$33**

FFA pennant, felt, 1950s, excellent condition, 22". This was common among members and not at all rare as the listing indicated; however, most of these old pennants have long been tossed away, folded or damaged in some fashion **$37.50**

A common Chapter Farmer pin **$5**

A similar pin **$5**

Lot of four pins, including two FFA pins **$5.50**

Lot of nine pins: six 4-H pins and three FFA pins **$47.50**

Lot of 11 4-H and FFA pins, including four award pins, what looked like a Gold Star pin, and others ... **$13**

Metal sign, says "FFA Member Lives Here," circa 1950s-60s, clean condition, no major bends or dents, solid paint, 13-1/2" x 9-1/2". FFA members often hung these in front of the farm **$31**

U.S. stamps, commemorating the 25th anniversary of the FFA in 1953, with a beautiful stamp and plate blocks of this stamp **$10**

A ten-year vocational agricultural advisor pin, from 1956, marked 10k gold, presented to Lloyd Thor for his service to the FFA **$26**

FFA men's ring, sterling silver, large **$25**

My personal trophies for outstanding agricultural production projects for the Cedar Springs, Michigan Chapter, awarded two years in a row, 1964 and 1965, **$50+ each**. *Lewis Collection.*

Two of my personal officer pins for the FFA, **$10 each**. *Lewis Collection.*

My personal award pins dating from 1964-65, including the highest honor available at the state level: Gold Star State Farmer in Dairy, very rare, **$100+**. Regional pins are less rare and **$25+**. Also shown are two Dekalb corn awards for highest corn yields two years running, **$25+**. Corn award pins are even more common, but have nice advertising value as well.
Lewis Collection.

My personal pins for Chapter farmer: a record keeping award and a pin from Funks' seed corn for outstanding corn crop, **$5-$25 each**. *Lewis Collection.*

Pins and a nice patch from mypersonal FFA jacket, circa 1961, **$10** for the patch; pins range from **$5 to $100 each**. *Lewis Collection.*

My most significant award from the FFA was this 1 of 22,000 award for being the best dairy youth in the State of Michigan for 1965. The odd thing is that the actual award was an inexpensive plaque that actually broke. I removed the leather award emblem and have shown it here with the gold pin and the FFA emblem from my jacket. Again, the leather patch has little trade value but the pin is very rare and worth **$100 or more**. *Lewis Collection.*

My personal 4-H pins from 1958-60, **$5 each**. *Lewis Collection.*

Art Smith holds his personal FFA jacket from Coopersville, Mich., circa late 1960s, **$25+**. The front of Art's FFA jacket, at right, is a little washed out by the floodlights.

Art Smith's Star Green Hand award, given to the best of the new members of the FFA in the Coopersville, Mich., Chapter that year, fairly rare, **$50+**. *Art Smith Collection.*

A commemorative knife made by Schrade for the FFA and sold through farm stores in the early 1990s, **$25 in decent condition**; likely double if still mint on the card (it came in a clear plastic card with a small FFA patch). I use the one shown to cut strings on hay bales on our farm. *Lewis Collection.*

Art Smith's State Farmer trophy for 1970, very rare, **$50-$100**. He was one of the chosen few to get this award for being the best in the entire State of Michigan FFA organization for 1970.

❧ Chapter 12 ❧
Collectible Tractors

When selecting the title for this chapter, I could not help but think some might view it as "fighting words" because what is collectible to one person may not be to another.

However, I have made a somewhat arbitrary selection of tractors that are the most recognized to my generation of farmers, those of us in our 50s and 60s. Not that the other tractors are not collectible, as they certainly are; however, we all recognize a John Deere A or B and few of us recognize an old Rumely or even a very early green Allis-Chalmers.

I have also had to select only a few of the major producers of tractors and have slighted some only because I did not have access to all types or simply because some types were more popular than others in our region.

Here I am my wife's Farmall Cub on our new farm in the Lower Peninsula near Evart, Mich. This is our final move and we have all we need to raise sheep and horses, with more than 100 acres of hay ground. The Cub still works fine and does miscellaneous chores to earn its keep, from hauling a few hay bales to moving wood.

Thus, the lack of your favorite tractor being shown is not meant to indicate it is not valued, only that I did not have time to cover them all.

I think our interest in collecting tractors is caused to a very large extent by either what we had as children on the farm or what we wanted to have on the farm but could not purchase for some reason. I have documented this process well in my sporting collectibles books and I certainly believe the same process is at work with farm collectibles.

My earliest recollection of a tractor on our family farm was a Farmall BN and the fact that I not only rode on the square axle, but actually fell off once while my dad was plowing. Of course today we all see the dangers of that practice; however, at the time there was no greater thrill than riding along with dad while he did his chores. After the incident, I was relegated to following behind in the plow furrow and no longer allowed to ride along while plowing. A lesson was learned and farm safety then became more important to all of us.

Our family also had some early Allis-Chalmers tractors and my Uncle Ray had only Allis-Chalmers products. Eventually we purchased the powerful John Deere A and B (non-electric start). One of our early "modern" tractors was a Case low profile and when a Ford dealer came to town, we bought a Ford 5000 as our first ultra-modern tractor with newer hydraulics, live power, power steering and all of the modern conveniences. Somewhere along the way there were a couple of 8Ns and 9Ns used on the farm and in the woods for skidding logs, too. We also had some Oliver tractors in the family and one great-uncle relying on only that brand for motive power. Some neighbors thought that the Minneapolis-Moline brand was the only way to go, while others had the more unusual Cockshutt or Co-Op tractors.

Regardless of the brand, I am certain that many of my readers had similar experiences and memories based upon family and neighborhood usage.

I think the "big names" in tractor collecting from the vintage era of 1930 through about 1965 are as follows (in alphabetical order to avoid brawling): Allis-Chalmers, Case, Farmall, John Deere, and Oliver. I am certain some would add to the list Massey-Harris, Massey-Ferguson and Minneapolis-Moline; others might want to argue Cockshutt, Co-Op and others should be added. But from my observation, the "big five" are the first five listed. I believe they have the greatest brand recognition to the non-farm community as well, with John Deere undoubtedly having the greatest non-farm recognition due to its important role in history and its vigorous advertising in recent years for the lawn tractor market.

Yet, most non-farm folks will still recognize any of the other big five brands as being important in the horse-to-tractor-transition era.

I could spend an entire book on just this section, but there are already other books about tractors on the market; there are also a number of great Internet sites dedicated to antique and collectible tractors that should be on your favorite site lists.

I would begin by viewing the following Internet sites and then selecting any number of excellent books to read on the subject. Sites to view include, but are not limited to:

http://www.ssbtractor.com (a great source of history, parts, manuals, etc.)

http://www.atis.net (claiming to be the original Internet site for antique tractors since 1993, this site has an excellent bibliography of 23 different periodicals related to antique and collectible tractors and links to many of them)

http://www.tractorshed.com (this is The Antique Tractor Shed and has photos, history and information on antique tractors, also a guide to upcoming shows and events)

http://my.voyager.net (this Farm Life Page has many links of interest)

http://www.antiquetractorsonline.com (this page has many interesting links on antique tractors and farm collectibles in general)

http://www.antiquetractors.com (another complete site offering history, parts, discussion groups, show guides, events, and links to many other sites of interest)

Included in this chapter are a number of photos of some of the collectible tractors from this era with details provided as to value and age when known.

One of the most fun aspects of doing this book was my encounter with "Lefty" Laughlin, a fine old gentleman from whom we had purchased some hay for our sheep farm prior to me expanding our acreage of hay. I am certain that there is a book in just the life story of Lefty. He was a flight engineer on the Outlaw, one of the planes in the 509th that tested the atomic bomb in the Pacific and was the right wing guard on the flights to Japan of historic importance during the war. But he is also a man onto himself in the tractor business.

When I first purchased hay from him, he mentioned that his "newest" tractor was a 1950 John Deere B and I knew I was in for a treat. Lefty currently uses seven "antique" tractors in his daily farm operations and is the only person I know who can state with authority that he has invested less than $1,000 in buying and repairing these tractors.

His line includes: a pair of Oliver Row Crops; a 1948 Model 66 and a 1948 Model 77; two 1946 John Deere As and a 1950 John Deer B; a 1941 Farmall H; a T5 International crawler from the early 1940s; a 1945 Oliver Model 60 baler and an older Massey-Ferguson Model 12 baler; an Oliver 77 and Oliver 70 waiting to be repaired; and an Allis-Chalmers B in the restoration stage.

How many collectors of antique tractors could state they only use their collection? Lefty thought it was funny that I should consider his accumulation of tractors as antiques but fully understood the value of his prized possessions to the collector.

I have to share one story that is too good not to pass on: He told me about the time his neighbor wanted him to bale some hay but was unsure if Lefty could do it "with such old equipment." Lefty assured him that he had already baled thousands of bales that summer with the same equipment, but he was so insulted by his neighbor's demand to use newer equipment to bale his hay that the offer to bale hay was withdrawn by Lefty at that point. The moral of the story simply being many of us collect and use our equipment and its age is not a reflection of its ability to perform.

I used my wife's Cub to rake hay each year while doing at least two cuttings of 40 or more acres of hay. It used a cupful of gasoline and was fun to drive for such a job. A Cub cannot do everything on a modern farm but it still performs fine for some jobs and should be used if available, in my opinion.

Every tractor owner will have to decide the proper role for his/her collectibles, but I will drive and use my tractors as part of my farm and they will not just be placed in "retirement row."

The photos selected for this section are somewhat arbitrary inasmuch they are ones that were easily available to me due to the tractors in my own neighborhood. I thought it better to show what is commonly found, rather than what is a rare or difficult brand to find.

I hope the selection is enjoyed and that you fully understand that thousands of photos and dozens more models could have been shown if I would have unlimited space in the book and unlimited time to fill it.

I do think the photos are representative of vintage tractors that are in high demand by collectors and hope that it helps the beginner learn what people are seeking for their collections.

Lefty Laughlin's 1948 Oliver 77 Row Crop, with engine shield removed, hooked to a 1960s New Idea manure spreader. Again, this is a working collectible. Lefty found both of his Row Crop Oliver tractors with trees growing in front of both rear axles and had to "cut them out of the woods" before he could begin repairs, **$2,000.**

This is an Allis-Chalmers 1965 garden tractor Jerry Paulsen is restoring, showing two colors that will be corrected to the original when done. When completed, he estimates this tractor will bring between **$600 and $800.**

The Cub Jerry Paulsen received in a trade for an Allis-Chalmers B, after restoration work was complete. The tires are original and so give you an idea of the excellent shape this tractor was in when found. Also, you should hear it purr! A simple pull on the starter rod and it is off and running. Jerry Paulsen would not sell this particular Cub for less than $4,000.

A blade for the Paulsen Cub, $100-$200.

Some of the implements that go with the A-C 1965 garden tractor, shown on Page 224, or similar Simplicity models, **$25-$100 each.**

Lefty Laughlin's 1941 Farmall H with a modified loader that is used to feed round hay bales to his Hereford cattle. He has increased the hydraulic pressure as much as possible and told me that the tractor does just fine lifting the smaller 4-foot x 4-foot bales weighing 600-800 pounds. Again, it demonstrates that an antique tractor can be modified for modern needs. An interesting side note is that the chains seen on the tractor are from a 6-foot x 6-foot military craft Laughlin retrieved from the Pacific when discharged in 1945. This is yet another older item still seeing use on today's farm, **$1,200**.

One of the two 1946 John Deere As owned by Lefty Laughlin waiting to be used, **$1,500**.

Lefty Laughlin's nice 1950 John Deere B all tucked away for winter. All of his tractors will be stored in this or another shed for the winter, **$2,000**.

Lefty Laughlin's second 1946 John Deere A, **$1,500-$2,000**.

A Massey-Ferguson Model 12 baler that Lefty Laughlin purchased for under $500 in excellent working order that was used all summer baling hay. The baler did give him a little trouble until he discovered it was a simple spring on the hay dog that needed replacing and then it only missed one tie in about 150 bales. Not bad for a baler at least 40 years old, **$400**.

An Oliver Model 60 baler from 1945 also still used by Laughlin for hay baling, **$600-$800**.

Lefty Laughlin's 1948 Oliver 66 Row Crop next to his other 1946 John Deere A, **$2,000**.

Lefty's 1948 Oliver 66, **$2,000**.

An early 1940s IHC crawler belonging to Laughlin, **$3,000**.

An Oliver 77 Row Crop and an Oliver 70 wait for care and repair by Laughlin. Value "in progress."

An Allis-Chalmers B, with its front end already in the shop being repaired by Laughlin, waits to be pieced together and restored. Value "in progress."

Laughlin's older Allis-Chalmers side delivery rake is in need of repairs, but it can still be put into service when restored, **$75-$150**.

A Ford 8N owned by a neighbor was purchased at auction in Paris, Mich., and is used to mow the lawn, **$2,500**.

A John Deere B purchased by David VanAlstine's father is still in the family on the farm in Michigan, **$2,000**.

A Case garden tractor, with a nice snow blower on front, for sale by a neighbor, **$1,200**.

A Ford 8N that has been fully restored is owned by Burnips Equipment of Burnips and Big Rapids, Mich. The tractor may be viewed in the Big Rapids dealership, **$4,000+ in this condition**.

A Ford 8N selling at the large Yoder consignment sale in Mt. Pleasant, Mich. All of the following tractors through Page 238 were from that sale and many were "no sale" tractors bid back in by their owners and are so noted with the high bid also noted. This 8N was from 1948 or 1949 and the restoration job was noted by an obviously recent paint job, **$1,600**.

A crank-start Allis-Chalmers WC with spoke wheels received a high bid of $950 but was another "no sale"; an original 1940s Oliver Model 70 shown in the background sold for **$950.**

An Allis-Chalmers B wide front, **$900.**

This 1949 Case VAC had frozen gears and still sold for **$1,000.**

An Allis-Chalmers C with single plow received bids of $1,250 and was a no sale, with a minimum of $1,800 wanted.

A Farmall C, **$1,200.**

A Farmall Super H did not sell for $1,300, as the buyer wanted $1,800.

A Farmall Super C, above and in the top photo, with a 'fast hitch' nicely restored, **$1,800.**

A nice Ferguson Model 20 repainted with a nice engine, **$1,750.**

A ford 8N received bids of $2,400, but was still a "no sale." This should have been sold for that price, as that is about right according to my data, but some sellers put a premium on the restoration work they have done, as in this case.

A beautiful Ford 4000, all original and field ready with only 3,000+ hours, only received a high bid of $2,750 and was a "no sale." Items in the background that did sell include a John Deere 70 Diesel, **$1,225;** a John Deere AR, **$1,400;** a John Deere wide front 720 Diesel, **$3,300;** weights for the JD AR, **$550;** and a 3-point hitch for the JD 70, **$450.**

A John Deere B, **$1,325.**

A rough John Deere B, with original paint and a bad manifold (a new manifold was included), sold for only **$675.** A repainted John Deere B received bids of $1,050, but was yet another "no sale" that day.

This nice old John Deere B on spoke wheels could only muster a high bid of $1,500 and was a "no sale" also.

A John Deere Model 1010 from 1964, with donned fresh paint and a live PTO, **$3,050.**

A nice F-12 McCormick-Deering from 1935, ran fine, **$1,125.** This shows the low price some vintage tractors can bring.

An older McCormick-Deering on steel, **$1,025**.

A 1946 Oliver orchard model, **$850**.

To show how some folks value their antique tractors, I found the following four Farmall tractors for sale in my neighborhood and they are all beautiful, and nicely restored or in original condition. I would buy them all, but the asking prices are too high for the current market and they have already been reduced; nonetheless, it shows the current state of the market well. From top left they are: an H, Super H, M and Super M. The Super M Farmall from 1952 is **$2,600**. A Super MTA that was "show ready" did sell for $10,500 in 2003 showing the demand for some of the more unusual Farmalls. This M is a 1939 for **$2,800**, reduced from $3,800, which was far too high. This 1953 Super H is **$2,800** and was also reduced. A 1940 Farmall H is **$2,400** and was again reduced, but not yet enough to sell quickly.

John Deere hit and miss engines from the 1910s or early
1920s, 1-1/2 horse power each, were used by a vendor
to make ice cream at the Yoder consignment sale; what a
great use of old technology, **$2,000+ each.**

My wife's Farmall Cub, **$2,500**. I've used the Cub to rake many acres of hay on the farm.

The author on his newer Ford 4610 tractor in the machinery shed. My favorite tractors to use are Fords, and my newer 4630, to the right in the photo, and this 4610 are nearly twins. I also use a 1910 with a loader for barnyard duties and feeding chores. If properly cared for and stored from inclement weather, these may someday become collectible. In the meantime, they get the job done.

❧ Chapter 13 ❧

A History of Farm Advertising

This chapter is a review of many of the farm and agricultural items that are now collectible and features reprints of a number of advertisements from farm publications dating from 1903 until about 1965. Of special interest are all of the detailed ads from the 1903-05 period reproduced that show most of the items found in this book.

You should get an idea of how old many of the collectible items are. It will also become apparent that many farm items did not change greatly once invented in the late 1800s or early 1900s, for instance fence stretching tools, feeding equipment and implements, until the advent of the tractor in the 1920s.

Also, a review of the *Montgomery Ward Farm Catalog* of 1964 demonstrates that many of the early 1900s items are still in use and demand yet in the mid-1960s. This should also assist you in dating items to prevent you from buying "antique items" that are really only a few years old. Many of the items passed off online as "antique" are really only 30 to 40 years old and may not be all that rare. Ads from this catalog start on Page 281.

Of course, some of the more recent items are still highly collectible, but the buyer should be aware of how long many of the farm items of a collectible nature were actually manufactured. It is difficult to tell a hoof pick from 2006 from one from 1965, for instance.

This chapter is offered as a great way to familiarize yourself with changes through the ages of American agriculture.

I have selected items from catalogs from the 1930s, 1940s and 1950s as well. Again, they are reproduced as found in the catalogs. However, a careful study of the advertisements will result in viewing many items shown earlier in this book. For instance, kitchen roosters, the Jiffy Egg Scale, egg carrying baskets, a calf muzzle similar to the cribbing muzzle shown, a calf weaning device like the one shown, calls and decoys shown, similar tools, barn track and pulleys like the ones shown, and many early sleds, bicycles, and similar items, etc.

Rather than present the items in a chapter-by-chapter organization, I thought it better to show the advertisements as they actually appeared in the original publications. It is clear that the old magazines themselves from the early 1900s are now collectible, but the advertisements found in them are even more valued for the information provided to collectors and researchers.

It was amazing to me that many of the advertisements found were then documented with the same item being sold. For instance, a hay tedder advertisement from 1905 was found and the same hay tedder was sold at a recent horse-drawn farm implement auction in Michigan.

A close examination of this chapter will show you many items I did not have an opportunity to photograph, but have been described in the previous chapters. It will also show many items still to be discovered at those farm sales in the future.

I would like to give a special thanks to my wife, Wendy, for being the main researcher on the old farm advertisements from our collection of early 1900s *Breeder's Gazette* magazines.

She spent many hours pouring over the pages of these great old magazines looking for interesting advertisements to help other collectors.

We were fortunate to find two bound volumes of these magazines from friends in the Upper Peninsula that had had them for a number of years in their family. It is not common to find bound magazines from 1903 in nearly mint condition and it is lucky for us that we had these items for research purposes.

All of the advertisements featured on Pages 243 through 252 are from these *Breeder's Gazette* magazines.

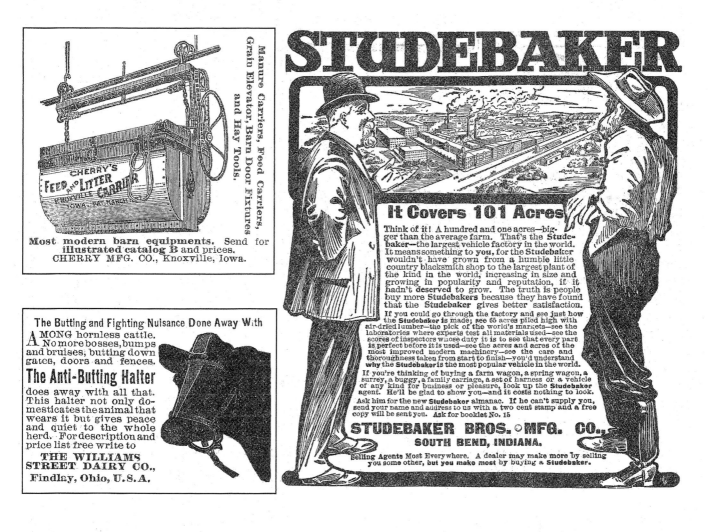

Low Down Wagons

soon earn their cost on any farm.

A low wagon at a low price. Handy for the farmer. Will carry a load anywhere a horse can travel.

Steel Wheels

for farm wagons. Straight or staggered spokes. Any size wanted, any width of tire. Hubs to fit any axle. For catalogue and prices, write to Empire Mfg. Co., Box 100 H Quincy, Ill.

FARMERS SAVE TIME & MONEY BY DOING BLACKSMITHING AND REPAIRING AT HOME

THIS STEEL FORGE WILL EASILY WELD A 4 INCH WAGON TIRE FULLY GUARANTEED

ANY FARMER CAN START a welding fire in this steel forge in two minutes and do repairing at home. **WE GUARANTEE** our steel forges to equal in every way any $10 forge and the as represented or money refunded. **Special Introductory Prices.** One forge complete $4.25, or 1 forge, 1 pr. of tongs and 1 anvil vice combined, all $6.00. Our forges have been used and endorsed by farmers in every state and Canada for the last years. Write for free catalog and testimonials. **C. A. S. FORGE WORKS, Saranac, Mich.**

The Coming Unloader!

Louden Hay Sling

The easiest and speediest means of unloading hay, bound grains, forage crops. **Can Be Used With Any Hay Carrier.** Raises

Half a Wagon Load

where there is barn room to handle it. Cleans the rack and deposits flat in the mow as it was on wagon. **Best Line Hay Tools in the World** for field, stack and barn. Hay Carriers. Hay Forks, Steel Tracks and Switches, Hay Rack Fixtures, Feed and Litter Carriers, etc. Our **Flexible Barn Door Hangers** are the best on Earth. Ask for complete catalog of Hay Tools, Appliances and Hardware Specialties. It is Mailed Free for the Asking.
LOUDEN MACHINERY COMPANY,
46 Broadway, Fairfield, Iowa.

THE **SMITH** **Great Western** Endless Apron **Manure Spreader**

SPREADS all kinds of manure, straw stack bottoms and commercial fertilizer regardless of their condition. Spreads as much in a day as 15 men can by hand. Spreads the largest load in 2 to 4 minutes. Makes the same amount of manure go three times as far and produce better results; makes all manure fine and immediately available for plant food.

NON-BUNCHABLE RAKE forms a hopper, holds all hard chunks in contact with beater until thoroughly pulverized.

ENDLESS APRON is one continous apron, (not a ½ apron) therefore always ready to load. You don't have to drive a certain distance to pull it back into position after each load or wind it back by hand; it is a great advantage in making long hauls.

THERE IS NO GEARING about our Endless Apron to break and cause trouble, it is always up out of the way of obstructions as it does not extend below axle. Spreads evenly from start to finish and cleans out perfectly clean.

HOOD AND END GATE keeps manure away from beater while loading; prevents choking of beater and throwing out a bunch when starting and acts as wind shield when spreading. It has a graduating lever and can be regulated while in motion to spread thick or thin, 3 to 25 loads per acre.

LIGHT DRAFT because the load is nearly equally balanced on front and rear axles. The team is as near the load as it can work. Front and rear axles are the same length and wheels track; beater shaft runs in ball and socket bearings, therefore no friction. Beater is 23 inches in diameter, seat turns over when loading. Machine turns in its own length.

SIMPLICITY There are only two levers on our machine. One which raises the hood, locks it and throws the machine in gear at the same time. It can then be thrown in and out of gear without lowering the hood. One lever which changes feed to spread thick or thin, making it so simple that a boy who can drive a team can handle it.

STRENGTH AND DURABILITY is one of the most important points to be considered in a manure spreader. The Great Western has a good, strong, durable wheel. Extra strong spoke and rim, heavy steel tires. Strong, well braced box with heavy oak sill. Oak tongue, hickory doubletrees, malleable castings, gears and sprockets all keyed on. Galvanized hood. Every part is made extra strong, regardless of cost. It is made for the man who wants the best; made in four sizes, 30, 50, 70 and 100 bushel capacity.

GUARANTEE Should any part break, wear out or get out of order within one year we replace free of charge. Send for free catalogue, showing latest improvements. It tells how to apply manure to secure best results.

SMITH MANURE SPREADER CO.
15 S. Clinton Street, CHICAGO, ILL.

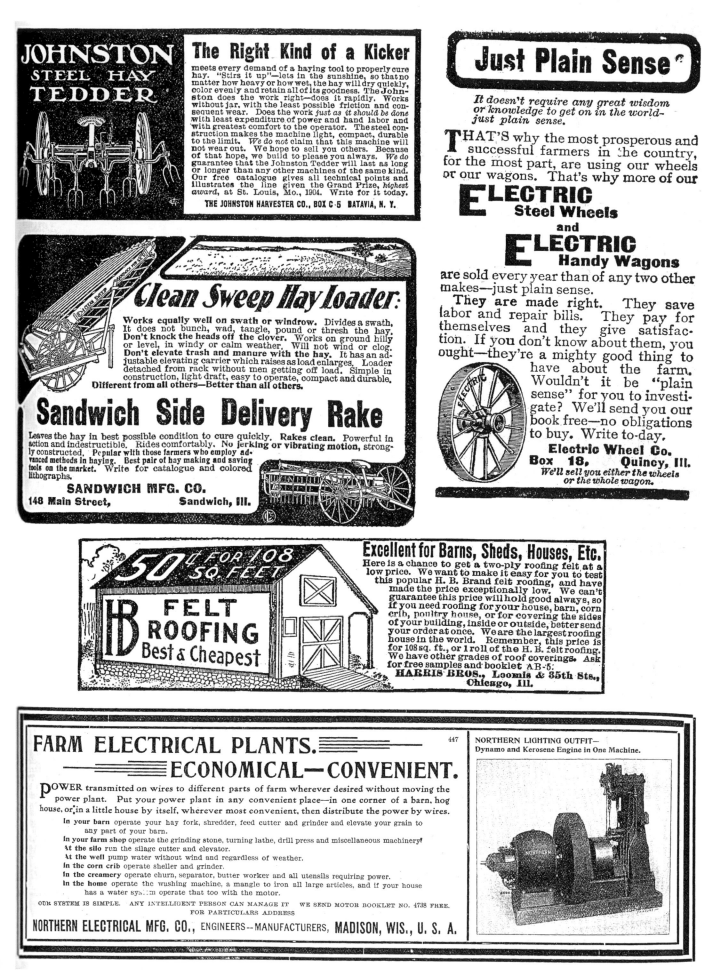

(Continued from page 543.)

public, sale June 7 are coming along nicely. I understand there will be a combination sale of North Dakota breeders in Fargo June 6, so that together we hope to get the largest crowd of breeders that ever attended a sale in that part of the country." See page 555.

W. H. Miller & Sons, Mulberry, Ind., write: "THE GAZETTE is the paper to stay with and so far it is worth the price. We have decided to offer our Polled Durham herd bull Royal Abbotsburn for sale. He is just past three years old, a good dehorner, splendid breeder and we guarantee him in every way. He is a show bull in first company. His calves are coming in his way and we offer him for no other reason. We also have a 20-months red polled bull out of a granddaughter of imp. Gay Monarch that is of the low-down thick meaty kind. He should head some choice herd. We also have a roan 12-months polled calf (out of a Scotch cow bred by F. Douglas, Canada) of the true Scotch type that will make a very valuable bull for some one. We have other younger ones that are very promising. All are sired by Royal Abbotsburn. Our herd numbers 75 head." See page 558.

ELDER LAWN SHORT-HORNS.

The reputation of T. K. Tomson & Sons, Dover, Kan., for breeding first-class Short-horn cattle is becoming widely known throughout the Middle West. They have recently made a very valuable sale to Mr. Nevius of Kansas on a choice bull and 10 females. However, they find themselves at this time with a splendid lot of young bulls on hand, both Scotch and Scotch-topped. They have at least 12 big strong useful bulls ready for service. They have issued a very neat little pamphlet giving the sire and dam of each of these bulls, as well as a brief description of each. They will be pleased to mail this to all GAZETTE readers who are interested in the purchase of a good young bull. Their herd is made up of the very best representatives of Scotch and American families, particular attention being paid to the milking qualities as well as the thick flesh qualities of their Short-horns. They have been conspicuous in the show-rings in the hottest company for a number of years, having over 200 prizes to their credit, won at State and National shows. The reputation gained by their chief herd bull, Gallant Knight, is certainly an enviable one of which any breeder could justly feel proud. This firm will furnish its stock with sufficient guarantees back of it. The announcement appears on page 553.

STEELE'S SHORT-HORN SALE.

On March 29 C. R. Steele, Ireton, Ia., will sell from his Willow Lane herd some 60 head of richly-bred Short-horns, including a large number of Scotch and imported Scotch cattle. He will be joined in this sale by O. F. Farrand, of the same place, who will sell 15 head. The cattle, however, are under the supervision of Mr. Steele, and it may practically be called his own sale. Mr. Steele has selected for this sale some of the best cattle in his herd, as well as some of the best from the Scotch standpoint. Since his last sale the herd has been very much strengthened in herd bulls. One of the best Scotch bulls in the West is Mr. Steele's chief herd bull, Grand Baron 2d, bred by A. & G. Davidson of Iowa. He was sired by Grand Baron, a straight Scotch bull by Glaucus. Grand Baron belonged to the famous Lavender family, having for his grandam imp. Lavender 38th by Dunblane. Grand Baron 2d's dam was the famous Duchess of Gloster cow, Duchess of Gloster 28th. She belongs to the best of this famous family, descending from imp. 12th Duchess of Gloster by Champion of England. This family in the hands of James I. Davidson of Ontario proved in all probability the most valuable family of Short-horn cattle that he ever owned. In Grand Baron 2d is found the typical old Baron Victor owned by Senator W. A. Harris, possessing practically all of Baron Victor's good points without his homely born. This bull has a beautiful head and horn, is very low and thick, carrying a thick-bedded back and loin, an exceedingly wide hind quarter, and is as smooth a bull at the tail head as ever it was our pleasure to see. We speak of this bull at some length from the fact that a large percentage of the females in Mr. Steele's offering are in calf to him. Those not in calf to him, aside from a very few, are bred to Red Gauntlet 2d, which is included in the sale. He was sired by the Harris-bred bull Red Gauntlet, a son of Scarlet Knight, while his dam, Geraldine, was by the Cruickshank bull imp. Chief Baron. She is out of Gardenia by Cumberland. This is a splendid Scotch bull, low and thick, a heavy flesh carrier and has proved himself an exceptionally good sire. Mr. Steele is selling him for no fault whatever, but simply because he has no use for so many herd bulls. He is a dark red, calved March 13, 1898. The females not bred to one of these bulls will be bred to two red sons of imp. Lord Banff. These two Lord Banff bulls are included in the sale. The choicest of the two was dropped July 15, 1903, and is out of imp. Contessa. She belongs to Mr. Cruickshank's famous Miss Gibson or Mary Anne (by Sillery) tribe. This bull is one of the choicest yearling bulls listed to pass under the auctioneer's hammer this spring. His stable companion is by the same bull and out of imp. Queen Elizabeth. This bull is perhaps not quite as attractive in all his make-up as his elder half-brother, but he is a corking good one. Either of them, however, is a choice bull and far above the average. Mr. Steele will offer a number of other good Scotch bulls, among which we note a son of H. D. Parsons' famous bull Victor Baron. This is a Mysie bull, royally bred, light red and is a very clever animal throughout. There are a number of other straight Scotch bulls of a little younger age, but the majority are ready for service this season. Mr. Steele is offering 19 long yearling heifers, the like of which is seldom offered by one breeder. They are bred to the Lord Banff bulls. Among Mr. Steele's straight Scotch cattle are two choice Orange Blossoms, two Mysies, two imported cows, one choice Canada-bred Scotch cow, two Louisas, one Spleenwort, one Sempstress, a richly-bred Secret and bull calf, and one beautiful daughter of Scottish Knight. The Secret cow with bull calf at foot is one of the best-bred Cruickshank Secrets living, and her beautiful red bull calf is one of the attractions of the sale. They too will be sold together. There are too many good cattle in the offering to endeavor to individualize on any of them. It is sufficient to say that no one who attends this sale can possibly be disappointed in the quality of the offering. The cattle with few exceptions are in fine sale condition. These exceptions as a rule are cows that are suckling calves that sell with them. Mr. Steele has endeavored to cut out all drones, and every animal that would need to have an apology offered for it. The sale will be conducted by Auctioneers Woods and Jones, and will be held March 29, allowing March 30 for breeders who attend this sale to reach the sale of John Lister at Conrad, Ia., on March 31. For catalogue address C. R. Steele at Ireton, Ia. See page 552.

HOW TO BUY A BUGGY

Just as You Would a Horse—Look It Over Carefully and "TRY IT OUT" on the Road

$50

IF YOU buy a buggy with your eyes shut, you will get a bad bargain every time. A buggy may look all right today and go all to pieces inside of a year. You wouldn't think of buying a horse with your eyes shut. You would look at his teeth to find out his age, wave your hands before his eyes to see if he had good eyesight, look him over for spavins and ringbones and "size him up" generally to be sure he was sound. Then you would drive him at a good gait to see if he was wind broken. Why not be even more careful in buying a buggy? We are selling our famous SPLIT HICKORY Buggies on a new plan, which allows the buyer to "try out" the vehicle as he would a horse, before concluding the purchase. Here is our offer made in absolute good faith to any responsible person.

We Will Ship Our 1905 Split Hickory Special Top Buggy, the Price of which is $50, Anywhere in the United States on 30 Days Free Trial. Guaranteed For Two Years.

We will tell you just how it is made, giving complete specifications, so that when you receive the buggy you can go over it part by part, and check up every item. You can compare it with the buggies sold in your neighborhood for nearly twice as much money. You can hitch up to it and use it just as though it were your own and if you do not find it just as represented, you can ship it back to us at our expense and your money will be refunded. *The Fourth National Bank of Cincinnati, Ohio,* will tell you we are responsible for our contracts and agreements and that you may be assured of fair and honest dealing.

Here are some points of merit of the SPLIT HICKORY SPECIAL.

Wheels are made of the very best selected second growth split hickory, with screws through the rims; axles are long distance, dust proof, best refined steel, with split hickory axle beds cemented and full clipped; oil tempered springs, 16 oz. imported all wool broadcloth upholstering; box frame spring cushion; solid polished panel spring back; water-proof top with No. 1 enameled leather quarters and leather back stays; 28 oz. water-proof rubber roof and back curtain; back curtain lined and reinforced; rubber side curtains; full length storm apron; padded patent leather dash; full length velvet carpet; split hickory, fully guaranteed, shafts. Painting, oil and lead process; all wood work carried 100 days in pure oil and lead, 16 coats, every coat rubbed out and dried before the next is applied.

Our 1905 Catalogue, containing 192 pages, is a regular Information Bureau on the subject of Vehicles and Harness. If there's anything you want to know about buggies you will find it there. We send it free and take pleasure in answering letters immediately.

THE OHIO CARRIAGE MFG. CO.,
(H. C. Phelps, Pres.)
STATION 7,   **CINCINNATI, O.**

MODERN COUNTRY LIFE

The rural mail delivery, the telephone and the suburban electric railway are working wonderful changes in the life of the farmer's family today. The former isolation which drove many of the young men and women from the farm to the city, has been banished by the many telephone lines now in use all over this country.

STROMBERG-CARLSON TELEPHONES

have brought the cost of building farmers lines within the means of every farmer. Time is near at hand when every farm will have its own telephone, and the farmer's family will be in close touch with the whole neighborhood, as well as the entire world. It is impossible to estimate the value, in dollars and cents, of the telephone to the rural home. Its influence on the boys and girls in keeping them contented and at home, is incalculable. The farmer will reap benefits every year worth considerably more than the entire cost to him—in keeping tab on the markets, in getting help in busy times and in many other ways. Write for free book F. 82 "Telephone Facts for Farmers"—giving information on how to organize and build a telephone line. Our book 82 tells how others have built rural telephone lines. Write today to nearest office.

STROMBERG-CARLSON TEL. MFG. CO.,
Rochester, N. Y.   **Chicago, Ill.**

STANDARD BOOKS

FOR THE FARMER AND BREEDER for sale at this office. Send for new catalogue. Address J. H. SANDERS PUBLISHING CO., Chicago, Ill.

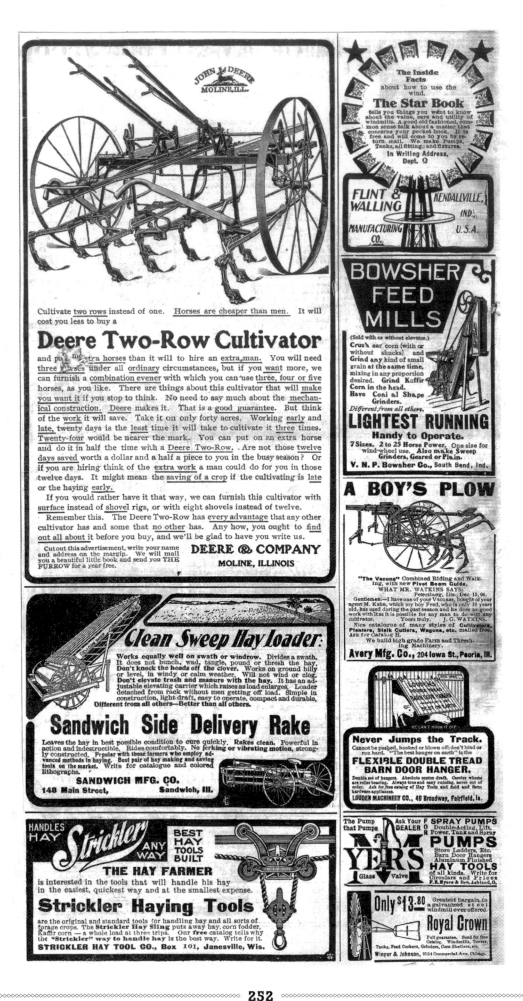

This is the cover of a 1930 *L.L. Bean Catalog.*

The Maine Snow-shoe

If there is a better Snow-shoe made we certainly would like to see it. The frames are especially selected State of Maine second growth white ash butts, seasoned so they will not warp.

The filling is the very best cowhide, cured by a secret process that positively prevents sagging. The workmanship is so well done that it gives the shoe a perfect balance. The models are designed especially for New England winter sports.

Both Men's and Ladies' are very sporty looking shoes. Wool tassels 60¢ extra. Initials on toe bar 60¢ extra. Regular orders filled same day received. With initials or tassels one week.

Ladies' $9.50

Men's $9.75

We recommend sizes as follows:
Men weighing 115 to 140, 12x48.
Men weighing 140 to 165, 13x48.
Men weighing 165 to 225, 14x48.
Ladies weighing 80 to 120, 10x50.
Ladies weighing 120 to 160, 11x50.
Price Men's $9.75. Ladies $9.50. Delivered free in the United States.

Bean's Snow-shoe Rigging

After experimenting with different Snow-shoe Riggings for over two seasons, we have settled on this one as the best and most practical for both men and ladies.

As we use waste pieces that are too small for our Hunting Shoes, we are able to make a light weight, high-grade rigging at the low price of $1.25.

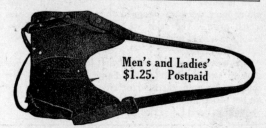

Men's and Ladies' $1.25. Postpaid

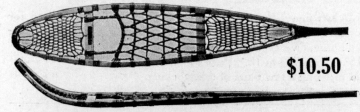

$10.50

The Pickerel

This new narrow shoe is made of the same high grade material used in the "Maine" Snow-Shoe as shown above.

This type of shoe had its origin in the far North where the Indians needed a light easy running shoe to track down their game on light drifting snow. Beginners can start right off in confidence for the narrow tread and high upturn eliminates interference and tripping.

It does not load and its bearing value is equal to other type of shoes 50% wider.

Note the special rawhide reinforcements at toe and around bars.

Filled with fine mesh in toe and heel and heavy coarse mesh in body.

Sizes 8"x56", "9x56", 10"x56". Price $10.50 delivered.

L. L. BEAN, FREEPORT, MAINE.

An ad for snow-shoes from the 1930 *L.L. Bean Catalog*.

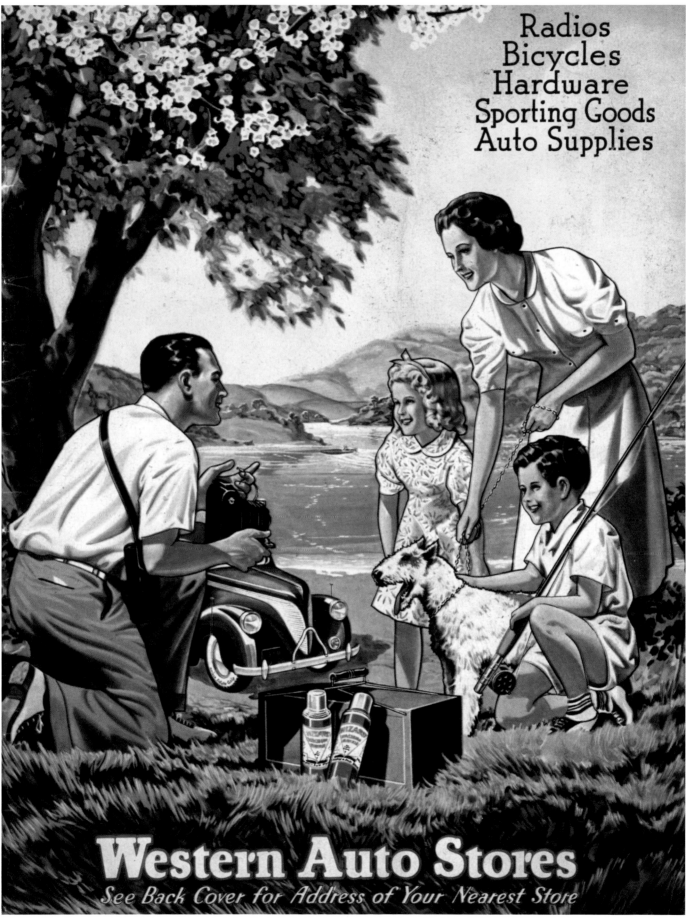

This is the cover of the 1938 *Western Auto Stores Catalog*.

The advertisements here and through
Page 262 are from the 1938 *Western
Auto Stores Catalog.*

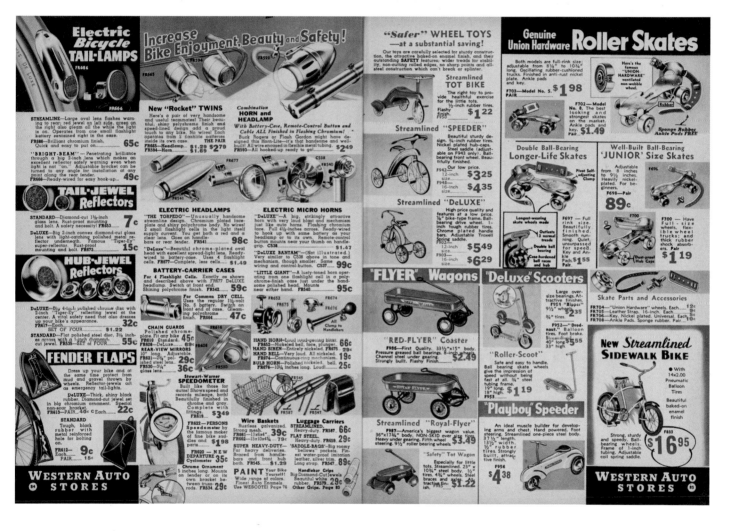

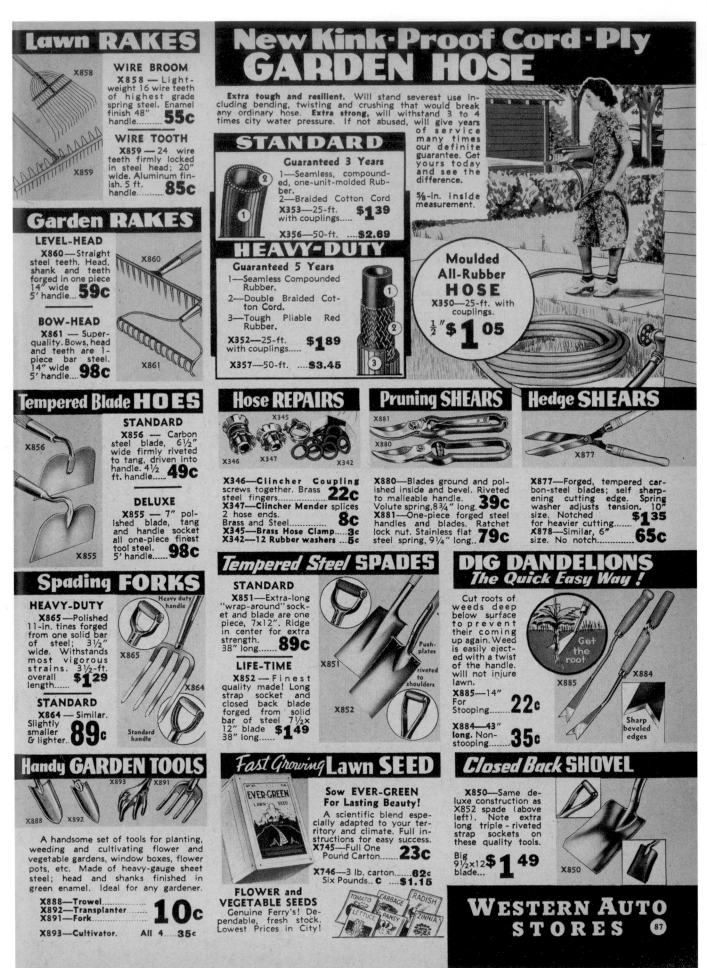

Lawn RAKES

WIRE BROOM
X858 — Lightweight 16 wire teeth of highest grade spring steel. Enamel finish 48" handle.......... **55c**

WIRE TOOTH
X859 — 24 wire teeth firmly locked in steel head; 20" wide. Aluminum finish. 5 ft. handle......... **85c**

Garden RAKES

LEVEL-HEAD
X860 — Straight steel teeth. Head, shank and teeth forged in one piece 14" wide 5' handle... **59c**

BOW-HEAD
X861 — Super-quality. Bows, head and teeth are 1-piece bar steel. 14" wide 5' handle.... **98c**

New Kink-Proof Cord-Ply GARDEN HOSE

Extra tough and resilient. Will stand severest use including bending, twisting and crushing that would break any ordinary hose. Extra strong, will withstand 3 to 4 times city water pressure. If not abused, will give years of service many times our definite guarantee. Get yours today and see the difference.

⅝-in. inside measurement.

STANDARD
Guaranteed 3 Years
1 — Seamless, compounded, one-unit-molded Rubber.
2 — Braided Cotton Cord
X353 — 25-ft. with couplings..... **$1 39**
X356 — 50-ft. ...**$2.69**

HEAVY-DUTY
Guaranteed 5 Years
1 — Seamless Compounded Rubber.
2 — Double Braided Cotton Cord.
3 — Tough Pliable Red Rubber.
X352 — 25-ft. with couplings..... **$1 89**
X357 — 50-ft. **$3.45**

Moulded All-Rubber HOSE
X350 — 25-ft. with couplings.
½" **$1 05**

Tempered Blade HOES

STANDARD
X856 — Carbon steel blade, 6½" wide firmly riveted to tang, driven into handle. 4½ ft. handle...... **49c**

DELUXE
X855 — 7" polished blade, tang and handle socket all one-piece finest tool steel. 5' handle...... **98c**

Hose REPAIRS

X346 — Clincher Coupling screws together. Brass steel fingers.................. **22c**
X347 — Clincher Mender splices 2 hose ends. Brass and Steel............ **8c**
X345 — Brass Hose Clamp....**3c**
X342 — 12 Rubber washers ..**5c**

Pruning SHEARS

X880 — Blades ground and polished inside and bevel. Riveted to malleable handle. Volute spring, 8¾" long. **39c**
X881 — One-piece forged steel handles and blades. Ratchet lock nut. Stainless flat steel spring, 9¼" long.. **79c**

Hedge SHEARS

X877 — Forged, tempered carbon-steel blades; self sharpening cutting edge. Spring washer adjusts tension. 10" size. Notched for heavier cutting....... **$1 35**
X878 — Similar, 6" size. No notch.............. **65c**

Spading FORKS

HEAVY-DUTY
X865 — Polished 11-in. tines forged from one solid bar of steel; 3½" wide. Withstands most vigorous strains. 3½-ft. overall length...... **$1 29**

STANDARD
X864 — Similar. Slightly smaller & lighter.. **89c**

Tempered Steel SPADES

STANDARD
X851 — Extra-long "wrap-around" socket and blade are one piece, 7x12". Ridge in center for extra strength. 38" long....... **89c**

LIFE-TIME
X852 — Finest quality made! Long strap socket and closed back blade forged from solid bar of steel 7½x12" blade 38" long..... **$1 49**

Push-plates riveted to shoulders

DIG DANDELIONS
The Quick Easy Way!

Cut roots of weeds deep below surface to prevent their coming up again. Weed is easily ejected with a twist of the handle. will not injure lawn.

X885 — 14" For Stooping........ **22c**

X884 — 43" long. Non-stooping........ **35c**

Get the root

Sharp beveled edges

Handy GARDEN TOOLS

A handsome set of tools for planting, weeding and cultivating flower and vegetable gardens, window boxes, flower pots, etc. Made of heavy-gauge sheet steel; head and shanks finished in green enamel. Ideal for any gardener.

X888 — Trowel.........
X892 — Transplanter....
X891 — Fork........ **10c**
X893 — Cultivator. All 4...**35c**

Fast Growing Lawn SEED

Sow EVER-GREEN For Lasting Beauty!
A scientific blend especially adapted to your territory and climate. Full instructions for easy success.
X745 — Full One Pound Carton....... **23c**
X746 — 3 lb. carton.......**62c**
Six Pounds..C ...**$1.15**

FLOWER and VEGETABLE SEEDS
Genuine Ferry's! Dependable, fresh stock. Lowest Prices in City!

Closed Back SHOVEL

X850 — Same deluxe construction as X852 spade (above left). Note extra long triple-riveted strap sockets on these quality tools.
Big 9½x12" blade... **$1 49**

WESTERN AUTO STORES

87

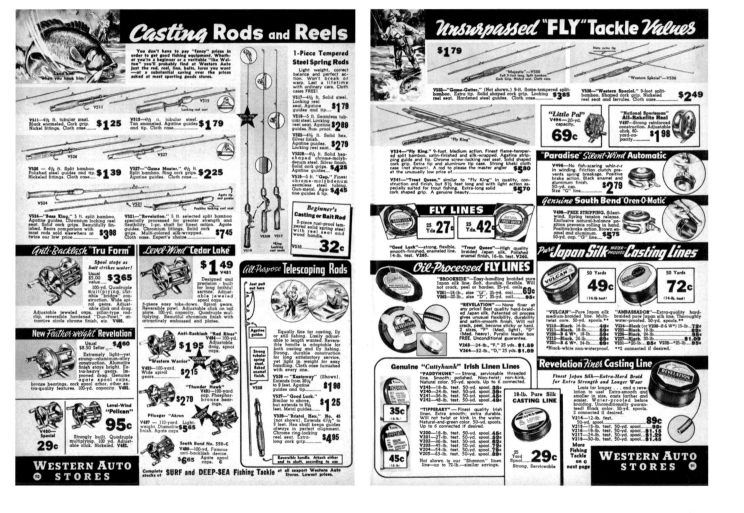

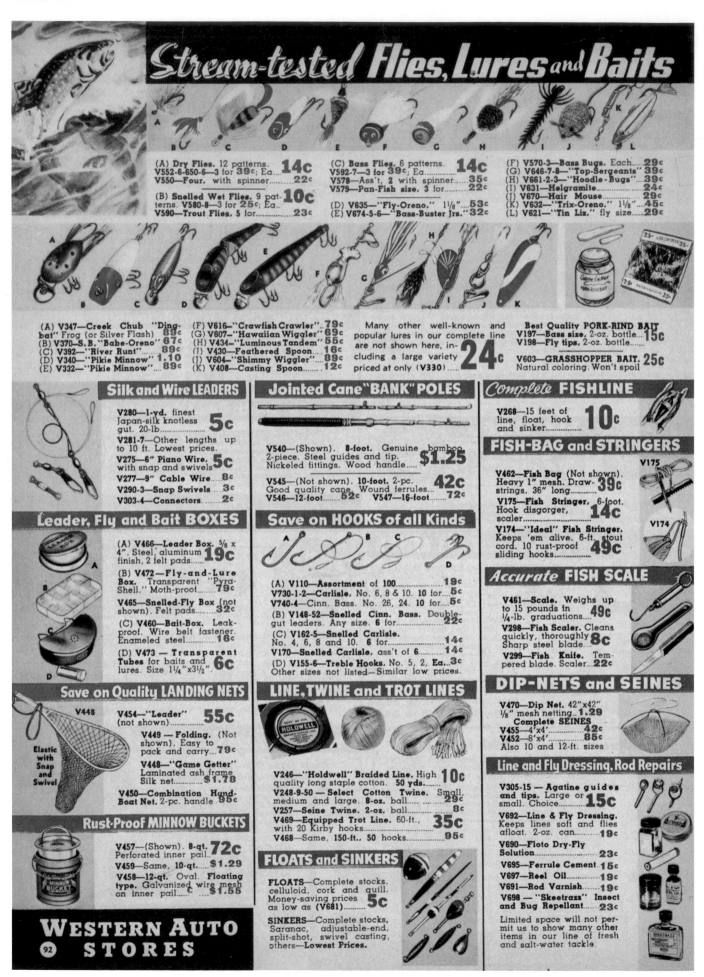

Stream-tested Flies, Lures and Baits

(A) **Dry Flies.** 12 patterns. **14c**
V552-6-650-6—3 for 39c; Ea.
V550—Four, with spinner..........**22c**

(B) **Snelled Wet Flies.** 9 patterns. V580-8—3 for 25c; Ea. **10c**
V590—Trout Flies, 5 for..........**23c**

(C) **Bass Flies.** 6 patterns. **14c**
V592-7—3 for 39c; Ea.
V578—Ass't, 2 with spinner.......**35c**
V579—Pan-Fish size. 3 for.........**22c**

(D) V635—"Fly-Oreno." 1⅛"....**53c**
(E) V674-5-6—"Bass-Buster Jrs."**32c**

(F) V570-3—Bass Bugs. Each....**29c**
(G) V646-7-8—"Top-Sergeants"**39c**
(H) V661-2-3—"Hoodle-Bugs"...**39c**
(I) V631—Helgramite..............**24c**
(J) V670—Hair Mouse............**29c**
(K) V632—"Trix-Oreno." 1⅛"...**45c**
(L) V621—"Tin Liz," fly size...**29c**

(A) V347—Creek Chub "Ding-bat" Frog (or Silver Flash) **89c**
(B) V370—S. B. "Babe-Oreno" **67c**
(C) V392—"River Runt"..........**89c**
(D) V340—"Pikie Minnow" **1.10**
(E) V332—"Pikie Minnow"......**89c**

(F) V616—"Crawfish Crawler"..**79c**
(G) V607—"Hawaiian Wiggler"**69c**
(H) V434—"Luminous Tandem"**55c**
(I) V430—Feathered Spoon......**16c**
(J) V604—"Shimmy Wiggler"..**89c**
(K) V408—Casting Spoon........**12c**

Many other well-known and popular lures in our complete line are not shown here, including a large variety priced at only (V330).... **24c**

Best Quality **PORK-RIND BAIT**
V197—Bass size, 2-oz. bottle...**15c**
V198—Fly tips, 2-oz. bottle......

V603—**GRASSHOPPER BAIT.** **25c**
Natural coloring. Won't spoil

Silk and Wire LEADERS

V280—1-yd. finest Japan-silk knotless gut. 20-lb. **5c**
V281-7—Other lengths up to 10 ft. Lowest prices.
V275—6" Piano Wire, with snap and swivels **5c**
V277—9" Cable Wire....**8c**
V290-3—Snap Swivels....**3c**
V303-4—Connectors........**2c**

Leader, Fly and Bait BOXES

(A) V466—Leader Box. ⅝ x 4". Steel, aluminum finish, 2 felt pads. **19c**
(B) V472—Fly-and-Lure Box. Transparent "Pyra-Shell." Moth-proof........**79c**
V465—Snelled-Fly Box (not shown). Felt pads........**32c**
(C) V460—Bait-Box. Leak-proof. Wire belt fastener. Enameled steel..........**16c**
(D) V473—Transparent Tubes for baits and lures. Size 1¼"x3½". **6c**

Save on Quality LANDING NETS

V454—"Leader" (not shown)........**55c**
V449—Folding. (Not shown). Easy to pack and carry....**79c**
V448—"Game Getter" Laminated ash frame Silk net......**$1.78**
V450—Combination Hand-Boat Net. 2-pc. handle..**95c**

Elastic with Snap and Swivel

Rust-Proof MINNOW BUCKETS

V457—(Shown). 8-qt. **72c** Perforated inner pail.
V459—Same, 10-qt. **$1.29**
V458—12-qt. Oval. Floating type. Galvanized wire mesh on inner pail........**$1.55**

Jointed Cane "BANK" POLES

V540—(Shown). 8-foot. Genuine bamboo 2-piece. Steel guides and tip. Nickeled fittings. Wood handle..... **$1.25**
V545—(Not shown). 10-foot. 2-pc. **42c** Good quality cane. Wound ferrules.
V546—12-foot...**52c** V547—16-foot...**72c**

Save on HOOKS of all Kinds

(A) V110—Assortment of 100..........**19c**
V730-1-2—Carlisle, No. 6, 8 & 10. 10 for....**5c**
V740-4—Cinn. Bass. No. 26, 24. 10 for....**5c**
(B) V148-52—Snelled Cinn. Bass. Double-gut leaders. Any size. 6 for..........**22c**
(C) V162-5—Snelled Carlisle. No. 4, 6, 8 and 10. 6 for..........**14c**
V170—Snelled Carlisle, ass't of 6........**14c**
(D) V155-6—Treble Hooks. No. 5, 2. Ea..**3c**
Other sizes not listed—Similar low prices.

LINE, TWINE and TROT LINES

V246—"Holdwell" Braided Line. High quality long staple cotton. 50 yds. **10c**
V248-9-50—Select Cotton Twine. Small, medium and large. 8-oz. ball......**29c**
V257—Seine Twine. 2-oz. ball......**8c**
V469—Equipped Trot Line. 60-ft., with 20 Kirby hooks....**35c**
V468—Same, 150-ft., 50 hooks..........**95c**

FLOATS and SINKERS

FLOATS—Complete stocks, celluloid, cork and quill. Money-saving prices as low as (V681)........ **5c**

SINKERS—Complete stocks, Saranac, adjustable-end, split-shot, swivel casting, others—Lowest Prices.

Complete FISHLINE

V268—15 feet of line, float, hook and sinker........ **10c**

FISH-BAG and STRINGERS

V462—Fish Bag (Not shown). Heavy 1" mesh. Draw-strings. 36" long...... **39c**
V175—Fish Stringer, 6-foot. Hook disgorger, scaler.......... **14c**
V174—"Ideal" Fish Stringer. Keeps 'em alive. 6-ft. stout cord. 10 rust-proof sliding hooks.......... **49c**

Accurate FISH SCALE

V461—Scale. Weighs up to 15 pounds in ¼-lb. graduations.... **49c**
V298—Fish Scaler. Cleans quickly, thoroughly. Sharp steel blade **8c**
V299—Fish Knife. Tempered blade. Scaler..**22c**

DIP-NETS and SEINES

V470—Dip Net. 42"x42" ⅛" mesh netting..**1.29**
Complete **SEINES**
V455—4'x4'..........**42c**
V452—8'x4'..........**85c**
Also 10 and 12-ft. sizes

Line and Fly Dressing, Rod Repairs

V305-15—Agatine guides and tips. Large or small. Choice..........**15c**
V692—Line & Fly Dressing. Keeps lines soft and flies afloat. 2-oz. can..........**19c**
V690—Floto Dry-Fly Solution..........**23c**
V695—Ferrule Cement..**15c**
V697—Reel Oil..........**19c**
V691—Rod Varnish..........**19c**
V698—"Skeetrazz" Insect and Bug Repellant..........**23c**

Limited space will not permit us to show many other items in our line of fresh and salt-water tackle.

WESTERN AUTO STORES
92

Firestone

EXTRA VALUE MERCHANDISE

FOR CAR AND TRUCK
HOME AND FARM
WORK AND RECREATION

BROOKFIELD TIRE & BATTERY CO.

120 N. Main St.   Phone: 30

BROOKFIELD, MO.

Fall AND *Winter* 1947

WEST

This is the cover of a 1947 *Firestone Catalog.* The advertisements on Pages 264 through 278 are from this catalog.

Have Fun This Winter

(A) GIRLS' JUVENILE FIGURE SKATES — Enjoy real skating ease and pleasure. Fine quality white leather uppers have reinforced eyelets and tops. Shoes have web instep reinforcement and leather heel protectors. Felt lining with felt-lined tongue and metal tipped shoe laces. Nickel-plated figure skates are riveted to durable sole and built-up heel. Sizes from 12 to 2.
10-D-36 .... **8.95**

(B) LADIES' WHITE FIGURE SKATES — An excellent quality ladies' figure skate with fine quality white elk top grain uppers, flared top, shearling tongue lining, felt sock lining. Professional type closed toe, extended leather counters for greater ankle support and oak-tanned soles. Hollow ground runners are nickel-plated. Steel shanks. Truly a fine buy for the lady skaters in your family. Sizes 3 to 9.
10-D-20 .... **13.95**

(C) MEN'S SUPREME QUALITY HARD TOE HOCKEY SKATES — The hockey skates experts prefer — built for speed and comfort. Extra heavy top grain elk uppers, elk trim, stitched sole construction. Fine quality shearling tongue lining, extra heavy sock lining. Heavy duty double box toe, professional last, brass Klondike eyelets; back stay, reinforced at instep with leather for extra protection. Extended leather counters, leather innersole, heavy sole. Supreme quality tubular skates, nickel-plated and electrically welded for strength. Steel shanks. Full sizes 7 to 12.
10-D-38 .... **15.95**

(D) MEN'S AND BOYS' HARD TOE HOCKEY SKATES — Good quality black top grain uppers, brown elk trim, heavy felt tongue lining. Reinforced at ankle and instep with leather for extra protection. Strong box toe, oak-tanned sole. Electrically welded tubular skates, bright nickel-plated, steel shanks. Boys' sizes 2 to 6. Men's sizes 7 to 12.
10-D-37 .... **11.95**

(E) MEN'S FIGURE SKATES — Built for skaters who enjoy fancy skating. Bright nickel-plated, one-piece hollow ground runners. Black shoes. Three web ankle reinforcement straps on inside. Felt-lined tongue and felt insoles. Sizes 6 to 11.
10-D-16 .... **13.45**

Firestone 42

Be Ready For Sledding

(D) (E) SILVER STREAK SLEDS — There's a Silver Streak Sled at our store for youngsters of every age — from 3 years old up — in sizes from 38 in. up to 54 in. Come in and see these speedsters with their scientifically grooved runners, turned up and supported by strong curved steel brace. They're built for speed. Specially built yoke assures easier steering control. Runners and undercarriage made of special tempered steel for maximum service, securely riveted to body. The body and cross bars are straight-grained hardwood with extra heavy coats of weather-resistant varnish to withstand roughest treatment. All metal parts silver finish, attractive red and blue trim.

10-L-7 — 38-in.		**4.98**
10-L-8 — 45-in.		**5.95**
10-L-9 — 54-in.		**6.95**

(F) 45-INCH ROYAL RACER SLED — A low priced, quality sled. Designed for easy steering with strong metal undercarriage supports, tempered flat steel runners. All metal parts are securely fastened together with heavy rivets. Bed, cross-members and steering handle made of hardwood, with weather-resistant varnish finish. Red baked enamel trim.

10-L-6 — 45-inch **4.45**

(A) (B) (C) YOUTH'S HOCKEY STICKS — When snow flies, and the pond freezes over, hockey is the sport every active boy enjoys. These sturdy, straight-grained, hardwood sticks are built for rough service. Easy to handle — proper weight and size. Attractively painted blade and lower shaft, smoothly sanded natural finish handle.

10-D-40 — Length 47 in **1.29**

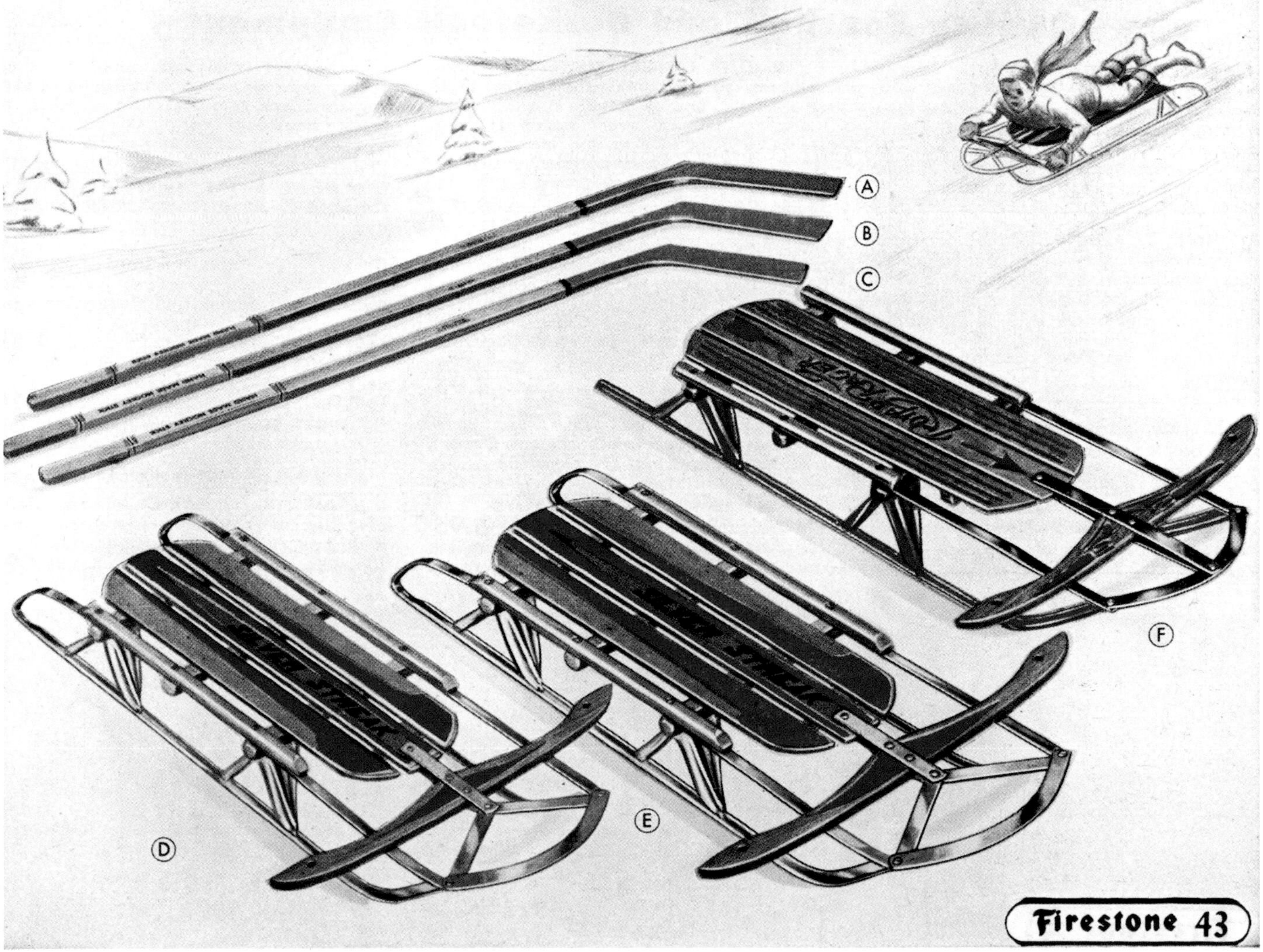

Firestone 43

265

Quality Football and Basketball Equipment

(A) FOOTBALL HELMET — Strong, rugged head protection for high school and sand lot players. Heavy top grain leather ears, front and back. Stiff, well-formed plastic fiber crown — thick felt lining. Carefully stitched seams provide long life. Adjustable snap button elastic chin strap.
10-J-24 .... **7.95**

(B) SHOULDER PADS — Designed for hard, competitive service — built to give maximum protection. Well-formed collar, shoulder and shock plates of stiff plastic fiber, lined with heavy felt and assembled with riveted wide leather straps. Strong web lacing in front and back, wide elastic arm bands.
10-J-22 .... **5.95**

(C) OFFICIAL FOOTBALL — The ideal low-priced ball for young players. It is cut- and scuff-resistant — DuPont Football Covering with pebble grain. Official in size and weight, sewed with tough waxed thread. One-piece molded bladder, leakproof rubber valve.
10-J-37 .... **3.95**

(D) VARSITY OFFICIAL FOOTBALL — Takes plenty of abuse on the sand lot or high school field. Double lined top grain, pebble grain leather, strong chain stitched seams. Official in size and weight. One-piece molded rubber bladder, leakproof rubber valve.
10-J-6 .... **6.95**

(E) SPALDING OFFICIAL FOOTBALL — A really fine ball — equal in quality to balls used by semi-pro and pro football players. Selected top grain leather, double vulcanized lined. Lock-stitched with tough waxed thread for rough use. Official in size, weight and shape. One-piece molded rubber bladder with leakproof rubber valve.
10-J-41 .... **8.95**

(F) OFFICIAL BASKETBALL — Easy to handle official size basketball, made with long-wearing, cut- and scuff-resistant DuPont basketball covering. Flat plastic laces eliminate bulging. One-piece molded bladder has leakproof rubber valve.
10-J-38 .... **5.95**

(G) "BLUE ARROW" BASKETBALL — For indoor or outdoor play. Tough, long-wearing rubber cover will take roughest playground service—resists scuffing on cement and unpaved surfaces. No stitches to break. Leakproof valve. Official in size and weight for accurate performance.
10-J-20 .... **8.95**

(H) MEN'S SWEAT SHIRT — Fine cotton yarns, fleece-lined. Jersey knit cuffs. Silver gray.
10-K-3 .... **1.59**

(J) KNIT "T" SHIRT — Attractive heathertone colors — tan, blue and yellow. Full cut, hemmed bottom and sleeves. In sizes to fit.
13-C-4 .... **1.59**

(K) WHITE "T" SHIRT — Full cut — rib knit neck. Made of combed cotton.
13-C-5 .... **1.19**

(L) SPORT SOCKS — Good-quality combed yarn socks. Made of 50% wool, 25% cotton, 25% rayon.
10-K-8 — Pair **59c**

(M) ATHLETIC SUPPORTER — Elastic Neoprene synthetic rubber belt and leg straps. Rayon pouch has elastic edges.
10-K-1 .... **69c**

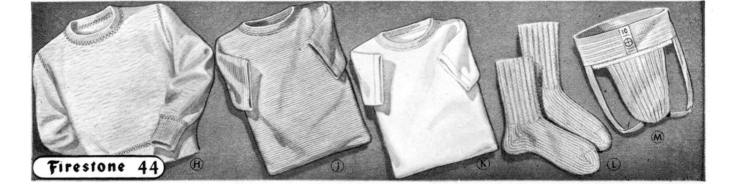

Firestone 44

Choose Your Fun — Indoors or Out

(A) TABLE TENNIS BALLS — Official size and weight. Celluloid. Meets U. S. Table Tennis Association specifications.
10-J-14 — Each............................... **10c**

(B) STANDARD TABLE TENNIS SET — Ideal for beginners or occasional players. Includes four 3-ply rubber-faced, basswood paddles with wood handles; official 60-inch net with table mounting brackets; 3 lively balls.
10-J-17 — Complete........................... **4.95**

(C) DE LUXE TABLE TENNIS SET — A good set with four 3-ply genuine basswood paddles with rubber faces for top-spin, laminated wood handles. Official 60-inch net, adjustable mounting posts. Six lively balls, official rule book included.
10-J-16 — Complete........................... **5.95**

(D) SUPREME TABLE TENNIS SET — Regulation size net. Four professionally balanced, rubber-faced, 5-ply paddles, smoothly sanded edges and handles. 60-inch tape-bound net ties on sturdy screw-on posts. 12 table tennis balls, complete rule book included.
10-J-15 — Complete........................... **7.95**

(E) STRIKING BAG — Genuine sheepskin leather bag that will take any and all punches. Official size and shape. Lock-stitched, reinforced, welted seams. Valve-type rubber bladder. Sturdy steel swivel hanger with leather thong. Fits standard platform.
10-J-18 — Complete........................... **5.95**

(F) BOXING GLOVES — High quality, full-sized boxing gloves made of wine-colored sheepskin. Just right for active boys, with plenty of padding. Double-stitched thumb, built-up wrist. Heavy fabric trim and laces. Four gloves to a set.
10-J-4 — Set of 4,............................ **7.95**

(G) ROLLER SKATES — Real outdoor exercise for young fry on these speedy all-steel, ball-bearing roller skates. Sturdy nickel-plated, channel steel frames, adjustable from 8¼ to 11 inches. Adjustable streamlined toe clamps. Rubber-cushioned trucks. Adjustable leather ankle strap.
10-D-22 — With key........................... **3.95**

(H) BEGINNER'S ROLLER SKATES — Good sturdy skates for children 3 to 7 years old. Long life rubber wheels and steel axles. Strap for toe and ankle. Rich looking satin silver finish — rustproof.
10-D-21.. **2.69**

Firestone 45

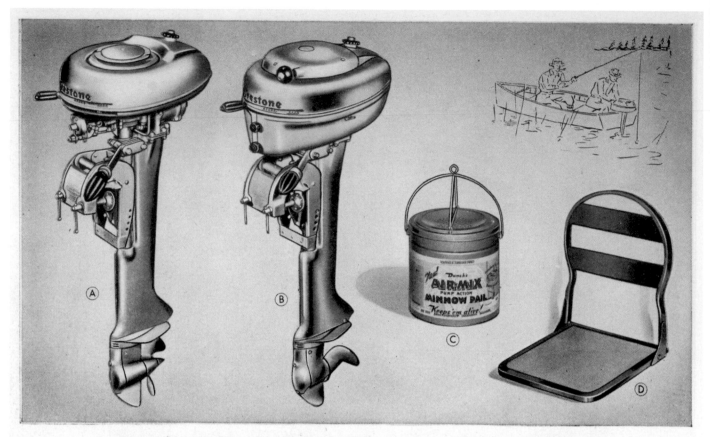

Everything for the Outdoor Man

(A) THE NEW FIRESTONE STANDARD 3½ H.P. SINGLE CYLINDER OUTBOARD MOTOR — Add hours of pleasure and convenience to your fishing and boating enjoyment. The new Firestone 3½ H.P. Single Cylinder Motor has new positive action water pump, drop-forged hardened steel connecting rods with roller bearings for friction-free operation. Scientifically designed counter-balanced crankshaft, high intensity magneto that gives hotter spark for quicker starting and lower idling speed. Positive non-flooding choke. New hydraulic jet silencer for quieter operation. Hardened, ground gears. Streamlined gas tank with full one gallon capacity. Handy carrying handle.

All castings especially treated for corrosion resistance. Weighs only 40 lbs.
10-A-1 .... **99.50**

3½ H.P. DE LUXE QUALITY SINGLE CYLINDER OUTBOARD MOTOR — Same type as 10-A-1 above except has these added features: Self-winding starter rope; all enclosed mechanism to protect cylinder block, spark plug, gas lines from weather and damage. Weighs only 42 lbs. — easy to handle.
10-A-2 — (Not illustrated) **112.50**
Only 4.75 a Week on Budget Terms

(B) 7½ H.P. DE LUXE QUALITY TWIN CYLINDER OUTBOARD MOTOR — For maximum performance, smoothest operation, greatest speed and life, choose this De Luxe Quality Twin Cylinder Motor. Has all the features of the 10-A-1 and 10-A-2 at left plus the following: Powerful 7½ H.P. twin cylinder motor; alternate firing for smooth operation at all speeds. Approved by the National Outboard Association.
10-A-3 .... **164.50**
Only 6.75 a Week on Budget Terms

(C) 12-QT. MINNOW BUCKET — Keeps minnows alive longer without changing water.
10-M-155 .... **3.95**

(D) METAL BOAT SEAT — A safe, comfortable seat for fishermen.
10-A-5 .... **4.49**

FIRESTONE IS FISHING HEADQUARTERS

SUPERIOR STEEL CASTING RODS — A fine quality casting rod — made of tapered, precision-ground, carbon alloy steel, oil-tempered and heat-treated. Stainless steel guides and tip, "Duo-Loc" reel seat. Screw type lock. Complete with cloth cover with protective wood insert.
10-M-195 — 5-ft. Length. Natural green finish **8.95**
10-M-196 — 4½-ft. Length. Pearl gray finish **8.95**

DE LUXE STEEL CASTING RODS — Solid taper, precision-ground silicon-chrome steel, heat-treated and oil-tempered. Cast-aluminum handle, comfortable cork grip. Finished in non-glare cream enamel, red trim. Complete with cloth sack with wood insert.
10-M-224 — 4½- or 5-ft. lengths **6.45**
10-M-194 — 47-inch length **4.98**

STANDARD STEEL CASTING ROD — Solid steel, two-piece rod, with jeweled guides and tip. Cast aluminum handle has black ribbed grip. Removable reel clamp.
10-M-223 — 4¼ feet long **4.98**

INTERSTATE CASTING REEL — Handsomely designed, sturdily constructed fresh water reel. Satin chrome finish. Lightweight oilite cushioned spool and worm bearings permit greater yardage on casts with less backlash. Handy adjustable brake. Line capacity 100 yards.
10-M-169 .... **7.98**

NILE CASTING REEL — Highly polished chrome-plated finish. Adjustable drag and "S" shaped handle with tenite knobs. Oilite bearings and quadruple multiplying gears. Line capacity 100 yards.
10-M-170 .... **5.95**

FISHING FLIES, LURES, MINNOWS, PLUGS — Equip your tackle box with the proven flies, lures, minnows and plugs successful fishermen use. You'll find a quality selection of famous brands at our store, reasonably priced. Come in and look them over today — select what you need and be ready to head for that favorite fishing spot.

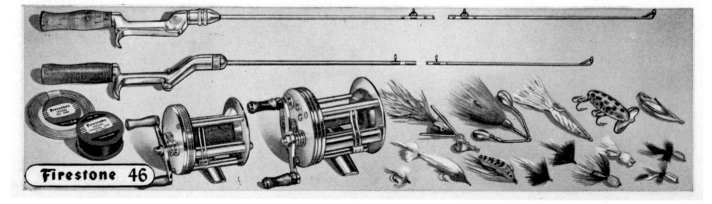

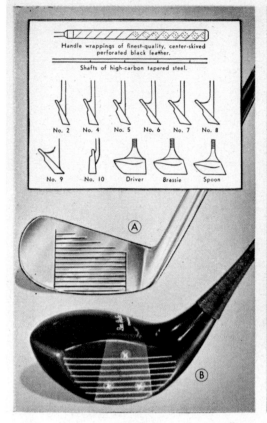

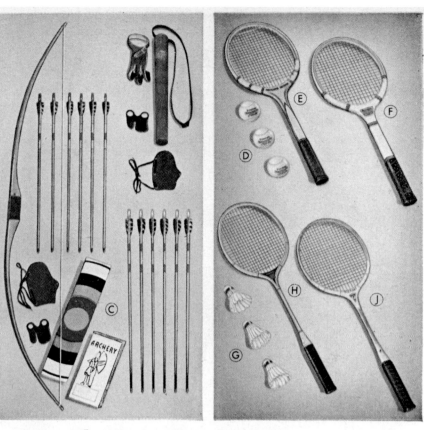

For Outdoor Fun That Keeps You Fit

(A) (B) FIRESTONE "DON MacDOUGAL" CHAMPION GOLF CLUBS — Designed to give you greater control, more power, a freer swing. Made from finest materials. Woods expertly designed, made of seasoned persimmon with Keystone fiber inserts on hitting face. Irons arch-back design, placing weight where it is needed most. Heads of irons are forged steel, chromium-plated over copper and nickel. All face scorings conform with P.G.A. specifications. All

shafts of high carbon tapered steel. Shafts of woods chromium-plated, irons are hickory sheathed. Non-slip, perforated black leather handles. All clubs matched and registered, swing-weighted and balanced.

(A) 10-H-16 — Set of 8 irons (see illustration above) **59.75**
(B) 10-H-11 — Set of 3 woods (see illustration above) **29.75**

(C) SUPREME QUALITY ARCHERY EQUIPMENT — More and more archery enthusiasts are finding the many fine quality archery supplies they need at Firestone. Whether it's a complete target archery set you're looking for, a hunting bow, a set of arrows, gloves, finger tabs, quiver, target face or stand, see the exceptionally fine display and price range of equipment at our store before you buy.

(D) FIRESTONE CHAMPIONSHIP TENNIS BALLS — Approved by U. S. Lawn Tennis Association. Vacuum packed cans.
10-E-22 — White .... 3 for **1.79**

(E) PROFESSIONAL CHAMPION TENNIS RACKET — Truly the racket choice of those who demand the best. The eight-ply, laminated wood frame with its full flake overlay at the throat and six throat windings gives you the finest frame available. Strung with new, strong, red nylon. Leather handle grip.
10-E-21 .... **11.45**

(F) FIRESTONE "VICTORY" TENNIS RACKET — Nine-ply; laminated wood frame, tightly strung with clear nylon. Full-flake overlay and six throat windings. Perforated leather grip.
10-E-7 — Choice of weights **10.95**

(G) BADMINTON SHUTTLECOCKS—Selected white hand trimmed feathers.
10-E-19 — Indoor .... 3 for **1.19**
10-E-18 — Outdoor. Weighted .... 3 for **1.49**

(H) "VICTORY" BADMINTON RACKET — Five-ply laminated wood frame. Full-flake overlay at throat and shoulders. Clear nylon strings. Leather grip.
10-E-3 .... **5.75**

(J) "DRIVER" BADMINTON RACKET — Three-ply, laminated wood frame with "Pyralin" plastic overlay. Strung with clear nylon. Imitation leather grip.
10-E-11 .... **4.79**

(K) BASEBALL CAPS — 70% wool, 30% cotton. Size 6¾ through 7½.
10-F-34 — Royal Blue **98c**
10-F-35 — Scarlet **98c**

(L) SUPREME BASEBALL — Used by many leagues. Top quality cork and rubber center.
10-F-13 — Pearl horsehide cover **2.19**

(M) SUPREME SOFTBALL — Official. 100% Kapok core. Triple-stitched, horsehide cover.
10-F-11 .... **2.29**

(N) "BOB DOERR" AUTOGRAPHED FIELDER'S

GLOVE — Genuine horsehide leather. Welted seams. Fully lined.
10-F-15 .... **4.69**
(P) SOFTBALL MITT — Combination softball catcher's and baseman's mitt. Genuine horsehide leather, full laced except at wrist. Rawhide face webbing between thumb and ball pocket.
10-F-19 .... **4.49**
(R) "BOB DOERR" AUTOGRAPHED FIELDER'S GLOVE — A good quality, selected cowhide leather glove with tunnel loops. Hand formed. Fully lined. Rawhide lacing.
10-F-3 .... **5.29**
(S) SOFTBALL GLOVE — Genuine horsehide with half lined back. Raised padding.
10-F-18 .... **3.69**
(T) "RUDY YORK" AUTOGRAPHED BASEMAN'S MITT — Top-grain leather. Rawhide webbing between thumb and forefinger. Fully lined.
10-F-6 .... **5.95**
(U) BASEBALL BAT — Famous "Louisville Slugger" professional model.
10-F-33 — Assorted lengths and weights... **2.65**
(V) SOFTBALL BAT — Ash with taped handle.
10-F-9 — Assorted weights and lengths... **1.59**
(W) SOFTBALL BAT — Good-grade ash.
10-F-10 — Red finish **1.25**

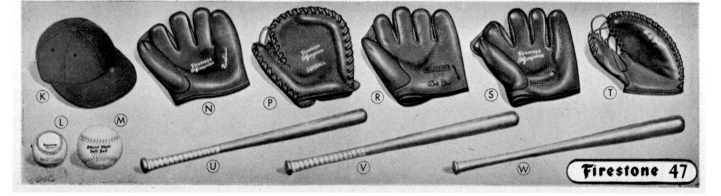

Firestone 47

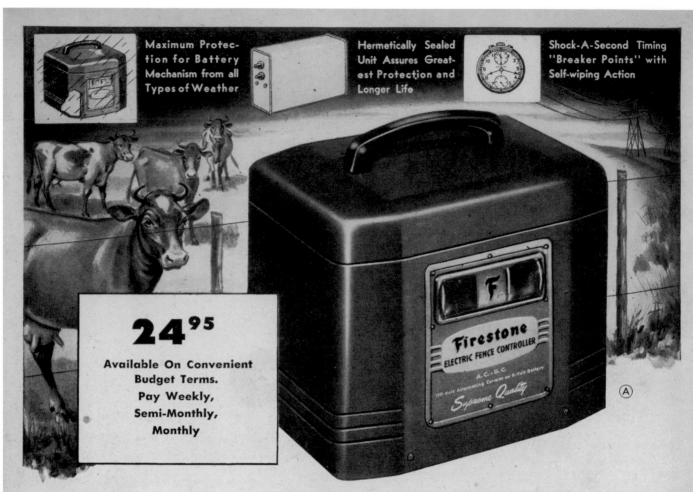

Maximum Protection for Battery Mechanism from all Types of Weather

Hermetically Sealed Unit Assures Greatest Protection and Longer Life

Shock-A-Second Timing "Breaker Points" with Self-wiping Action

24⁹⁵

Available On Convenient Budget Terms. Pay Weekly, Semi-Monthly, Monthly

Safe, Dependable Fence Controllers

The modern, practical way of fencing in your stock. Protects valuable crop acreage from straying livestock. Will handle up to 15 miles of barbed or smooth wire fence. Firestone Electric Fence Controllers are made to withstand any and all weather conditions. Can be used inside and out, with a hermetically sealed air-tight unit housed in a heavy 18-gauge weatherproof steel case, finished in smooth baked enamel. Dirt, dust, moisture and insects can't get in to foul unit. Scientifically engineered with convenient "off-and-on" switch, "dry" and "wet" terminals, shock-a-second timing, "breaker points" with self-wiping action, lightning arrester, filter to avoid radio and phone interference, trouble-signal light. Cases designed to house either a 6-volt hot shot battery or a 6-volt Willard fence controller battery. Firestone

Fence Controllers comply with Electrical National Safety code and are approved by Wisconsin Industrial Commission. Terminal wires, brackets, instructions are included.

(A) SUPREME AC-DC BATTERY MODEL — Will operate from Battery or 110-volt, 60-cycle AC. Simple to convert from Battery to AC—permanently attached cord furnished for AC. Light indicator flashes off and on when fence is operating correctly. Guaranteed.
16-D-8 — Battery extra.................. **24.95**

(E) DE LUXE 6-VOLT BATTERY MODEL — Same quality as 16-D-8 above, but will not operate on AC. Has special built-in meter to test battery condition and is also equipped with light indicator to show if unit is operating correctly. Guaranteed.
16-D-7 — Battery extra.................. **20.95**

(D) STANDARD 6-VOLT BATTERY MODEL — Operates on battery only. Equipped with a single light indicating if controller and fence are operating correctly.
16-D-6 — Battery extra.................. **14.95**

(B) 6-VOLT HOT SHOT BATTERY — For use with any 6-volt electric fence controllers. Approximate battery life in normal use is four months.
16-D-1 — Each............................ **2.39**
(C) FENCE TESTER—With neon flasher.
16-D-11................................... **75c**

Fence Controller Accessories
WARNING SIGN — Meets state regulation.
16-D-12.................................. **8c**
LEATHER WASHERS — For wood posts.
16-D-5 — 100 for.......................... **16c**
WIRE FASTENER — Holds wire on insulator.
16-D-9 — 100 for.......................... **39c**
INSULATOR FASTENER — For mounting porcelain insulators on steel fence posts.
16-D-13 — 50 for.......................... **22c**
GATE HANDLE — Wooden.
16-D-10................................... **26c**
WOOD POST INSULATOR — Includes washer and nail.
16-D-2 — 3 for............................ **10c**
STEEL POST INSULATOR — Porcelain.
16-D-3 — 2 for............................ **5c**
CORNER KNOB — Porcelain insulator.
16-D-4.................................... **5c**

Firestone 48A

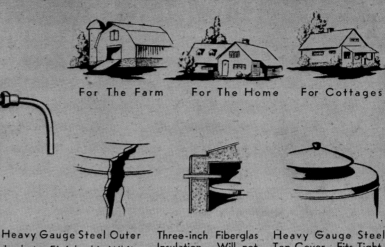

For The Farm   For The Home   For Cottages

Heavy Gauge Steel Outer Jacket—Finished in White Baked Enamel

Three-inch Fiberglas Insulation—Will not Rot or Absorb Moisture

Heavy Gauge Steel Top Cover—Fits Tightly. Keeps Heat In, Dirt Out

ELECTRIC DAIRY HOT WATER HEATER

Designed for use in dairy barns to supply hot water for washing dairy utensils, sterilizing milking machines, furnishing adequate hot water when rapid milking system is used. Even though running water is not available, this heater will operate manually. With running water, heater can be made fully automatic. Extra-large water capacity — two sizes, 10- and 15-gallon. Special fill tank increases capacity to 12 and 17 gallons.

CHECK THESE EXTRA QUALITY FEATURES

Removable flange for easy cleaning. Brass swivel faucet—eliminates dripping caused by heated water expanding. Heavy gauge steel top cover—fits tightly—keeps heat in, dirt out. Steel outer shell and legs. Tank solid copper. Three-inch Fiberglas insulation, will not rot or absorb moisture; odorless and verminproof. Submersion-type heating element for quick, easy heating. Heavy-duty automatic thermostat turns current on when needed, off when water reaches correct temperature. Heavy-gauge steel bottom cover. Entire unit is easy to clean. Attractively finished in white baked enamel, trimmed in red. Heating element, rubber cord and plug, Underwriters' listed. Designed for 110-120 alternating current. Guaranteed one year.

16-A-41 — 12-gal. size........**50.95**
16-A-42 — 17-gal. size........**57.95**

FLOAT VALVE—Enables heater to be converted into a fully automatic unit. (Not illustrated.)
16-A-45........**2.95**

(A) **DAIRY FLY SPRAY**—Will not taint foods.
16-A-77 — Qt.........................**45c**
16-A-78 — Gallon...................**1.19**
16-A-79 — 5-Gallon................**4.95**

(B) **FILTER DISKS**—Famous Johnson and Johnson.
16-A-6 — 6" Plain..................**49c**
16-A-7 — 6" Gauze.................**75c**
16-A-8 — 6½" Plain................**55c**
16-A-9 — 6½" Gauze...............**85c**

(C) **SUPREME DAIRY PAIL**—12-qt. heavy duty. Tin-plated sheet steel. Sides and bottom seamless. Dome bottom.
16-A-11........**2.79**

(D) **TIN DAIRY PAIL** — 12-qt. Recessed bottom, riveted bail ears. Zinc base plating.
16-A-10........**79c**

(E) **PELOUSE DAIRY SCALE**—Accurate. Seven-inch dial, graduating reading of 1/12 lb. up to 40 lbs.
16-A-24........**4.19**

(F) **DAIRY STRAINER** — Heavy-gauge, tin-plated steel. Seamless construction — easy to clean. Perforated disc bottom and removable high-speed dome. 16-qt. capacity.
16-A-16........**3.49**

(G) **WOOD BUTTER CHURN** — Three-gallon capacity. Sturdily built. Handle for manual operation. Platform base for stability while in operation.
16-A-38........**4.50**

(H) **ONE-GALLON DAISY BUTTER CHURN** — Strong, durable glass withstands rapid temperature changes. Efficient washer, easy to clean. Streamlined gear case — makes churning fast and easy. Patented removable strainer.
16-A-13........**3.25**

Firestone 48 F

BE ASSURED OF PURE, SAFE MILK

High Speed Dome Perforated To Allow Rapid Flow

Electro-magnetic Agitation Means Constant Movement

Milk Automatically Heated To 143 Degrees

Firestone Electric Milk Pasteurizer

Farm families and families living in communities where pasteurized milk is not available can be assured of safe, pure milk for those growing youngsters, disease-free milk for the entire family. Avoid the danger of transmittal of undulant fever, typhoid fever, scarlet fever and diphtheria by pasteurizing your milk. Actual tests prove that the Firestone Electric Milk Pasteurizer kills or renders harmless all disease organisms which may be transmitted through milk. Meets pasteurizing requirements of the U. S. Public Health Service. Operates at the efficiency of large commercial units, yet priced within the reach of every farm family.

Pasteurizes two gallons of milk in one hour by simple water-bath principle. Electrically heated. Milk automatically heated to 143 degrees during pasteurization. Temperature and timing regulated automatically by timer and high-efficiency 4-inch Fenwall thermostat. Electro-magnetic agitator keeps milk and water in constant movement, assuring uniform pasteurizing temperature, avoids "cooked" taste.

Finished in snowy white, baked-on enamel with red trim. Water jacket coated with rustproof lacquer. Milk container heavy tinplated steel. Operates from 110-120 volt AC outlet; 1250-watt heating element. Complete with cord, plug and operating instructions.

16-A-43 _____ **47.95**

(A) **SUPREME CREAM OR MILK CANS** — Top quality, handy containers made of heavy gauge steel. Heavy tin coated after forming.
16-A-17—8-qt. **3.89** 16-A-18—12-qt. **4.49**

(B) **STANDARD MILK CAN** — Heavy gauge steel, sanitary seamless sides, durable rolled edges. Heavy tin coated after forming. Sanitary, seamless plug cover.
16-A-14 — 10-gal. capacity _____ **6.95**

(C) **MILK STOOL**—Sturdy construction—.065 gauge steel, torch-welded and practically "tip-proof" due to 3-leg construction. Circular brace on legs adds rigidity.
16-A-80 _____ **1.19**

(D) **MILK STOOL** — All-steel, tubular legs securely riveted to seat. Convenient height, no-tip design.
16-A-15 _____ **1.45**

(E) **MILK CAN BRUSH** — Winged-type. Bassine and Tampico fibers. Hardwood handle.
16-A-5 _____ **59c**

(F) **MERCURY TUBE THERMOMETER** — Finest quality, guaranteed accurate. Easy-to-read scale. Registers 10° F., to 230° F.
16-A-22 — 11-in. long _____ **69c**

(G) **RED SPIRIT TUBE THERMOMETER** —Reliable, good quality. Graduated scale from 30° F., to 230° F.
16-A-23 — 11-in. long _____ **38c**

(H) **STANDARD MILK BOTTLE BRUSH** — Horsehair bristles. Will not scratch.
16-A-4 _____ **29c**

(J) **SUPREME MILK BOTTLE BRUSH** — Fine quality. Horsehair bristles and end tufts.
16-A-3 _____ **79c**

(K) **MILK BOTTLE CAPS** — Strong, tab-pull, sprucewood cardboard. Fit all standard half-pint, pint and No. 2 qt. bottles. Paraffin coated.
16-A-2 — Tube of 500 _____ **49c**

Firestone 48G

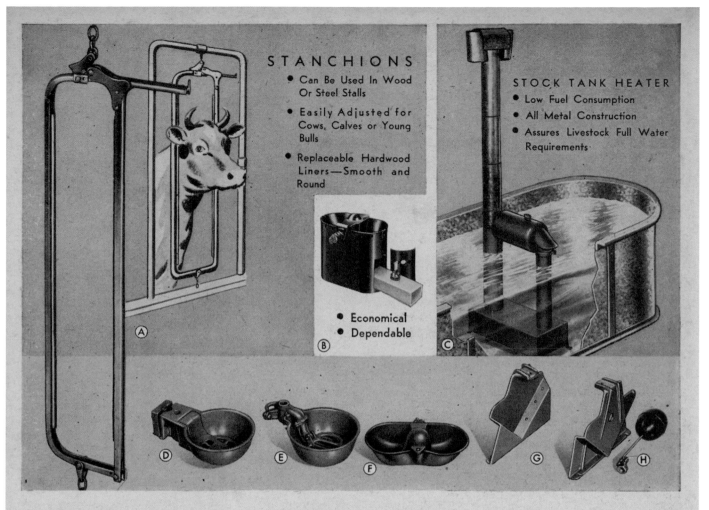

STANCHIONS

- Can Be Used In Wood Or Steel Stalls
- Easily Adjusted for Cows, Calves or Young Bulls
- Replaceable Hardwood Liners—Smooth and Round

- Economical
- Dependable

STOCK TANK HEATER

- Low Fuel Consumption
- All Metal Construction
- Assures Livestock Full Water Requirements

(A) OVAL-TYPE STANCHIONS — Fine-quality oval stanchions for use in either wood or steel stalls. Easily adjusted to needed width for cows, calves or young bulls. The steel bars, 1-5/16 by 7/8 by 3/16 in., have replaceable hardwood liners, smooth and rounded. Height inside 43 in., width at top 17½ in. Bottom adjustable to two widths for added comfort. Heavy malleable lock is cowproof — easily released.
16-J-3 — Stanchion...................... **3.95**

(B) HEATED STOCK WATERER — Removes chill from water during winter months — serves as water bowl year around. Heavy cast iron. Lead-coated kerosene or fuel oil reservoir holds 2½ pts. Easily connected to any tank or barrel. Over-all

dimensions 15 by 12 in., drinking space 7 by 14 by 4½ in.
16-J-32.................................. **8.95**

(C) STOCK TANK HEATER — Economical, efficient, all-metal kerosene-type water heater. Keeps water free from ice in coldest weather; encourages livestock to drink their full requirement of water. Low fuel consumption. Easily assembled.
16-J-23 — Instructions included...... **20.95**

(D) SUPREME DAIRY WATER BOWL — Regulates flow of water from either high-pressure or gravity water system — no splash, no overflow. Positive-acting, long-wearing, brass-type valve.
16-J-44.................................. **4.95**

(E) WATER BOWL — Trouble-free, simple valve mechanism operates by slight

pressure of animal's muzzle. Easily mounted.
16-J-2 — Tapped for ¾-in. pipe....... **3.95**

(F) STOCK OR HOG WATERER — Cast iron drinking bowl. Over-all size 14 by 7 by 4 in. Automatic float and valve prevent overflow. Strainer prevents valve from clogging.
16-J-1 — Tapped for ¾-in. pipe........ **3.25**

(G) (H) HOG WATERER KIT — Farmers — Construct your own automatic hog water trough! Kit complete except for lumber. Includes cast iron trough ends (G), automatic float valve and float (H). Zinc-plated hinges and lock nuts, bolts, leather washers, door hooks and nails.
16-J-29 — Instructions included...... **5.49**

(J) CALF WEANER — Swings out of way when animal is eating or drinking. Rustproof, cadmium-plated steel. Malleable iron nose piece.
16-A-34................................... **49c**

(K) YEARLING WEANER — Same as above except slightly smaller.
16-A-35................................... **45c**

(L) COW HOBBLE — Copper-finished chain, with clamp on each end. Easy to adjust.
16-A-33................................... **35c**

(M) GLASS ROOF WINDOW — Gives livestock and poultry much needed sunlight for better health and growth. Heavy, rust-resisting galvanized steel frame. One light. 20 by 28 in.
16-G-11 — Instructions included....... **2.69**

(N) REVOLVING HEAD ROOF VENTILATOR — Ideal for hog houses and poultry houses. Weather-resistant, aluminum painted, galvanized steel. Vent is 15 by 12 in. with grille to keep out birds. Base is 16 by 16 in., has 12-in. flue.
16-G-5 — With instructions............ **9.45**

Firestone 48 H

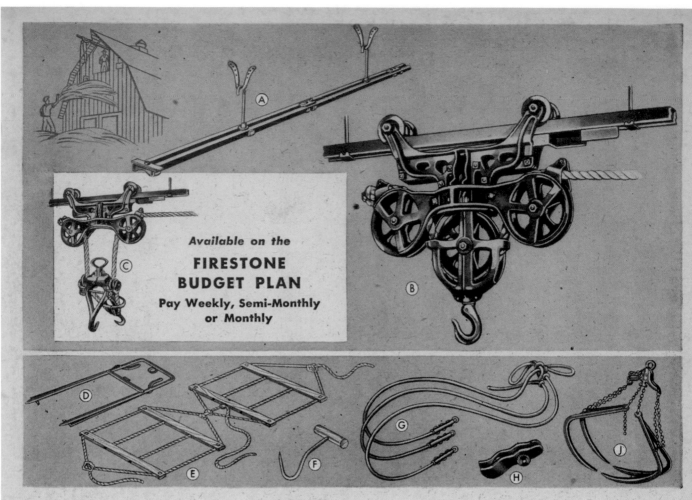

Available on the

FIRESTONE BUDGET PLAN

Pay Weekly, Semi-Monthly or Monthly

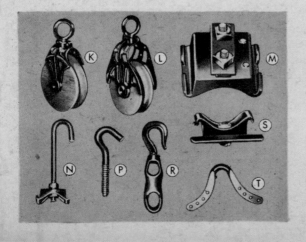

(A) STEEL TRACK — Smooth, positive joints permit easy movement of heaviest loads. 90-degree angle — steel 1 by 1 by 5/32 in.
16-J-10 — 10-ft..............................**1.29**
16-J-18 — 5-ft................................**59c**

(B) HAY CARRIER — Heavy duty, malleable iron with swivel base that permits reversing without removing from track. Large 7-in. pulleys are mounted on oilite bearings for long-life and easy operation. Fork pulley, 7-in. diameter, accommodates 1 in. rope or smaller. Long wheel base distributes load on track. Trip block furnished with each carrier to fit steel tracks.
16-J-9...**19.95**

(C) HAY SLING CARRIER — Big 7-in. sheaves handle up to 1 in. rope. Double swivel and

reversible, allowing complete reversal of direction while suspended. Pulley can be engaged from any angle. Constructed of heavy malleable iron, mounted on 17-in. wheelbase. Sturdy 3-in. track wheels, equipped with oilite bearings.
16-J-34...**21.95**

Use Our Easy Budget Terms

(D) HARPOON FORK — Loads fast, trips easily. Long-tine, double-harpoon type. 17-in. wide, 25-in. or 31-in. long, as available.
16-J-17...**4.25**

(E) WAGON SLINGS — Adaptable for 20-ft. racks but fully adjustable for shorter racks. Center trip permits easy removal of hay. Positive action trip will release when trip rope is pulled regardless of angle.
16-J-35 — 5-ft. wagon sling. 12-ft. 8-in. long. With 1/2-in. manila rope...**7.95**
16-J-36 — 6-ft. wagon sling. 13-ft. 8-in. long. With 1/2-in. manila rope...............................**9.45**

(F) HAY HOOK — Heavy-gauge, tough steel, 3/8 by 8 1/2-in. hook. Hardwood handle.
16-J-22...**39c**

(G) ROPE SLINGS — Handle hay this economical way. Fully adjustable in lengths up to 20 ft. Equipped with 1/2-in. manila rope. Eyelets prevent fraying of rope ends. Malleable iron adjustment and pulley adapter.
16-J-37 — Two-Rope Sling. 20-in. long, iron adjustment and pulley adapter.......**2.19**
16-J-38 — Three-Rope Sling. 20-in. long..........................**3.19**

(H) ROPE SLING HOLDER — Malleable iron positive grip construction permits use with two- or three-rope slings.
16-J-39...**1.49**

(J) GRAPPLE FORK — Simple, rugged, safe and fast. Spreads to full 6 ft. for faster loading. Four 1 1/2 by 1/2 in. high-carbon steel tines. Malleable iron pulley, chain-operated release. Malleable iron trip lock.
16-J-40...**14.95**

(K) REGULAR PULLEY — Malleable iron frame, swivel eye, heavy axle. 5 1/2-in. maple wheel.
16-J-15...**1.05**

(L) WIDE-MOUTH PULLEY — Flanged malleable iron frame. Large swivel eye permits splices to pass through easily. Heavy axle. 5 1/2-in. maple wheel.
16-J-16...**1.19**

(M) TRACK COUPLING — Malleable iron with interlocking lugs.
16-J-19...**37c**

(N) TRACK HANGING HOOK — Used with 16-J-13 Rafter Bracket to install steel track.
16-J-11...**25c**

(P) FLOOR HOOK — For use when installing regular or wide-mouth pulleys.
16-J-12...**25c**

(R) SWIVEL ROPE HITCH
16-J-14...**49c**

(S) END BUMPER — Bolts securely to end of track to stop carrier.
16-J-20...**25c**

(T) RAFTER BRACKET — Used with 16-J-11 Track Hanging Hook to install steel track.
16-J-13...**9c**

Firestone 48 J

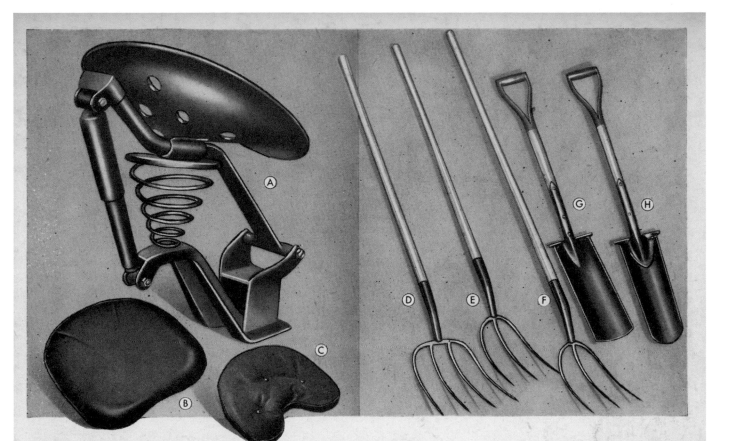

(A) MONROE E-Z-RIDE HYDRAULIC TRACTOR SEAT — Added comfort for the tractor rider. It cushions the jolts and bumps, makes your day easier. This tractor seat consists of a comfortably formed steel saddle mounted on one end of a lever bar supported by a special variable rate spring. Operating in conjunction with this is a Monroe Double-Action Hydraulic Shock Absorber to absorb jolts, jars and shock. The other end of the lever arm is attached through a pivot bearing to the stabilizer, minimizing side thrust and sway. Fits all popular makes of tractors from 1938. **29.95**

EASY BUDGET TERMS AVAILABLE

(B) DE LUXE SEAT CUSHION — Fits Monroe tractor seat and over 60% of all tractors. Waterproof fabric.
16-Z-20.................................... **1.98**

(C) STANDARD SEAT CUSHION — Canvas duck covering waterproofed. Cloth lined.
16-Z-18.................................... **1.39**

(D) SUPREME QUALITY 4-TINE MANURE FORK — Finest quality hot-rolled steel with polished tempered tines. Tested for strength and uniformity.
16-H-20 — 4-ft. handle............... **1.98**
16-H-26 — 4½-ft. handle............. **2.09**

(E) SUPREME QUALITY 3-TINE HAY FORK — Fine quality, hot-rolled steel with 12-inch oval polished, tempered tines.
(E) 16-H-25 — 4-ft. handle.......... **1.79**
(F) 16-H-19 — 4½-ft. handle........ **1.98**

(G) DE LUXE QUALITY DITCHING SPADE — Heat-treated steel blade 6¼ by 15¾ in. with two foot rests securely riveted to blade. Northern ash "D" handle, 27 in. long.
16-H-12.................................... **2.49**

(H) DE LUXE QUALITY DRAIN SPADE — Heat-treated blade 4¾ by 15½ in. — rounded cutting edge. Northern ash "D" handle.
16-H-13 — Handle 27 in. long...... **2.49**

(J) HEAVY-DUTY ELECTRIC ANIMAL CLIPPER — Ideal for dairy farmers in removing excess hair from dairy herd udders for clean milk production. Designed for easy clipping. Simple to operate. Operates on 110-120 volt AC-DC, all cycles. Specially hardened cutting blades—highly polished. Plastic case.
16-Z-31.................................... **29.45**
AVAILABLE ON EASY BUDGET TERMS

(K) 12-GAL. WHEELBARROW SPRAYER — Heavy sheet steel tank, galvanized after forming. 16-in. by 2-in. steel wheel. Pressure tank 6⅜ in. by 12 in. Fitted with 300-lb. pressure gauge, 6 ft. of ⅜-in. spray hose, automatic shut-off with trigger "quick spray" lock and 2-ft. brass extension rod with nozzle.
16-Z-28 — 12 gal....................... **27.95**
16-Z-29 — 18 gal....................... **45.95**

(L) GENERAL PURPOSE WHEELBARROW — Easy to handle — strong, long-wearing. Heavy steel legs, riveted braces — smooth, comfortable grip wood handles. One-piece 16-gauge pressed steel tray, rolled edges. Capacity 3 cu. ft. Eight-spoke steel wheel, cold-rolled steel axle, 16-in. diameter.
16-H-6..................................... **9.95**

(M) PNEUMATIC-TIRED STEEL WHEELBARROW — Same as 16-H-6 except with ball-bearing disc wheel with 10 by 2.75-in. pneumatic rubber tire for easy rolling.
16-H-30.................................... **14.95**

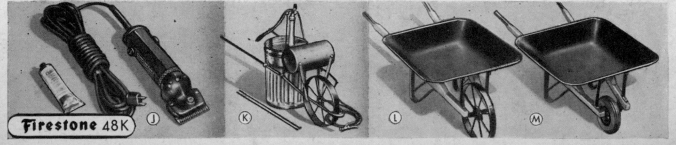

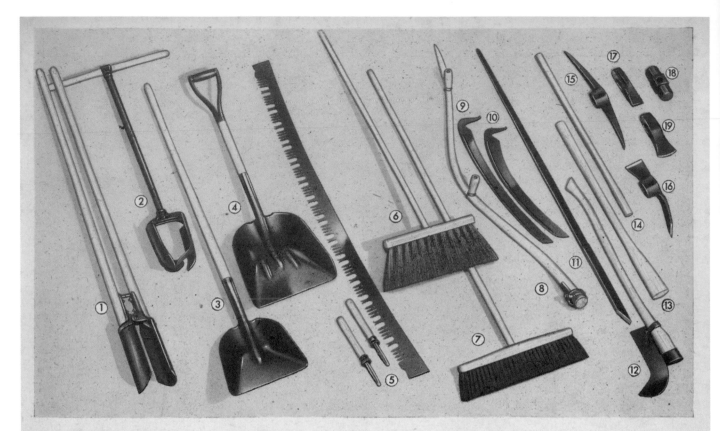

(1) **POSTHOLE DIGGER** — Hinged type. Malleable iron shanks, carbon steel blades. 10-in. length, 6-in. diameter.
16-H-28 — 48-in. handle **2.98**

(2) **8-INCH POSTHOLE AUGER** — Sharp crucible steel blades interlock and twist into earth like a drill. Iron pipe handle. 47″ length.
16-H-29 . . . . **3.09**

(3) **UTILITY SCOOP** — Long handled barn and utility scoop. Stamped steel blade 11¾″ x 14¾″. 50″ straight ash handle.
16-H-10 . . . . **1.89**

(4) **"D" HANDLED GRAIN SCOOP** — Popular No. 10 size. Well balanced, light and durable. "D" handle attached by 6½″ ferrule and rivets.
16-H-11 . . . . **2.39**

(5) **DE LUXE NARROW CROSSCUT SAW** — 5½-ft. High-carbon oil-tempered steel blade. Smooth in action.
7-A-4 — Handles extra **4.19**

CROSSCUT SAW LOOP HANDLES — Select hardwood.
7-A-5 — Pair **98c**

(6) **PUSH BROOM** — 14″ hardwood head — fiber bristles. 5-ft. handle.
16-H-15 . . . . **1.59**

(7) **PUSH BROOM** — 16″ extra durable broom. 60″ sturdy handle.
16-H-14 . . . . **1.85**

(8) **SNATH** — White ash, properly balanced snath. Malleable iron fittings. Fits grass or weed scythe blades.
16-H-3 . . . . **2.79**

(9, 10) **SCYTHE BLADES** — Special high-carbon steel to hold keen edge. Polished cutting edge.
16-H-4 — 28″ Grass Blade **2.19**
16-H-5 — 26″ Weed Blade **2.19**

(11) **60″ PINCH-POINT CROWBAR** — Hand-forged, high-carbon steel.
7-A-12 — Black finish **3.39**

(12) **BUSH HOOK** — Curved, forged-steel blade, 2¾″ x 11″. Bolted with steel strips to 36″ handle.
16-H-24 . . . . **2.59**

(13) **PICK AND MATTOCK HANDLE** — 36″ white straight-grained hickory.
7-A-28 — Wax finished **75c**

(14) **SLEDGE HAMMER HANDLE** — 36″ white straight-grained hickory.
7-A-142 — Wax finished **49c**

(15) **DE LUXE 6-LB. CLAY PICK**
7-A-7 . . . . **1.55**

(16) **DE LUXE 5-LB. CUTTER MATTOCK**
7-A-8 . . . . **1.59**

(17) **DE LUXE 4-LB. SQUARE HEAD WEDGE**
7-A-9 . . . . **79c**

(18) **DE LUXE 8-LB. DOUBLE-FACED BLACK-SMITH SLEDGE**
7-A-11 . . . . **1.98**

(19) **DE LUXE 6-LB. OVAL EYE WOOD CHOPPER'S MAUL**
7-A-10 . . . . **1.98**

(20) **TRUCK AND TRACTOR FUNNEL** — Heavy gauge, galvanized steel, fine copper strainer.
16-Z-30 . . . . **1.13**

(21) **HAND SPRAYER** — Delivers fine spray with easy operating long-life pump.
16-Z-27 — Capacity 2½ qts **3.19**

(22) **NEATSFOOT OIL** — Softens, renews and preserves leather.
16-K-40 — 1 pt . . . **69c**   16-K-41 — 1 qt . . . **1.09**

(23) **FLOODLIGHT** — Swivel base, die-formed highly polished aluminum reflector. Weather-tight seal and heat-resisting glass lens. 4-in. steel base with mounting holes. Uses 100-watt bulb.
16-G-6 — Six-ft. cord **3.49**

(24) **BENCH SICKLE GRINDER** — Power operated, with two grinding wheels. Sickle holder included. Cone is 5½ by 3½ in., with ⅝ in. bore. For electric motor or gas engine.
16-H-9 — Motor not included **10.95**

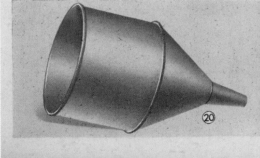

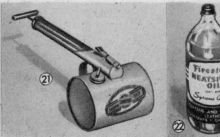

(A) PREMIER ELECTRIC BROODER

Starts up to 400 chicks — efficient, trouble-free. Big electric heating element assures plenty of warmth when needed. Built for long-life operation. Adjustable thermostat maintains uniform temperature, turning current off and on as needed. Accurate thermometer. Legs are adjustable, permitting raising of canopy edge 7 to 12 in. off floor, to accommodate growing chicks. Galvanized, rust-resistant steel canopy. Securely bolted. Ventilators in top of canopy. Heavy denim drop curtains. Masonite insulation throughout.
16-B-31 — 200 chick size. 36 by 36 in............. **17.45**
16-B-34 — 400 chick size. 48 by 48 in............. **22.95**

(C) KEROSENE CHICK BROODER

400 chick capacity. Efficient drum-type brooder maintains uniform heat. Galvanized steel canopy easily removed for cleaning. Burns either kerosene or 34-40 distillate oil. Thermostatically controlled die-cast valve regulates flow of fuel, heavy cast-iron burner has draft equalizer. Six-gallon fuel tank is equipped with glass sediment cup, flexible copper tubing, metal stand.
16-B-33 — 400 chick capacity.................. **17.45**

> **Buy the Farm Supplies You Need Now on the Convenient Firestone Budget Plan. Pay Weekly, Semi-Monthly or Monthly.**

(B) ALUMINUM 10-HOLE HEN NEST — Can't rust. Cuts down cleaning time — easy to handle. Two decks—accommodates a flock of 50 hens. Removable nest trays. Wood perches are mounted on hinged steel supports. Sloping roof discourages roosting. Nests each 10½ by 13 in.
16-B-61_____ **12.95**
(D) POULTRY FOUNT — Rust-resistant steel, hot-dipped galvanized after forming, top-fill water fountain. Water released by brass spring shut-off valve; vacuum action controls water flow.
16-B-15 — 5-gal........... **3.39**
16-B-14 — 3-gal........... **2.49**
(E) STEEL FOUNTAIN—Five-gallon capacity, top-fill water fountain. Heavy-gauge gal-

vanized steel double walls hold the heat when used with Heater No. 16-B-12. Heavy strap steel carrying handle. Brass spring valve governs water level. Water for 100 full grown chickens for 24 hours.
16-B-11_____ **3.19**
(F) OIL HEATER FOR 16-B-11 FOUNT — With fuel tank that covers entire base. Holds three-week fuel supply. Brass kerosene burner.
16-B-12_____ **2.39**
(G) CHICKEN FOUNTAIN — Heavy gauge, galvanized steel walls and pan. Double walls. Top-fill type makes filling easy. Rolled edges. Vacuum action keeps pan at constant level.
16-B-7 — 3-gal. capacity_____ **1.89**

(H) GALLON GLASS JAR POULTRY FOUNTAIN — Sanitary. Easy to fill or clean. Galvanized steel drinking pan. Water remains at correct level.
16-B-10_____ **65c**
(J) CHICK FOUNT — For baby chicks. Hot-dipped after forming, galvanized. Top handle.
16-B-9 — 5-qt. capacity_____ **79c**
(K) GLASS FOUNT BASE — Heavy, clear glass base accommodates pint, quart or two-quart mason jars. Vacuum action prevents overflowing. Ideal when addition of chemicals to water is desired.
16-B-8_____ **10c**

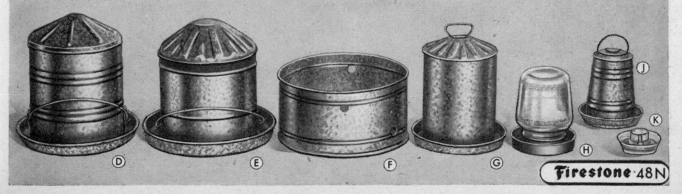

BE ASSURED OF PURE, SAFE MILK
High Speed Dome Perforated To Allow Rapid Flow
Electro-magnetic Agitation Means Constant Movement
Milk Automatically Heated To 143 Degrees

Firestone Electric Milk Pasteurizer

Farm families and families living in communities where pasteurized milk is not available can be assured of safe, pure milk for those growing youngsters, disease-free milk for the entire family. Avoid the danger of transmittal of undulant fever, typhoid fever, scarlet fever and diphtheria by pasteurizing your milk. Actual tests prove that the Firestone Electric Milk Pasteurizer kills or renders harmless all disease organisms which may be transmitted through milk. Meets pasteurizing requirements of the U. S. Public Health Service. Operates at the efficiency of large commercial units, yet priced within the reach of every farm family.

Pasteurizes two gallons of milk in one hour by simple water-bath principle. Electrically heated. Milk automatically heated to 143 degrees during pasteurization. Temperature and timing regulated automatically by timer and high-efficiency 4-inch Fenwall thermostat. Electro-magnetic agitator keeps milk and water in constant movement, assuring uniform pasteurizing temperature, avoids "cooked" taste.

Finished in snowy white, baked-on enamel with red trim. Water jacket coated with rustproof lacquer. Milk container heavy tinplated steel. Operates from 110-120 volt AC outlet; 1250-watt heating element. Complete with cord, plug and operating instructions.
16-A-43 **47.95**

(A) **SUPREME CREAM OR MILK CANS** — Top quality, handy containers made of heavy gauge steel. Heavy tin coated after forming.
16-A-17—8-qt. **3.89** 16-A-18—12-qt. **4.49**

(B) **STANDARD MILK CAN** — Heavy gauge steel, sanitary seamless sides, durable rolled edges. Heavy tin coated after forming. Sanitary, seamless plug cover.
16-A-14 — 10-gal. capacity **6.95**

(C) **MILK STOOL**—Sturdy construction—.065 gauge steel, torch-welded and practically "tip-proof" due to 3-leg construction. Circular brace on legs adds rigidity.
16-A-80 **1.19**

(D) **MILK STOOL** — All-steel, tubular legs securely riveted to seat. Convenient height, no-tip design.
16-A-15 **1.45**

(E) **MILK CAN BRUSH** — Winged-type. Bassine and Tampico fibers. Hardwood handle.
16-A-5 **59c**

(F) **MERCURY TUBE THERMOMETER** — Finest quality, guaranteed accurate. Easy-to-read scale. Registers 10° F., to 230° F.
16-A-22 — 11-in. long **69c**

(G) **RED SPIRIT TUBE THERMOMETER** —Reliable, good quality. Graduated scale from 30° F., to 230° F.
16-A-23 — 11-in. long **38c**

(H) **STANDARD MILK BOTTLE BRUSH** — Horsehair bristles. Will not scratch.
16-A-4 **29c**

(J) **SUPREME MILK BOTTLE BRUSH** — Fine quality. Horsehair bristles and end tufts.
16-A-3 **79c**

(K) **MILK BOTTLE CAPS** — Strong, tab-pull, sprucewood cardboard. Fit all standard half-pint, pint and No. 2 qt. bottles. Paraffin coated.
16-A-2 — Tube of 500 **49c**

Firestone 48G

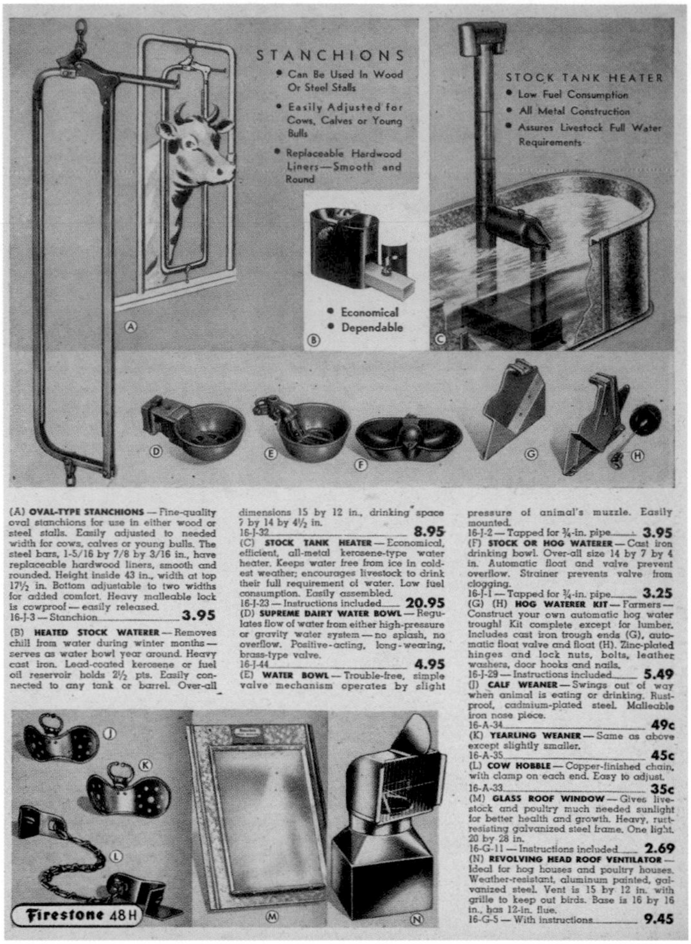
STANCHIONS
• Can Be Used In Wood Or Steel Stalls
• Easily Adjusted for Cows, Calves or Young Bulls
• Replaceable Hardwood Liners—Smooth and Round
• Economical
• Dependable
STOCK TANK HEATER
• Low Fuel Consumption
• All Metal Construction
• Assures Livestock Full Water Requirements

(A) **OVAL-TYPE STANCHIONS** — Fine-quality oval stanchions for use in either wood or steel stalls. Easily adjusted to needed width for cows, calves or young bulls. The steel bars, 1-5/16 by 7/8 by 3/16 in., have replaceable hardwood liners, smooth and rounded. Height inside 43 in., width at top 17½ in. Bottom adjustable to two widths for added comfort. Heavy malleable lock is cowproof — easily released.
16-J-3 — Stanchion **3.95**

(B) **HEATED STOCK WATERER** — Removes chill from water during winter months — serves as water bowl year around. Heavy cast iron. Lead-coated kerosene or fuel oil reservoir holds 2½ pts. Easily connected to any tank or barrel. Over-all dimensions 15 by 12 in., drinking space 7 by 14 by 4½ in.
16-J-32 **8.95**

(C) **STOCK TANK HEATER** — Economical, efficient, all-metal kerosene-type water heater. Keeps water free from ice in coldest weather; encourages livestock to drink their full requirement of water. Low fuel consumption. Easily assembled.
16-J-23 — Instructions included **20.95**

(D) **SUPREME DAIRY WATER BOWL** — Regulates flow of water from either high-pressure or gravity water system — no splash, no overflow. Positive-acting, long-wearing, brass-type valve.
16-J-44 **4.95**

(E) **WATER BOWL** — Trouble-free, simple valve mechanism operates by slight pressure of animal's muzzle. Easily mounted.
16-J-2 — Tapped for ¾-in. pipe **3.95**

(F) **STOCK OR HOG WATERER** — Cast iron drinking bowl. Over-all size 14 by 7 by 4 in. Automatic float and valve prevent overflow. Strainer prevents valve from clogging.
16-J-1 — Tapped for ¾-in. pipe **3.25**

(G) (H) **HOG WATERER KIT** — Farmers — Construct your own automatic hog water trough! Kit complete except for lumber. Includes cast iron trough ends (G), automatic float valve and float (H). Zinc-plated hinges and lock nuts, bolts, leather washers, door hooks and nails.
16-J-29 — Instructions included **5.49**

(J) **CALF WEANER** — Swings out of way when animal is eating or drinking. Rust-proof, cadmium-plated steel. Malleable iron nose piece.
16-A-34 **49c**

(K) **YEARLING WEANER** — Same as above except slightly smaller.
16-A-35 **45c**

(L) **COW HOBBLE** — Copper-finished chain, with clamp on each end. Easy to adjust.
16-A-33 **35c**

(M) **GLASS ROOF WINDOW** — Gives livestock and poultry much needed sunlight for better health and growth. Heavy, rust-resisting galvanized steel frame. One light. 20 by 28 in.
16-G-11 — Instructions included **2.69**

(N) **REVOLVING HEAD ROOF VENTILATOR** — Ideal for hog houses and poultry houses. Weather-resistant, aluminum painted, galvanized steel. Vent is 15 by 12 in. with grille to keep out birds. Base is 16 by 16 in., has 12-in. flue.
16-G-5 — With instructions **9.45**

Firestone 48H

Available on the
FIRESTONE BUDGET PLAN
Pay Weekly, Semi-Monthly or Monthly

(A) **STEEL TRACK** — Smooth, positive joints permit easy movement of heaviest loads. 90-degree angle — steel 1 by 1 by 5/32 in.
16-J-10 — 10-ft. **1.29**
16-J-18 — 5-ft. **59c**

(B) **HAY CARRIER** — Heavy duty, malleable iron with swivel base that permits reversing without removing from track. Large 7-in. pulleys are mounted on oilite bearings for long-life and easy operation. Fork pulley, 7-in. diameter, accommodates 1 in. rope or smaller. Long wheel base distributes load on track. Trip block furnished with each carrier to fit steel tracks.
16-J-9 **19.95**

(C) **HAY SLING CARRIER** — Big 7-in. sheaves handle up to 1 in. rope. Double swivel and reversible, allowing complete reversal of direction while suspended. Pulley can be engaged from any angle. Constructed of heavy malleable iron, mounted on 17-in. wheelbase. Sturdy 3-in. track wheels, equipped with oilite bearings.
16-J-34 **21.95**

Use Our Easy Budget Terms

(D) **HARPOON FORK** — Loads fast, trips easily. Long-tine, double-harpoon type. 17-in. wide, 25-in. or 31-in. long, as available.
16-J-17 **4.25**

(E) **WAGON SLINGS** — Adaptable for 20-ft. racks but fully adjustable for shorter racks. Center trip permits easy removal of hay. Positive action trip will release when trip rope is pulled regardless of angle.
16-J-35 — 5-ft. wagon sling. 12-ft. 8-in. long. With ½-in. manila rope **7.95**
16-J-36 — 6-ft. wagon sling. 13-ft. 8-in. long. With ½-in. manila rope **9.45**

(F) **HAY HOOK** — Heavy-gauge, tough steel, ⅜ by 8½-in. hook. Hardwood handle.
16-J-22 **39c**

(G) **ROPE SLINGS** — Handle hay this economical way. Fully adjustable in lengths up to 20 ft. Equipped with ½-in. manila rope. Eyelets prevent fraying of rope ends. Malleable iron adjustment and pulley adapter.
16-J-37—Two-Rope Sling. 20-in. long, iron adjustment and pulley adapter **2.19**
16-J-38—Three-Rope Sling. 20-in. long **3.19**

(H) **ROPE SLING HOLDER** — Malleable iron positive grip construction permits use with two- or three-rope slings.
16-J-39 **1.49**

(J) **GRAPPLE FORK** — Simple, rugged, safe and fast. Spreads to full 6 ft. for faster loading. Four 1½ by ½ in. high-carbon steel tines. Malleable iron pulley, chain-operated release. Malleable iron trip lock.
16-J-40 **14.95**

(K) **REGULAR PULLEY** — Malleable iron frame, swivel eye, heavy axle. 5½-in. maple wheel.
16-J-15 **1.05**

(L) **WIDE-MOUTH PULLEY** — Flanged malleable iron frame. Large swivel eye permits splices to pass through easily. Heavy axle. 5½-in. maple wheel.
16-J-16 **1.19**

(M) **TRACK COUPLING** — Malleable iron with interlocking lugs.
16-J-19 **37c**

(N) **TRACK HANGING HOOK** — Used with 16-J-13 Rafter Bracket to install steel track.
16-J-11 **25c**

(P) **FLOOR HOOK** — For use when installing regular or wide-mouth pulleys.
16-J-12 **25c**

(R) **SWIVEL ROPE HITCH**
16-J-14 **49c**

(S) **END BUMPER** — Bolts securely to end of track to stop carrier.
16-J-20 **25c**

(T) **RAFTER BRACKET** — Used with 16-J-1T Track Hanging Hook to install steel track.
16-J-13 **9c**

Firestone 48J

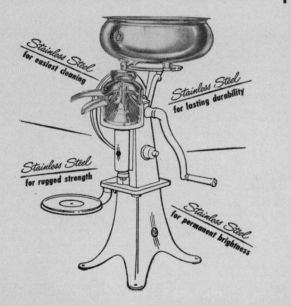

NEW DE LAVAL WORLD'S STANDARD SERIES CREAM SEPARATORS

Stainless Steel for easiest cleaning

Stainless Steel for lasting durability

Stainless Steel for rugged strength

Stainless Steel for permanent brightness

In the new De Laval World's Standard Series Separators every part that is touched by the milk and cream is made of tough, permanently bright and rust-proof stainless steel. Supply can, bowl and covers with new, open discharge type spouts —all are of gleaming, highly polished stainless steel which is the "friendliest" of all metals to milk and easiest to wash and keep clean. De Laval is noted for its especially high quality manufacture of stain-

less steel parts and you will find the stainless steel parts of the new De Laval World's Standard Series Separators to be beautiful examples of this outstanding skill.

NEW SUPER-SKIMMING BOWL

The new World's Standard Series stainless steel, Super-Skimming Bowl has been further refined in design and construction. It is the cleanest skimming device available to the farm producer of

18

Stainless steel, streamlined Super-Skimming Bowl —cleanest skimming, easiest cleaning.

Stainless steel covers with open type spouts—see how easy they are to wash!

butterfat . . . not only the first time you use it but throughout many long, profitable years. It produces cream of the highest quality and separates more milk in less time with less effort.

MECHANICALLY REFINED AND IMPROVED

The driving mechanism has been refined and improved for easiest operation and longest service. All ball bearings are of the fully enclosed and protected type to exclude any foreign matter. Gears are cut from special, long-wearing metals to highest precision standards. Lubrication is fully automatic and a new type plastic indicator shows oil level and condition at a glance.

Stainless steel, seamless, anti-splash supply can with visible flow "quick-clean" faucet.

Made in three sizes—hand or motor drive:
No. 514— 550 lbs. per hour
No. 518— 800 lbs. per hour
No. 519—1150 lbs. per hour

19

A De Laval advertisement for cream separators.

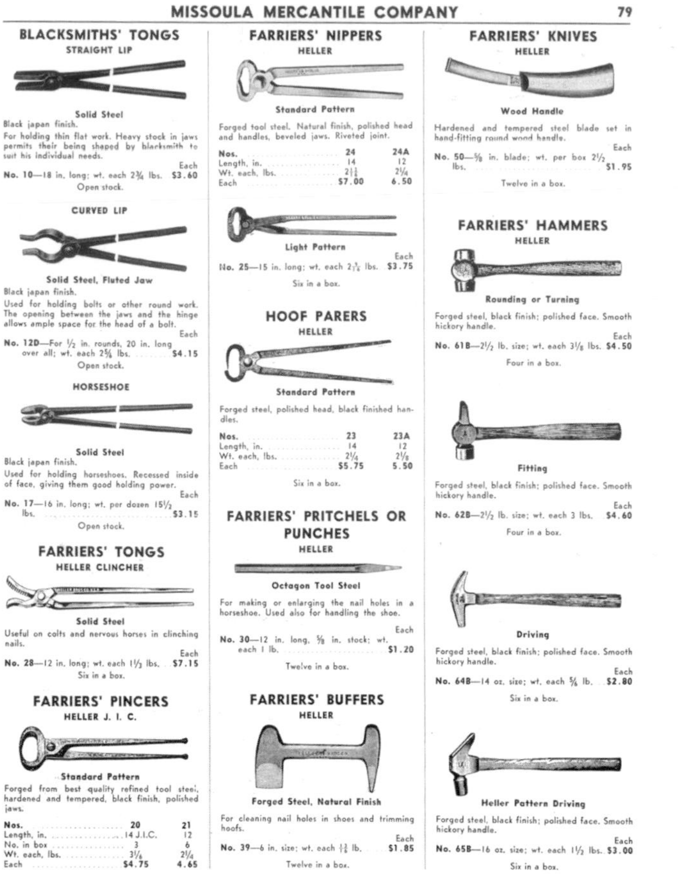

MISSOULA MERCANTILE COMPANY 79

BLACKSMITHS' TONGS

STRAIGHT LIP

Solid Steel

Black japan finish.

For holding thin flat work. Heavy stock in jaws permits their being shaped by blacksmith to suit his individual needs.

Each

No. 10—18 in. long; wt. each 2¾ lbs. $3.60

Open stock.

CURVED LIP

Solid Steel, Fluted Jaw

Black japan finish.

Used for holding bolts or other round work. The opening between the jaws and the hinge allows ample space for the head of a bolt.

Each

No. 12D—For ½ in. rounds, 20 in. long over all; wt. each 2⅝ lbs. $4.15

Open stock.

HORSESHOE

Solid Steel

Black japan finish.

Used for holding horseshoes. Recessed inside of face, giving them good holding power.

Each

No. 17—16 in. long; wt. per dozen 15½ lbs. $3.15

Open stock.

FARRIERS' TONGS

HELLER CLINCHER

Solid Steel

Useful on colts and nervous horses in clinching nails.

Each

No. 28—12 in. long; wt. each 1⅓ lbs. $7.15

Six in a box.

FARRIERS' PINCERS

HELLER J. I. C.

Standard Pattern

Forged from best quality refined tool steel, hardened and tempered, black finish, polished jaws.

Nos.	20	21
Length, in.	14 J.I.C.	12
No. in box	3	6
Wt. each, lbs.	3⅙	2¼
Each	$4.75	4.65

FARRIERS' NIPPERS

HELLER

Standard Pattern

Forged tool steel. Natural finish, polished head and handles, beveled jaws. Riveted joint.

Nos.	24	24A
Length, in.	14	12
Wt. each, lbs.	2 11/16	2¼
Each	$7.00	6.50

Light Pattern

Each

No. 25—15 in. long; wt. each 2 5/16 lbs. $3.75

Six in a box.

HOOF PARERS

HELLER

Standard Pattern

Forged steel, polished head, black finished handles.

Nos.	23	23A
Length, in.	14	12
Wt. each, lbs.	2¼	2⅛
Each	$5.75	5.50

Six in a box.

FARRIERS' PRITCHELS OR PUNCHES

HELLER

Octagon Tool Steel

For making or enlarging the nail holes in a horseshoe. Used also for handling the shoe.

Each

No. 30—12 in. long, ⅝ in. stock; wt. each 1 lb. $1.20

Twelve in a box.

FARRIERS' BUFFERS

HELLER

Forged Steel, Natural Finish

For cleaning nail holes in shoes and trimming hoofs.

Each

No. 39—6 in. size; wt. each 13/16 lb. $1.85

Twelve in a box.

FARRIERS' KNIVES

HELLER

Wood Handle

Hardened and tempered steel blade set in hand-fitting round wood handle.

Each

No. 50—⅝ in. blade; wt. per box 2½ lbs. $1.95

Twelve in a box.

FARRIERS' HAMMERS

HELLER

Rounding or Turning

Forged steel, black finish; polished face. Smooth hickory handle.

Each

No. 61B—2½ lb. size; wt. each 3⅛ lbs. $4.50

Four in a box.

Fitting

Forged steel, black finish; polished face. Smooth hickory handle.

Each

No. 62B—2½ lb. size; wt. each 3 lbs. $4.60

Four in a box.

Driving

Forged steel, black finish; polished face. Smooth hickory handle.

Each

No. 64B—14 oz. size; wt. each ⅝ lb. $2.80

Six in a box.

Heller Pattern Driving

Forged steel, black finish; polished face. Smooth hickory handle.

Each

No. 65B—16 oz. size; wt. each 1½ lbs. $3.00

Six in a box.

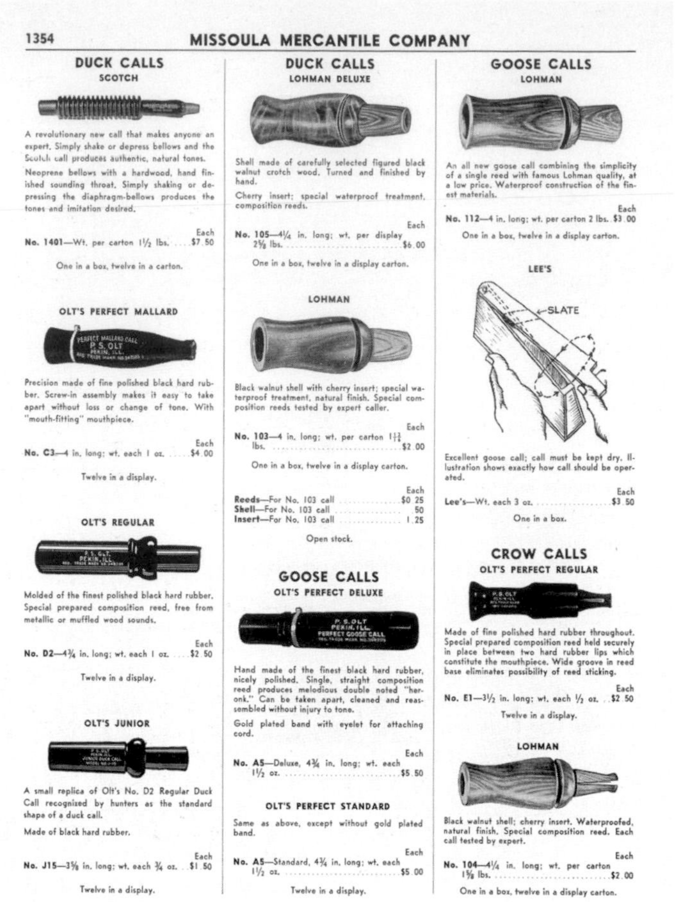

1354 MISSOULA MERCANTILE COMPANY

DUCK CALLS

SCOTCH

A revolutionary new call that makes anyone an expert. Simply shake or depress bellows and the Scotch call produces authentic, natural tones.

Neoprene bellows with a hardwood, hand finished sounding throat. Simply shaking or depressing the diaphragm-bellows produces the tones and imitation desired.

Each

No. 1401—Wt. per carton 1½ lbs. $7.50

One in a box, twelve in a carton.

OLT'S PERFECT MALLARD

Precision made of fine polished black hard rubber. Screw-in assembly makes it easy to take apart without loss or change of tone. With "mouth-fitting" mouthpiece.

Each

No. C3—4 in. long; wt. each 1 oz. $4.00

Twelve in a display.

OLT'S REGULAR

Molded of the finest polished black hard rubber. Special prepared composition reed, free from metallic or muffled wood sounds.

Each

No. D2—4¾ in. long; wt. each 1 oz. $2.50

Twelve in a display.

OLT'S JUNIOR

A small replica of Olt's No. D2 Regular Duck Call recognized by hunters as the standard shape of a duck call.

Made of black hard rubber.

Each

No. J15—3⅝ in. long; wt. each ¾ oz. $1.50

Twelve in a display.

DUCK CALLS

LOHMAN DELUXE

Shell made of carefully selected figured black walnut crotch wood. Turned and finished by hand.

Cherry insert; special waterproof treatment, composition reeds.

Each

No. 105—4¼ in. long; wt. per display 2⅝ lbs. $6.00

One in a box, twelve in a display carton.

LOHMAN

Black walnut shell with cherry insert; special waterproof treatment, natural finish. Special composition reeds tested by expert caller.

Each

No. 103—4 in. long; wt. per carton 1 11/16 lbs. $2.00

One in a box, twelve in a display carton.

Each

Reeds—For No. 103 call $0.25

Shell—For No. 103 call .50

Insert—For No. 103 call 1.25

Open stock.

GOOSE CALLS

OLT'S PERFECT DELUXE

Hand made of the finest black hard rubber, nicely polished. Single, straight composition reed produces melodious double noted "her-onk." Can be taken apart, cleaned and reassembled without injury to tone.

Gold plated band with eyelet for attaching cord.

Each

No. A5—Deluxe, 4¾ in. long; wt. each 1½ oz. $5.50

OLT'S PERFECT STANDARD

Same as above, except without gold plated band.

Each

No. A5—Standard, 4¾ in. long; wt. each 1½ oz. $5.00

Twelve in a display.

GOOSE CALLS

LOHMAN

An all new goose call combining the simplicity of a single reed with famous Lohman quality, at a low price. Waterproof construction of the finest materials.

Each

No. 112—4 in. long; wt. per carton 2 lbs. $3.00

One in a box, twelve in a display carton.

LEE'S

Excellent goose call; call must be kept dry. Illustration shows exactly how call should be operated.

Each

Lee's—Wt. each 3 oz. $3.50

One in a box.

CROW CALLS

OLT'S PERFECT REGULAR

Made of fine polished hard rubber throughout. Special prepared composition reed held securely in place between two hard rubber lips which constitute the mouthpiece. Wide groove in reed base eliminates possibility of reed sticking.

Each

No. E1—3½ in. long; wt. each ½ oz. $2.50

Twelve in a display.

LOHMAN

Black walnut shell; cherry insert. Waterproofed, natural finish. Special composition reed. Each call tested by expert.

Each

No. 104—4¼ in. long; wt. per carton 1⅝ lbs. $2.00

One in a box, twelve in a display carton.

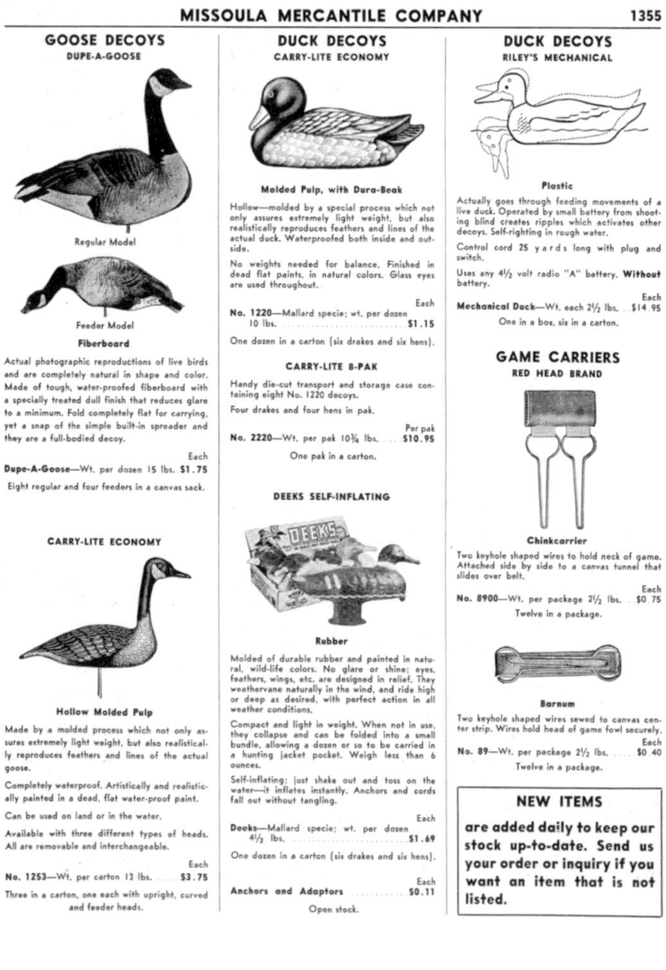

MISSOULA MERCANTILE COMPANY 1355

GOOSE DECOYS

DUPE-A-GOOSE

Regular Model

Feeder Model

Fiberboard

Actual photographic reproductions of live birds and are completely natural in shape and color. Made of tough, water-proofed fiberboard with a specially treated dull finish that reduces glare to a minimum. Fold completely flat for carrying, yet a snap of the simple built-in spreader and they are a full-bodied decoy.

Each

Dupe-A-Goose—Wt. per dozen 15 lbs. $1.75

Eight regular and four feeders in a canvas sack.

CARRY-LITE ECONOMY

Hollow Molded Pulp

Made by a molded process which not only assures extremely light weight, but also realistically reproduces feathers and lines of the actual goose.

Completely waterproof. Artistically and realistically painted in a dead, flat water-proof paint.

Can be used on land or in the water.

Available with three different types of heads. All are removable and interchangeable.

Each

No. 1253—Wt. per carton 13 lbs. $3.75

Three in a carton, one each with upright, curved and feeder heads.

DUCK DECOYS

CARRY-LITE ECONOMY

Molded Pulp, with Dura-Beak

Hollow—molded by a special process which not only assures extremely light weight, but also realistically reproduces feathers and lines of the actual duck. Waterproofed both inside and outside.

No weights needed for balance. Finished in dead flat paints, in natural colors. Glass eyes are used throughout.

Each

No. 1220—Mallard specie; wt. per dozen 10 lbs. $1.15

One dozen in a carton (six drakes and six hens).

CARRY-LITE 8-PAK

Handy die-cut transport and storage case containing eight No. 1220 decoys.

Four drakes and four hens in pak.

Per pak

No. 2220—Wt. per pak 10¾ lbs. $10.95

One pak in a carton.

DEEKS SELF-INFLATING

Rubber

Molded of durable rubber and painted in natural, wild-life colors. No glare or shine; eyes, feathers, wings, etc. are designed in relief. They weathervane naturally in the wind, and ride high or deep as desired, with perfect action in all weather conditions.

Compact and light in weight. When not in use, they collapse and can be folded into a small bundle, allowing a dozen or so to be carried in a hunting jacket pocket. Weigh less than 6 ounces.

Self-inflating; just shake out and toss on the water—it inflates instantly. Anchors and cords fall out without tangling.

Each

Deeks—Mallard specie; wt. per dozen 4½ lbs. $1.69

One dozen in a carton (six drakes and six hens).

Each

Anchors and Adaptors $0.11

Open stock.

DUCK DECOYS

RILEY'S MECHANICAL

Plastic

Actually goes through feeding movements of a live duck. Operated by small battery from shooting blind creates ripples which activates other decoys. Self-righting in rough water.

Control cord 25 yards long with plug and switch.

Uses any 4½ volt radio "A" battery. **Without** battery.

Each

Mechanical Duck—Wt. each 2½ lbs. $14.95

One in a box, six in a carton.

GAME CARRIERS

RED HEAD BRAND

Chinkcarrier

Two keyhole shaped wires to hold neck of game. Attached side by side to a canvas tunnel that slides over belt.

Each

No. 8900—Wt. per package 2½ lbs. $0.75

Twelve in a package.

Barnum

Two keyhole shaped wires sewed to canvas center strip. Wires hold head of game fowl securely.

Each

No. 89—Wt. per package 2½ lbs. $0.40

Twelve in a package.

NEW ITEMS

are added daily to keep our stock up-to-date. Send us your order or inquiry if you want an item that is not listed.

These three advertisements are from the 1956 Missoula Mercantile Company Catalog.

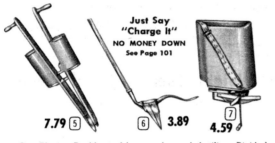

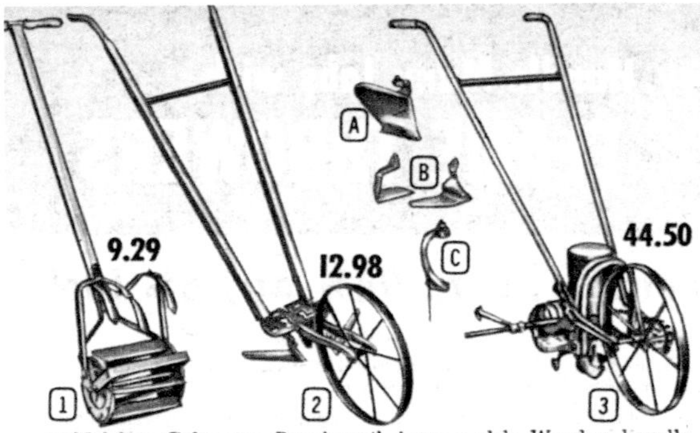

24-Inch High Wheel Cultivator

- **Time-Proven, Efficient Tool for Row-Crop Gardening**

④ **Cultivates Rapidly, Efficiently Between Rows.** 24-in. wheel runs smoothly and easily. Over-the-axle drive lessens handle load—no wheel wobble. Hardwood handles. Includes 5-tooth weeder, turning hill plow, reversible shovel and wrench. *Mailable.*
89 FB 1771YO—Shipping weight 22 lbs........**$9.39**

Tools for Standard High Wheel Cultivators. Important: These tools fit only cultivators with a slotted foot.

Ⓓ **Reversible Shovel.** Cuts 2- or 3-in. furrows.
89 FB 1777—Ship. wt. 1 lb..............Each **65c**

Ⓔ **Weeder-Scuffer.** Reversible 4-tooth end; 8-in. wide blade cuts roots, forms mulch.
89 FB 1778—Ship. wt. 2 lbs.............Each **$1.69**

Ⓕ **Turn Plow.** Hills and furrows. Plows 4 in. deep.
89 FB 1780—Ship. wt. 1 lb. 8 oz.........Each **69c**

Ⓖ **8-in. Sweep.** Triangular blade cultivates, hills, weeds.
89 FB 1776—Ship. wt. 1 lb. 4 oz.........Each **75c**

Ⓗ **Disc Hoe.** Two 3 blade gangs. 4½-in. wide. 5½ in. diameter disc blades. Adjustable.
89 FB 1775—Ship. wt. 8 lbs...............Set **$5.89**

5-tooth Weeder. (Not Shown.) Cuts roots 6 in. wide.
89 FB 1779—Ship. wt. 3 lbs..................**$2.49**

Just Phone Your Order

Only $9.39

Ideal for Nurseries and Vegetable Gardens

① **Mulcher, Cultivator.** Breaks soil, forms mulch. Wooden handle.
89 FB 1751Y—Ship. wt. 14 lbs. *Mail.* Eight 10-in. blades. .**$9.29**

② **Speed Hoe.** Use between rows. Large steel wheel. Includes 2 weeding hoes, 3 duckfeet, 1 turn plow, steel wrench.
89 FB 1766YO—Ship. wt. 21 lbs. *Mail.* Wooden handle.....**$12.98**

③ **Seeder and Cultivator.** Steel handles, rubber grips. Includes 2 weeding plows, 2 hilling plows, 4 duckfeet, row marker.
89 FB 1755YO—Ship. wt. 57 lbs. *Mailable.*...........Cash **$44.50**

ⒶⒷⒸ **Tools for Speed Hoe (2) and Cultivator (3).** *Mailable.*
Ⓐ **Single Turn Plow.** Right-hand, landslide bolt.
89 FB 1783—Plows 4 in. wide and deep. Wt. 3 lbs.......Each **$2.39**
Ⓑ **6-in. Weeding Hoes.** Staggered to clear trash, etc. With bolts.
89, FB 1786—Ship. wt. 2 lbs...........................Pair **$2.39**
Ⓒ **Cultivator Duckfeet.** 6 in. long. For roots, etc. With bolts.
89 FB 1785—Ship. wt. 8 oz............................Each **75c**

Just Say "Charge It"
NO MONEY DOWN
See Page 101

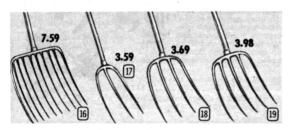

⑤ **Corn Planter.** Double steel hoppers for seed, fertilizer. Divided steel jaws prevent fertilizer from contacting seed. Convenient adjustable drop. Sturdy hardwood frame. *Mailable.*
89 FB 2271M—Ship. wt. 7 lbs. 8 oz.........................**$7.79**

Single Hopper Corn Planter (Not shown). Like (5) above but with steel hopper for seed only—not to be used for fertilizer.
89 FB 2273M—Ship. wt. 6 lbs. *Mailable.*...................**$5.98**

⑥ **Potato Planter.** Steel jaws, hardwood hdle. For home, trk. garden.
89 FB 2272M—Ship. wt. 3 lbs. 8 oz.........................**$3.89**

⑦ **Canvas Bag Seeder.** Broadcasts grass seed 10 to 18 ft.; small grains 18 to 25 ft.—lever controls rate. Side crank; adj. strap.
89 FB 2274—Ship. wt. 4 lbs. 8 oz. *Mail.* About ½-bu. cap....**$4.59**

Sturdy, Handy Service Tools

⑧ **Long Handle Grass Hook.** 11-inch high carbon steel blade with extra long, easy-to-work with 44-inch handle.
89 FB 812M—Ship. wt. 2 lbs. 8 oz.....**$1.75**

⑨ **Mattock Blade.** 3½-in. hoe blade and 2¾-in. cutter blade. Forged steel construction for long life. Use handle (10).
89 FB 1917 M—Ship. wt. 5 lbs........**$3.29**

⑩ **Pick or Mattock Handle.** Made from extra strong hickory wood.
84 FB 7095 M—36 in. Ship. wt. 2 lbs......**79c**

⑪ **Railroad Pick.** Heat treated, forged steel. Approx. 24 inches long. Ship. wt. 6 lbs.
89 FB 1916 M—Use with Handle (10)..**$3.15**

⑫ **Scythe Blades.** Forged steel. Tempered—fit on handle (13). Ship. wt. 3 lbs.
89 FB 1900 M—Grass. Approx. 30 in.....**$3.98**
89 FB 1904 M—Weed. Approx. 26 in..... 3.98
89 FB 1905—Bush. Approx. 20 in..... 3.98

⑬ **Snaths.** Ash. About 55 in. Fits Scythes (12).
89 FB 1907M—For Grass. Wt. 4 lbs.**$3.29**
89 FB 1909M—Weed and Bush. Wt. 5 lbs. 3.59

⑭ **Bush Hook.** Blade approx. 3¾x13 in.
89 FB 1910M—Ship. wt. 5 lbs.......**$4.49**

⑮ **Cutter—Mattock.** 3½-in., 1¾-in. forged blades. 54-in. fire-hardened wood handle.
89 FB 1914 M—Ship. wt. 3 lbs. 3 oz.....**$3.29**

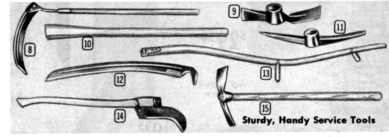

Farm Forks for Every Need . . . Low as **$3.59**

⑯ **Ensilage Fork.** Finest quality 1-piece forged head with ten 16-in. tines. 15½ inches wide at points. 30-inch Ash handle with steel "D" grip. *Mailable.*
89 FB 1922 MO—Ship. wt. 6 lbs......................**$7.59**

⑰ **Hay Fork.** Three 12-inch forged oval tines. 4-ft. select Ash handle. Sturdy—made to last. *Mailable.*
89 FB 1920 MO—Ship. wt. 3 lbs......................**$3.59**

⑱⑲ **Manure Forks.** Finest quality. Strong 12¼-in. forged tines. 10 in. wide at points. 4-ft. selected Ash handle with steel ferrule. Choose either 4 or 5-tine fork. *Mailable.*
(18) 89 FB 1921 MO—With 4 Tines. Ship. wt. 3 lbs.....**$3.69**
(19) 89 FB 1923 MO—With 5 Tines. Ship. wt. 4 lbs..... 3.98

For Added Convenience Just Phone Your Order Or Visit Your Nearest Ward Catalog Store. Remember Too, No Money Down on Any of Your Purchases . . . See Page 101

Husky and Durable Spades, Shovels and Scoops . . . Low as **$1.61**

- **Solid Steel Shanks for Maximum Reinforcement Where a Shovel Needs It Most**

⑳ **Post Hole Spade.** 6¼x16-in. blade. 27-in. "D" grip handle. *Mailable.*
89 FB 1870M—Ship. wt. 5 lbs. 8 oz.**$4.85**

㉑ **Drain Spade.** 4¼x16-in. forged tapered blade. 27-in. Ash "D" handle.
89 FB 1869M—Wt. 5 lbs. *Mail.*...**$4.85**

㉒ **Round Point Dirt Shovel.** 8⅞x11½-in. forged blade. 47-in. straight handle.
89 FB 1831MO—Wt. 4 lbs. *Mail.*..**$3.49**

㉓ **Good Quality General Purpose Shovel.** Stamped steel blade. 46½-in. hardwood handle. 11½x13¾-in. blade.
89 FB 1832MO—Wt. 5 lbs. *Mail.*..**$1.61**

㉔ **Dairy Barn Scoop.** Deep bowl design. 10¼x15¼-in. blade. 44½-in. handle.
89 FB 1847MO—Wt. 5 lbs. 8 oz. *Mail.***$4.39**

㉕㉖ **Grain Scoops.** "D" grip. Approx. blade sizes: No. 10—14x17½ in.; No. 12—14½x18½ in.; No. 14—15x19 in.

(25) **Sturdy Steel.** Steel blade. 27-in. ash handle. Ship. wt. 5 lbs. *Mailable.*
89 FB 1849MO—No. 10 Size.......**$4.89**

(26) **Lightweight Aluminum.** 27-in. handle. Ship. wts. 4 lbs. 8 oz.; 5 lbs. *Mail.*
89 FB 1852MO—Size 12....**$6.19**
89 FB 1854MO—Size 14.... 6.59

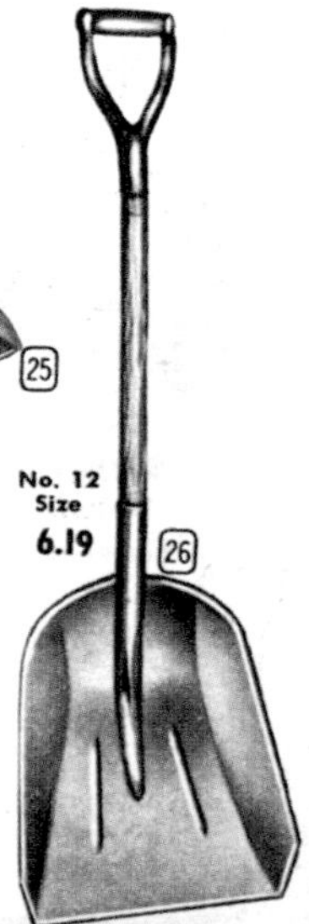

No. 10 Size **4.89**

No. 12 Size **6.19**

CBAKS **WARDS 79**

The remaining pages of advertisements are from the 1969 *Montgomery Ward Farm Catalog*.

7-HP* 18-IN. SAW
$181⁹⁵

9-HP* 21-IN. SAW
$196⁹⁵

Rubber Hand Grip for Handling Comfort

A

Grease Gun included at No extra cost.

Enclosed, High Positioned, Gravity-Drained Carburetor Helps Prevent Gumming . . . Keeps Carburetor Cleaner

Large, Easy to Clean Polyurethane Air Filter . . . Up-and-Out-of-the-Way

Large Pressure Type Thumb Oiler for Natural Ease of Operation

WARDS

NO MONEY DOWN

Fast Idle Hold Button Assures Easier, Fumble-Proof Starting

Large Anti-Spark Type Muffler Extinguishes Hot Exhaust Gasses for Added Protection

Reverse Side View

Full wrap-around handle for convenient handling. Hvy. duty rewind starter.

$236⁸⁵

14-in. Width
No Money Down

1

NOW! Take a Sawmill to the Tree

WITH ALASKAN CHAIN SAW LUMBERMAKER ATTACHMENT

- Cut Lumber Where the Tree Is Felled—Take It Ready-to-Use, to Market or Job
- Extra-Length Beams Bring Top Prices. "Alaskans" Cut Precise, Accurate Beams
- Farmers, Ranchers, Tree Farmers Can Harvest Their Own Timber Stands; Supply All Their Own Lumber Requirements for Fencing, Pens, Barns, Sheds, Etc.

Here Are a Few Jobs For the "Alaskan"

Cut Premium Length Beams; Extreme Length Bridge Sills; Railroad Track Cross Ties; Mine and Dam Special Timbers; Fence, Posts; Planks, Slabbing, Siding; Shoring and Sluice Box Material.

Turns snags, core rot or bug trees left in forest into valuable salvage lumber. Slab and sawdust left behind, increases hauling capacity.

1 **Amazing Performance** from this easy-to-use portable Mill—cut up to 1,200 board feet per day! Heavy production cutting right on-the-spot saves hauling time and helps reduce expense. Can be used with 1 or 2 chain saw engines—either direct or gear drive—minimum of 6 HP required. Direct-drive engine recommended for greater production. For highest volume, use 2 saw engines of equal size and power. Quantity of board feet depends on engine, HP, chain filing skill and width of lumber cut.

Precision-Machined of high alloy steel with nylon bearing rollers. Produces uniform, accurate and exact size lumber, cut smooth, ready to use. Simple, calibrated Risers allow cuts of any thickness from ½ in. to 12 in. Widths to 4 ft.

Complete Mill to Use with Chain Saw Power Unit. 6 cutting widths to meet specific needs. Includes: mill, dual end bar, specially ground ripping chain, helper handle with roller idler, auxiliary oil tank and deluxe chain sharpener (89 FB 24224, Page 110). We supply proper length bar for size of mill, regardless if used with one or two power units. No complicated fitting, no alterations to saw necessary. Ripping Chains are provided in .404, ⁷⁄₁₆-in., ½-in., ⁹⁄₁₆-in. pitch. Specify make and model of saw including pitch of chain wanted and sprocket size. Shipped, pay charges from Factory near Richmond, Calif.

Catalog No.	Cutting Width	Ship. Wt.	Cash
89 FB 24501KB	14 in.	38 lbs.	$236.85
89 FB 24502KB	20 in.	42 lbs.	267.50
89 FB 24503KB	26 in.	45 lbs.	283.50
89 FB 24504KB	32 in.	50 lbs.	299.50
89 FB 24505KB	38 in.	56 lbs.	318.50
89 FB 24506KB	48 in.	73 lbs.	359.95

2 **Guide Rail Bracket.** Make sturdy guide rail for slabbing cuts. Shouldered pegs anchor rail to log. Use your 2x4's plus 1 bracket every 4-5 ft. along rail.
89 FB 24510 K—Wt. 5 lbs.. Ea. $4.95

$4⁹⁵

2

108 CBAKSDF

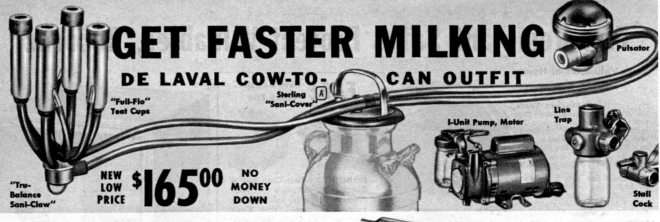

GET FASTER MILKING
DE LAVAL COW-TO- CAN OUTFIT

"Full-Flo" Teat Cups

Sterling "Sani-Cover" [A]

Pulsator

I-Unit Pump, Motor

Line Trap

Stall Cock

"Tru-Balance Sani-Claw"

NEW LOW PRICE $165.00 NO MONEY DOWN

- Milk Up To Twice As Many Cows in the Same Time with No Increase in Labor
- Easily Adapts to Any Barn Layout, Choose the Milker Operation You Want

Get Much Higher Milk Production, Bigger Profits with De Laval Cow-To-Can Milking. Cow-To-Can means fast, pleasant milking that gives maximum labor savings. For your present barn, it gives all benefits of mechanized milking without extensive alterations. For a new milk shed, it gives modern milking at lowest construction cost. Be sure to order De Laval Uni-filter with your outfit, for complete, modern, easy milk filtering. No milk pails needed, because milk flows from the cow to your 40-qt. cans. Simply transfer sani-cover to another can as can is filled.

[A] **Outfit with One Milker Unit.** Includes: FULL FLO TEAT CUPS—exclusive DE LAVAL cup with 1-piece tapered narrow bore neoprene liners. Automatically takes correct position on teat. Fits all size teats; TRU-BALANCE SANI-CLAW—perfect distribution, correct spacing of teat cups on udders of all sizes. 1-piece stainless steel. Brushes straight through for easier cleaning; STERLING OPERATING COVER—baffle keeps vacuum line milk-free. 1-piece stainless steel; STERLING PULSATOR—efficient, dependable, with only 2 moving parts. Never needs oiling. Pneumatically controlled. Plugs into stall cock, away from cow hair, etc.; DE LAVAL ¼-HP MOTOR AND VACUUM PUMP—engineered to give peak performance when needed. Provides large capacity, requires minimum maintenance. Starts easily; STERLING STALL COCK—automatic, designed for low cost installation, maximum efficiency; COMBINATION TRAP, VACUUM CONTROLLER—non-adjustable, maintains 12 to 13-in. vacuum. Outfit also includes rubber tube and plug for vacuum line. See "Ship. Note" at right.
89 FB 20042 F—Ship. wt. 63 lbs. No Money Down...Was $172.50; Now, Cash **$165.00**

Extra Cow-To-Can Milker Unit. With teat cup assembly, operating cover, pulsator.
89 FB 20044 K—Ship. wt. 15 lbs. No Money Down. ....Was $96.50; Now, Cash **$89.50**

Outfit with Two Milker Units. (See view at right.) Offers all the advantages of the more expensive milking systems, yet easily adaptable to your present setup. Outfit includes: Two TRU-BALANCE SANI-CLAW assemblies with FULL FLO TEAT CUPS, Two STERLING OPERATING COVERS, Two STERLING PULSATORS, Two STALL COCKS, ONE COMBINATION TRAP AND CONTROLLER and a DE LAVAL ½-HP MOTOR AND PUMP (same as (C), right), and ONE RUBBER PLUG for vacuum line. See "Shipping Note", right.
89 FB 20043 F—Ship. wt. 107 lbs. No Money Down...Was $308.00; Now, Cash **$293.00**

[B] **Easy-to-Use DE LAVAL Uni-Filter $14.00**

[B] Here's the really convenient way to filter milk. Simply install in milk line between teat cup assembly and operating cover. Preparing complicated filters is entirely eliminated with this modern up-to-date method. Saves lifting and pouring time without exposing milk to barn dirt and odors.
89 FB 20045 K—Ship. wt. 2 lbs. (Order Filter Tubes from Page 155) ...**$14.00**

DE LAVAL ½ OR ¼-HP MOTOR WITH PUMP

Make up your own outfits or replace worn pumps.

$150.00 2-Unit Pump, Motor

$85.50 1-Unit Pump, Motor

[C] De Laval ½-HP Motor and Pump for two milkers. Extra powerful, long lasting, engineered to provide large capacity and require minimum maintenance. Not Mailable. No Money Down, 89FB20047 R—Wt. 57 lbs. Cash **$150.00**

De Laval ¼-HP Motor and Pump to handle one milker, (pictured with (A) above). No Money Down.
89FB20046 MB—Wt. 38 lbs. Cash **$85.50**

Using Two Milker Units

IMPORTANT SHIPPING NOTE

De Laval Cow-to-Can Outfits and Uni-Filter shipped from Factory in Chicago, Ill. and Poughkeepsie, N.Y. You pay Freight charges from nearer. Pump-Motors above shipped from Stock.

LARGE VACUUM PUMPS TO SPEED MILKING TIME

Choose the Proper Size Pump to Assure Maximum Efficiency of Your Milking System

- The completely functional features incorporated in these pumping outfits assure you of sufficient vacuum reserve at all times to do a thorough job of milking.
- Get top vacuum per revolution with rotary vane pumps plus large vacuum tank.

[D] **Large Vacuum Tank with Belt Driven 1 or 1½-HP Pump.** Tank is hot dip galvanized inside and out for long, satisfactory service; 17-gal. capacity. Drain valve at bottom permits condensation to drain when pump is not in operation. Cleanout port with removable cover permits easy inspection and airing out.

$310.00 1 HP

148 WARDS CBAKSDF

NO MONEY DOWN

Efficient Rotary Vane Pumps are precision products—vanes take up their own wear. Pumps are air cooled for efficient operation, longer life. Transparent oil reservoir automatically dispenses correct amount of oil to pump. Oil level is visible—check at a glance. Muffler reduces noise. Vacuum power assembly includes fan cooled pump, motor belt and pulley, piping from pump to vacuum tank, automatic vacuum controller, drain valve, motor insulator and vacuum gauge. Check valve between pump and tank keeps pump from running backward when switched off.

With 1½-HP Pump you can milk more cows faster or have reserve capacity for future expansion. For 110–120-volt or 220–240 volt, 60-cycle AC. Shipped from Factory near Springfield, Mass. You pay freight charges from there. Order your Dairy needs Today. No Money Down on Easy Terms—see Page 101 for further details.

89 FB 20050 F—VACUUM TANK WITH 1-HP PUMP produces 11 cu. ft. air per minute—12-in. vacuum will handle 8 to 10 conventional units. Ship. wt. 170 lbs. Cash **$310.00**

89 FB 20051 F—VACUUM TANK WITH 1½-HP PUMP produces 16 ft. air per minute. 12-in. vacuum handles 10 to 14 conventional units. Ship. wt. 180 lbs......Cash **$435.00**

RITE-WAY FLOOR MODEL PAIL-TYPE

Single Milking Unit

$139.50

NO MONEY DOWN

- Efficient Design, Quality Inflations
- Precision Built Pulsator—Smooth Action
- Gets Milk Without Hand Stripping
- Pulsator Control Regulates Speed

[E]

Speed Milking—Improve Quality

[E] **Conventional Pail-Type Milker Unit** of sanitary stainless steel, with scientific Rite-Way features that mean bigger yields—profits. Perfectly balanced pulsator has only 2 moving parts. Completely encased for smooth, uniform action. Calf-like action strokes—cow lets down milk naturally. 1-piece finest quality inflations; sanitary, well-balanced claw. Transparent milk tube shows flow—easy to keep clean. Precision built to do a thorough job in just 3 minutes without any hand stripping.

Unit includes stainless steel pail, pulsator, shells, tubing and all accessories. (Pump-Motor Units may be ordered separately, see numbers 89 FB 20047 R and 89 FB 20046 MB under item (C) above.) Shipped from Stock by Freight, Truck or Express. Ship. wt. 25 lbs. No Money Down on Wards convenient terms—see full details on Page 101.

99 FB 20030 R—Single Unit, 50-lb. capacity ..Cash **$139.50**

Index

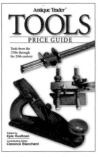

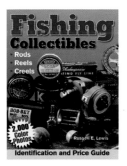
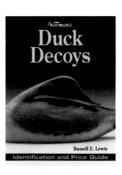
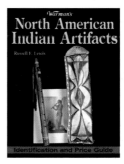

2/08

Subscribe Today

GET ONE FULL YEAR AT A GREAT LOW RATE! 1 YEAR (52 HUGE ISSUES) $38.00

That's right. Try *Antique Trader* today and discover the most authoritative voice in the antiques world. Each issue's filled to the brim with valuable information for your pursuit of antiques.

You'll find…

- Current prices and values
- Dolls, toys, furniture, clocks, glass and all special interests
- Exclusive antique market trends
- Auctions tips, techniques and strategies
- Expert appraisals
- And much, much more!

Don't pay $155.48 at the newsstand.

Subscribe Today & Save 76%!

DON'T WAIT–
Log on to www.antiquetrader.com
and subscribe today.

Call 877-300-0247; outside the U.S. & Canada, call 386-246-3434. Offer code: J7AHAD
Or write us at: P.O. Box 420235, Palm Coast, FL 32142-0235

In Canada: add $71 (includes GST/HST). Outside the U.S. and Canada: add $121 and remit payment in U.S. funds with order. Please allow 4-6 weeks for first-issue delivery. Annual newsstand rate $155.48.